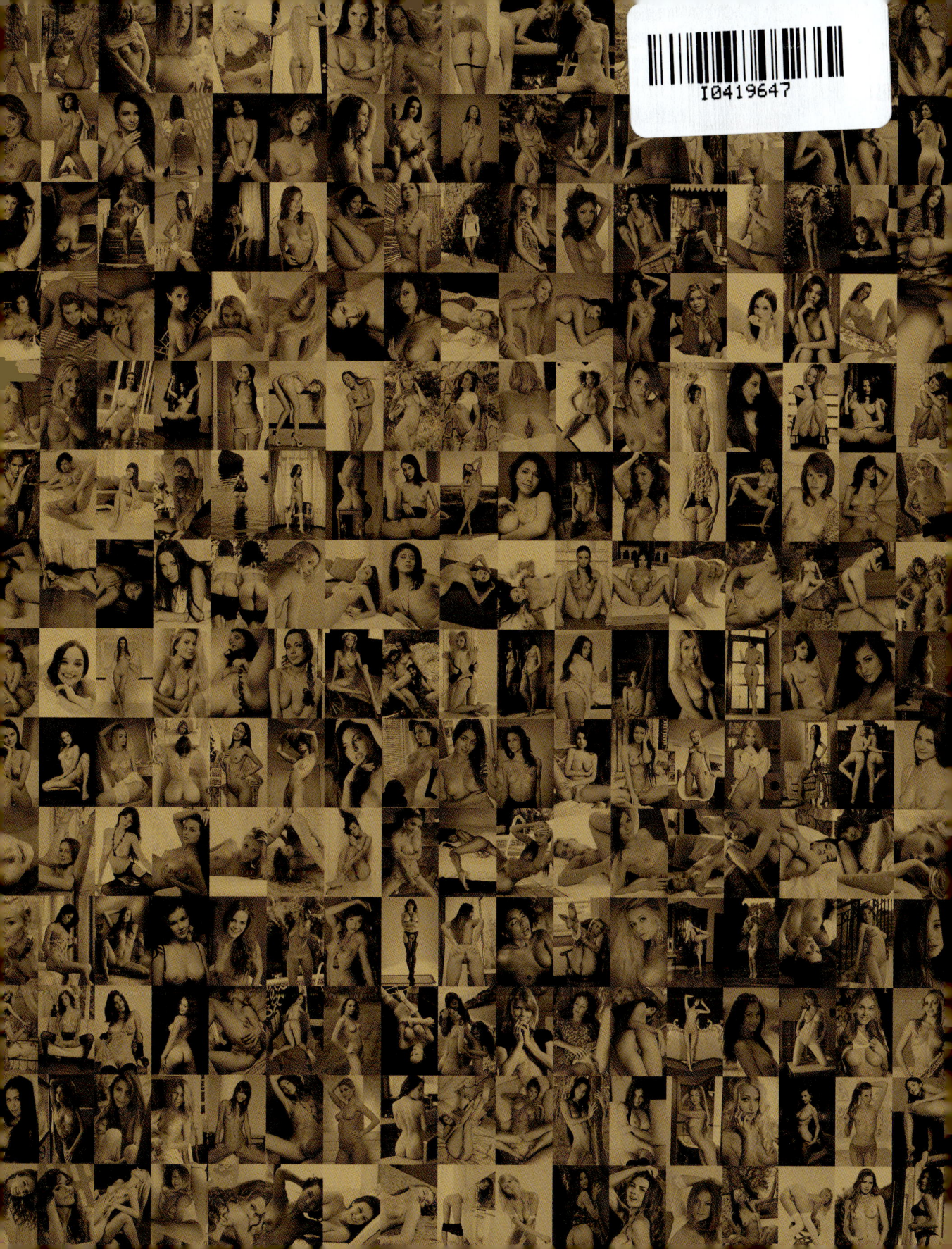

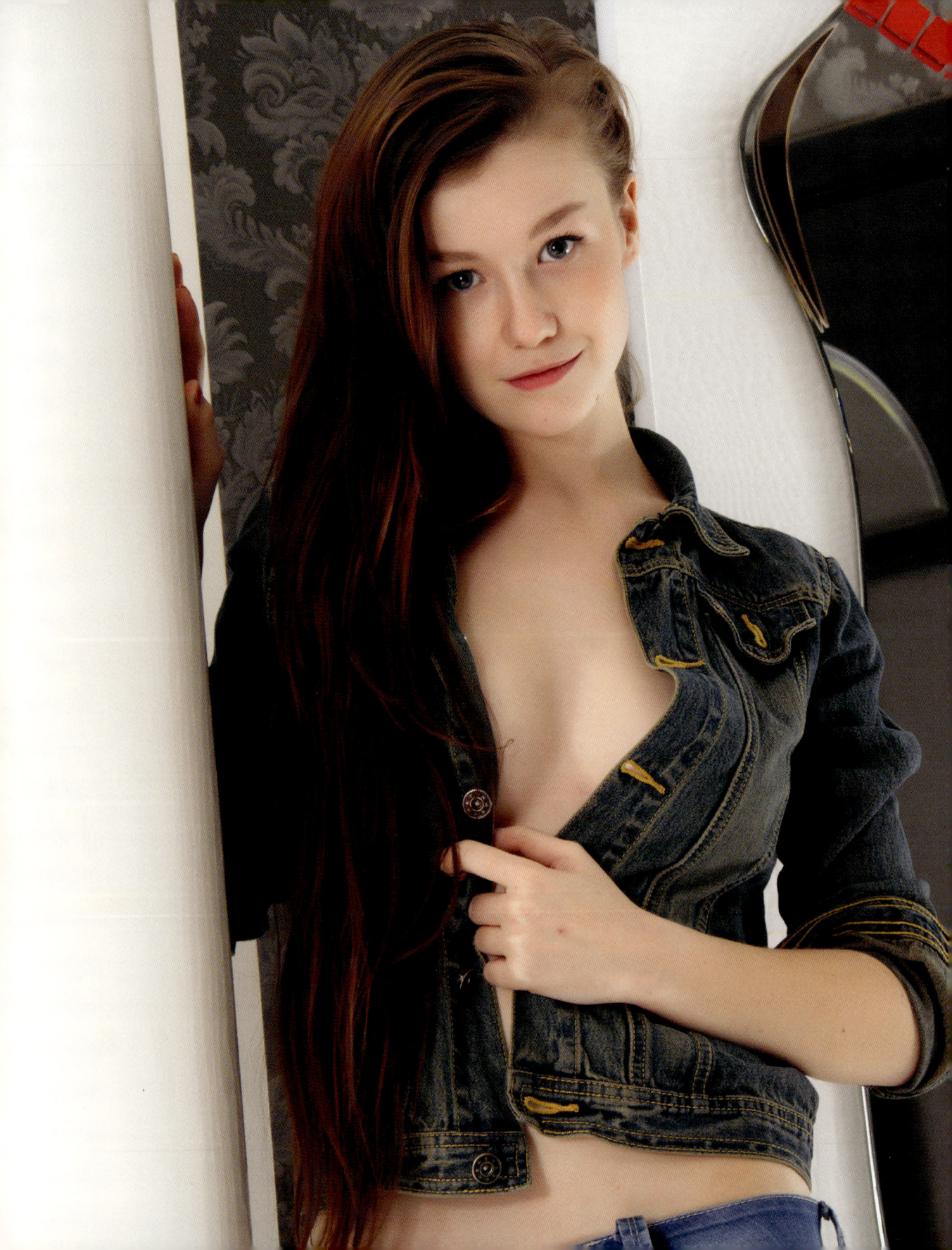

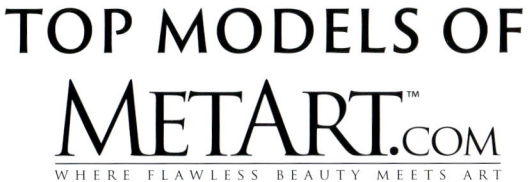

TOP MODELS OF
MetArt.com
WHERE FLAWLESS BEAUTY MEETS ART

EMILY
BLOOM

COLLECTED AND EDITED BY ISABELLA CATALINA

EDITION Skylight
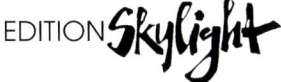

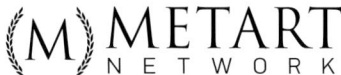

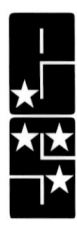

First edition 2024
Copyright © 2024 by Edition Skylight

EDITION SKYLIGHT
Rosengartenstrasse 13B
CH-8608 Bubikon / Zürich
Switzerland
info@edition-skylight.com
www.edition-skylight.com

ISBN 978-3-03766-704-0

Bibliographic information published by Die Deutsche Bibliothek
Die Deutsche Bibliothek lists this publication in the
Deutsche Nationalbibliografie; detailed bibliographic data
are available in the Internet at http://dnb.ddb.de.

Printed in Bosnia and Herzogovina

What a stunning and sexy fairy Emily Bloom is with her bright smile and deep blue eyes!

Youthful and tender, Ukrainian model Emily Bloom looks just like a fairy out of our fantasy. And what a sexy fairy she is! And a very flexible one too – as a former gymnast she can do spectacular exercises with her body. When Emily came into the picture, all in the crew at Metart were just stunned. She got everybody with her bright smile and deep blue eyes. Emily is a classic combination of naturally sexy and adorably cute. Her sweet face and sensational figure, particularly her beautiful breasts, make a lasting impression. Emily made her debut at the age of 19 in a "Presenting" photoset by Arkisi. To her surprise she has discovered that she gets turned on by modelling in the nude. No wonder she is deservedly popular throughout the MetArt Network, with multiple appearances on SexArt, Erotic Beauty, Errotica Archives, Goddess Nudes, Eternal Desire and Rylsky Art. So what is it that makes Emily so alluring? Well, her incredible figure is certainly eye-catching, with a tiny waist and big natural breasts, with just 168 cm and 49 kg, but it's the naughty expression in her bright blue eyes that really grabs the attention. She has a playful, fresh-faced girl-next-door appeal, with a sweet smile and an air of not-quite-innocent allure. She's talented, too, an accomplished singer, musician, artist and actress (see her playing piano and singing in "Sarada" by Alex Iskan); she is the epitome of smart sexiness. Still young and actively modeling as well as pursuing her creative dreams, it will be fascinating to see how Emily continues to 'bloom' – there's no doubt she is a sexual force to be reckoned with!

Jugendlich und zart, das ukrainische Model Emily Bloom sieht aus wie eine Fee aus einem Märchenland. Und was für eine sexy Fee sie ist! Und dazu noch sehr flexibel – als ehemalige Turnerin kann sie spektakuläre Übungen mit ihrem Körper machen. Als Emily ins Bild kam, waren alle im Team von MetArt einfach sprachlos. Sie hat alle mit ihrem strahlenden Lächeln und ihren tiefblauen Augen verzaubert. Emily präsentiert eine klassische Kombination aus natürlicher Sexiness und entzückender, gespielter Unschuld. Ihr süßes Gesicht und ihre sensationelle Figur, besonders ihre schönen Brüste, hinterlassen einen bleibenden Eindruck. Emily debütierte im Alter von 19 Jahren in einem „Presenting" Fotoset von Arkisi. Und sie hat zu ihrer Überraschung entdeckt: es erregt sie immer wieder, nackt zu posieren. Kein Wunder, dass sie im gesamten Metart-Netzwerk verdientermaßen beliebt ist, mit zahlreichen Beiträgen auch auf SexArt, Erotic Beauty, Errotica Archives, Goddess Nudes, Eternal Desire und Rylsky Art.

Was macht Emily also so verlockend? Nun, ihre unglaubliche Figur ist sicherlich auffällig, mit einer schmalen Taille und großen natürlichen Brüsten, und nur 168 cm und 49 kg, aber es ist der freche Ausdruck in ihren leuchtend blauen Augen, der wirklich die Aufmerksamkeit auf sich zieht. Sie hat einen verspielten, frischen Mädchen-von-nebenan-Reiz, mit einem süßen Lächeln und einer Aura von nicht ganz unschuldiger Anziehungskraft. Sie ist vielseitig talentiert, eine versierte Sängerin, Musikerin, Künstlerin und Schauspielerin (man schaut erstaunt wie sie Klavier spielt und singt in „Sarada" von Alex Iskan); sie ist der Inbegriff von smarter Verführung. Noch jung und aktiv als Model sowie in der Verfolgung ihrer kreativen Träume, wird es faszinierend sein zu sehen, wie Emily weiterhin „aufblüht" – es besteht kein Zweifel, sie besitzt sexuelle Kraft, die wohl jeden überwältigt!

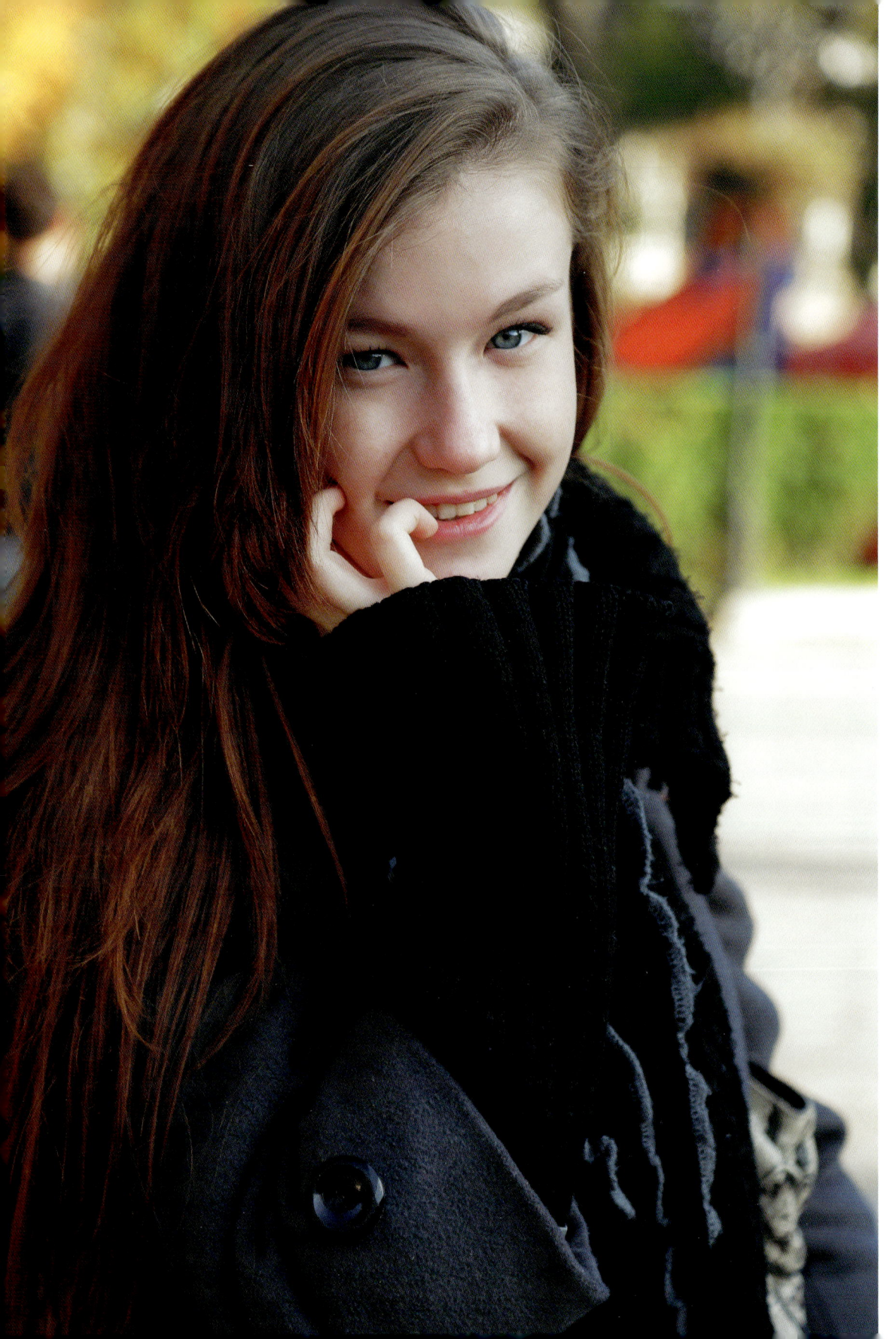

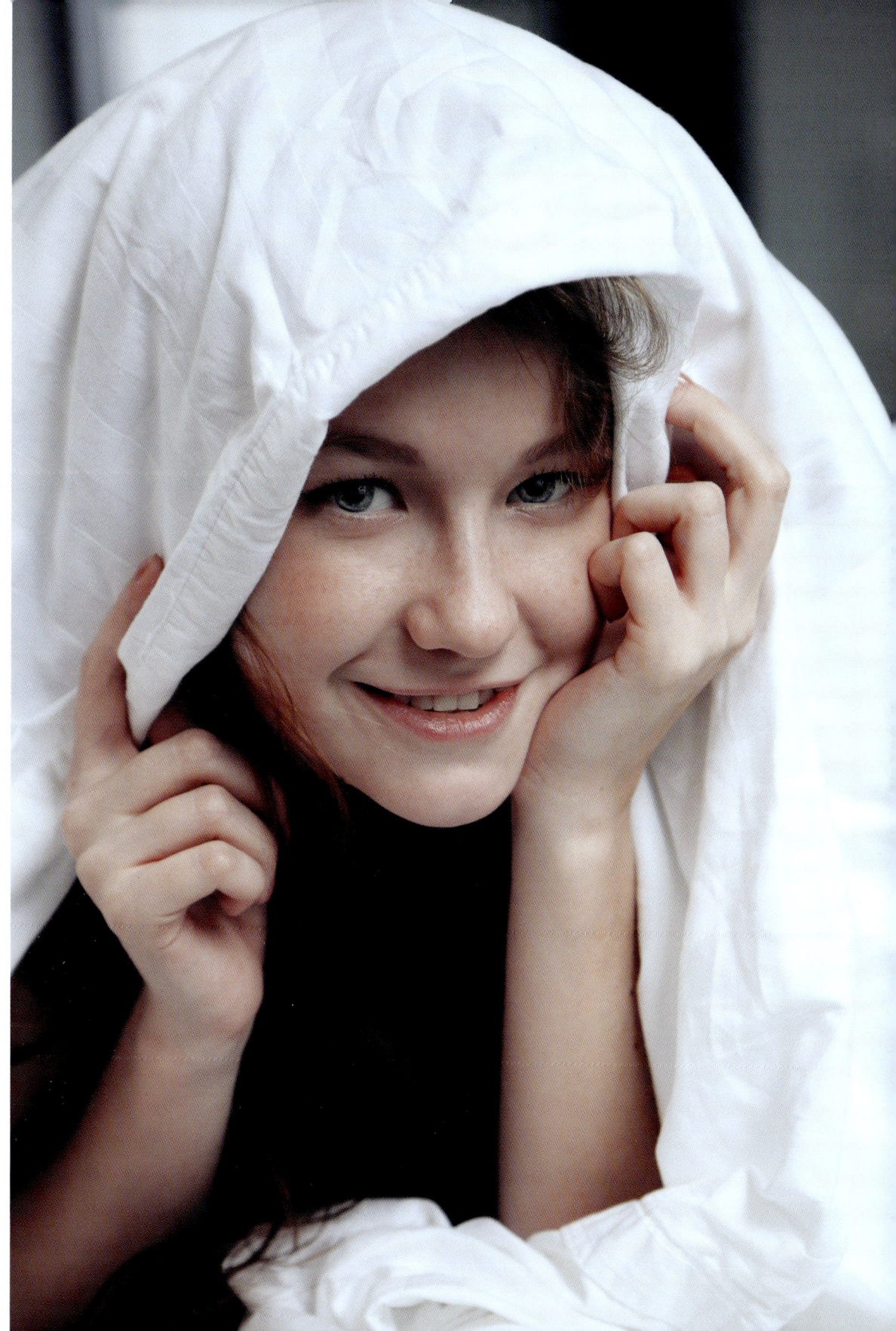

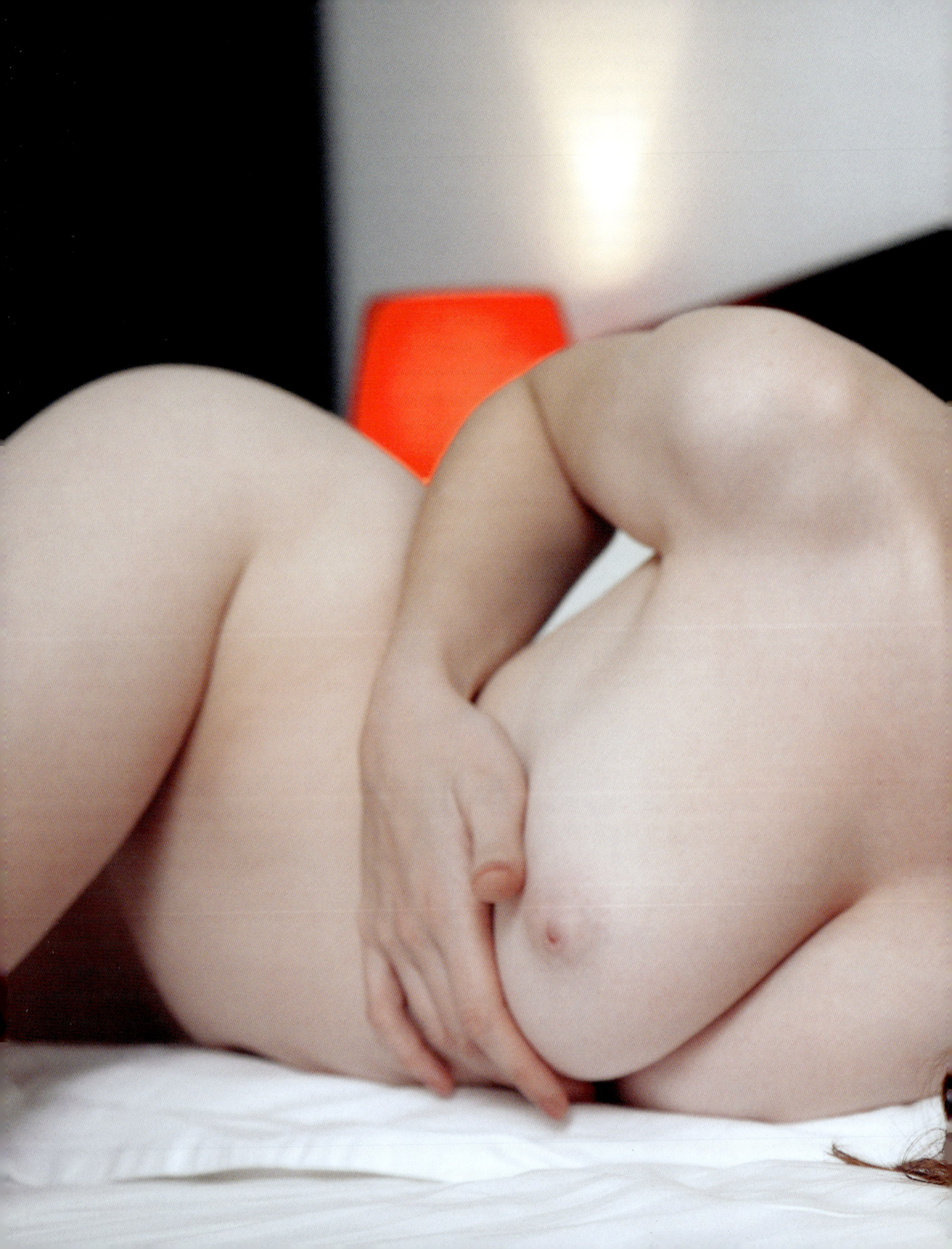

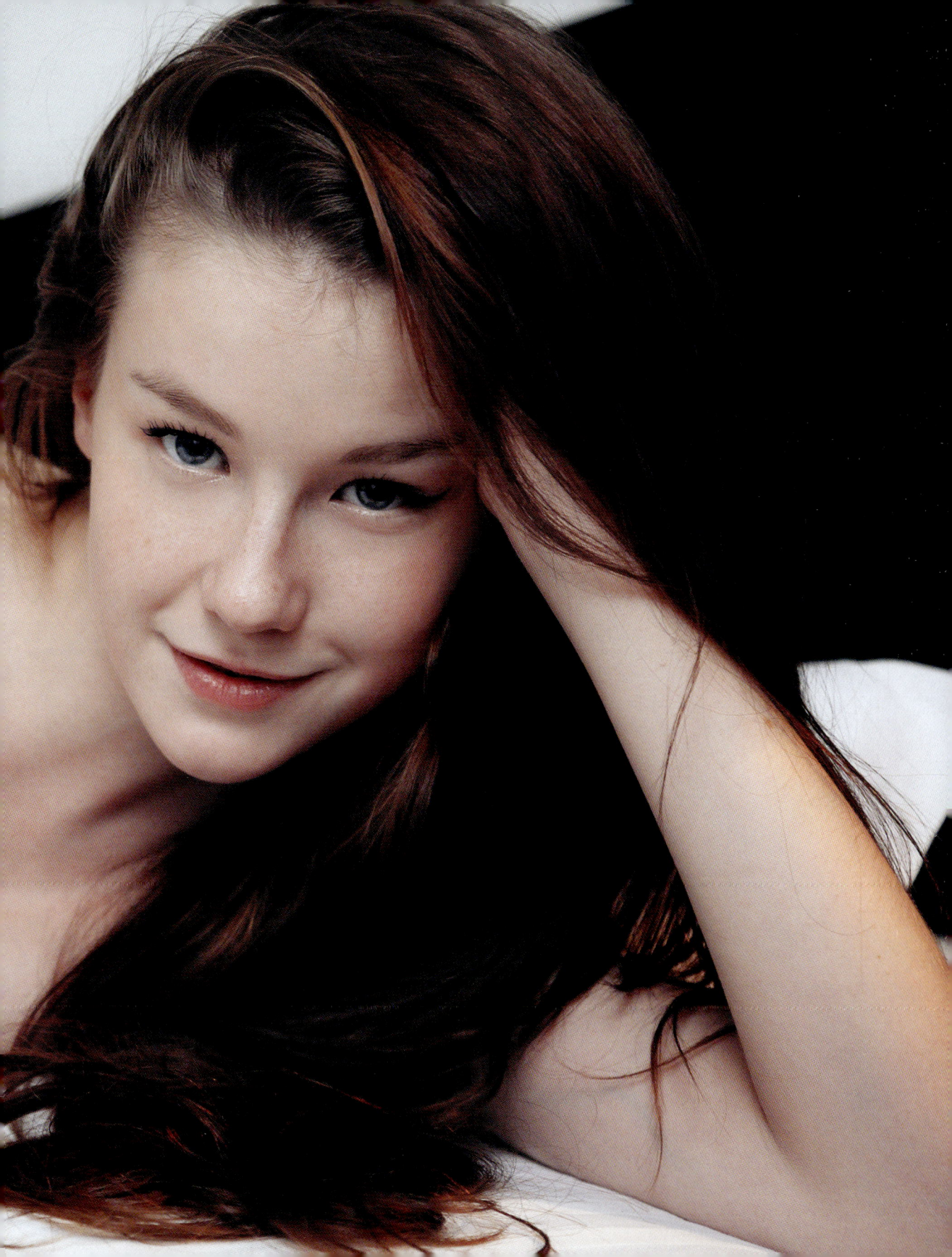

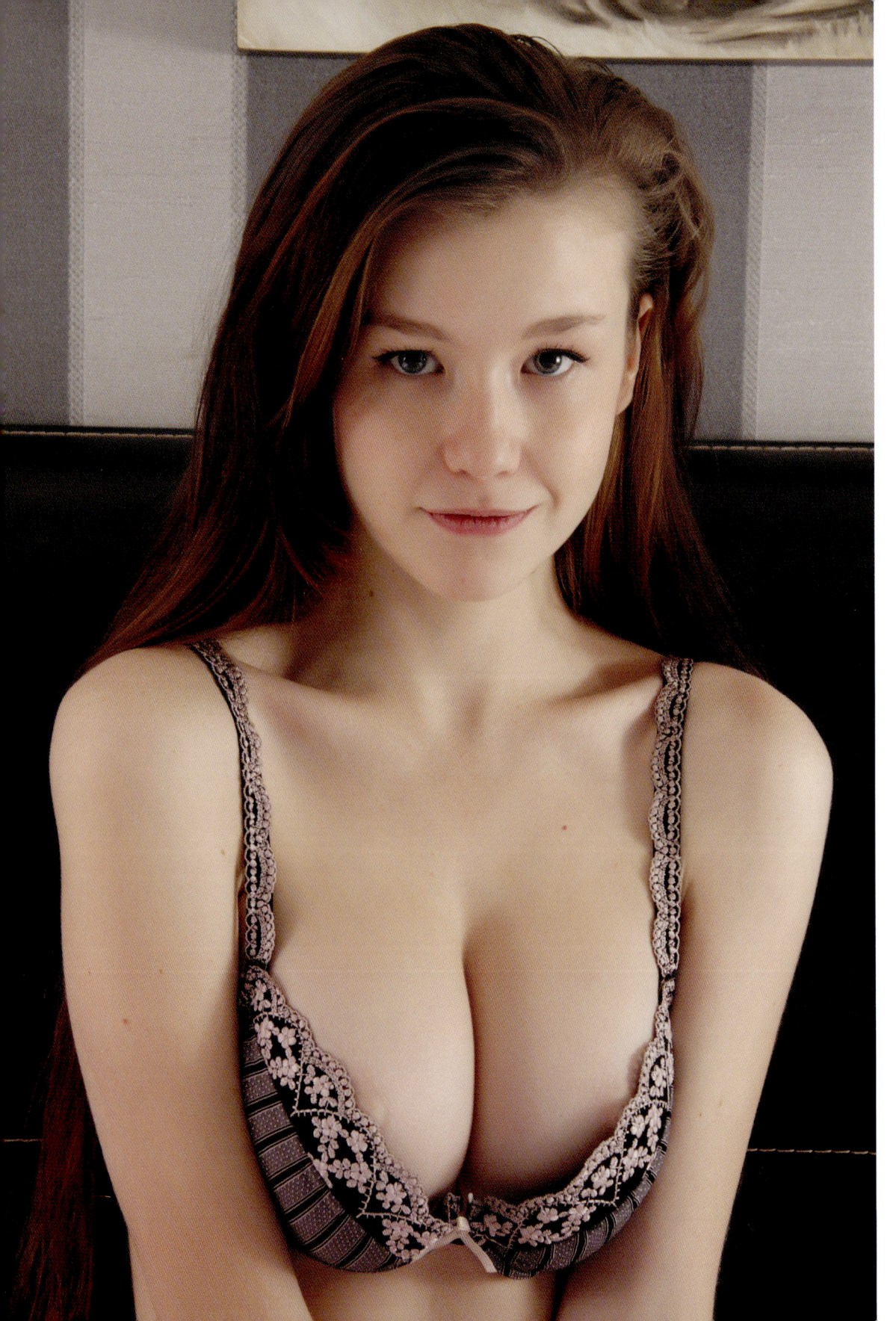

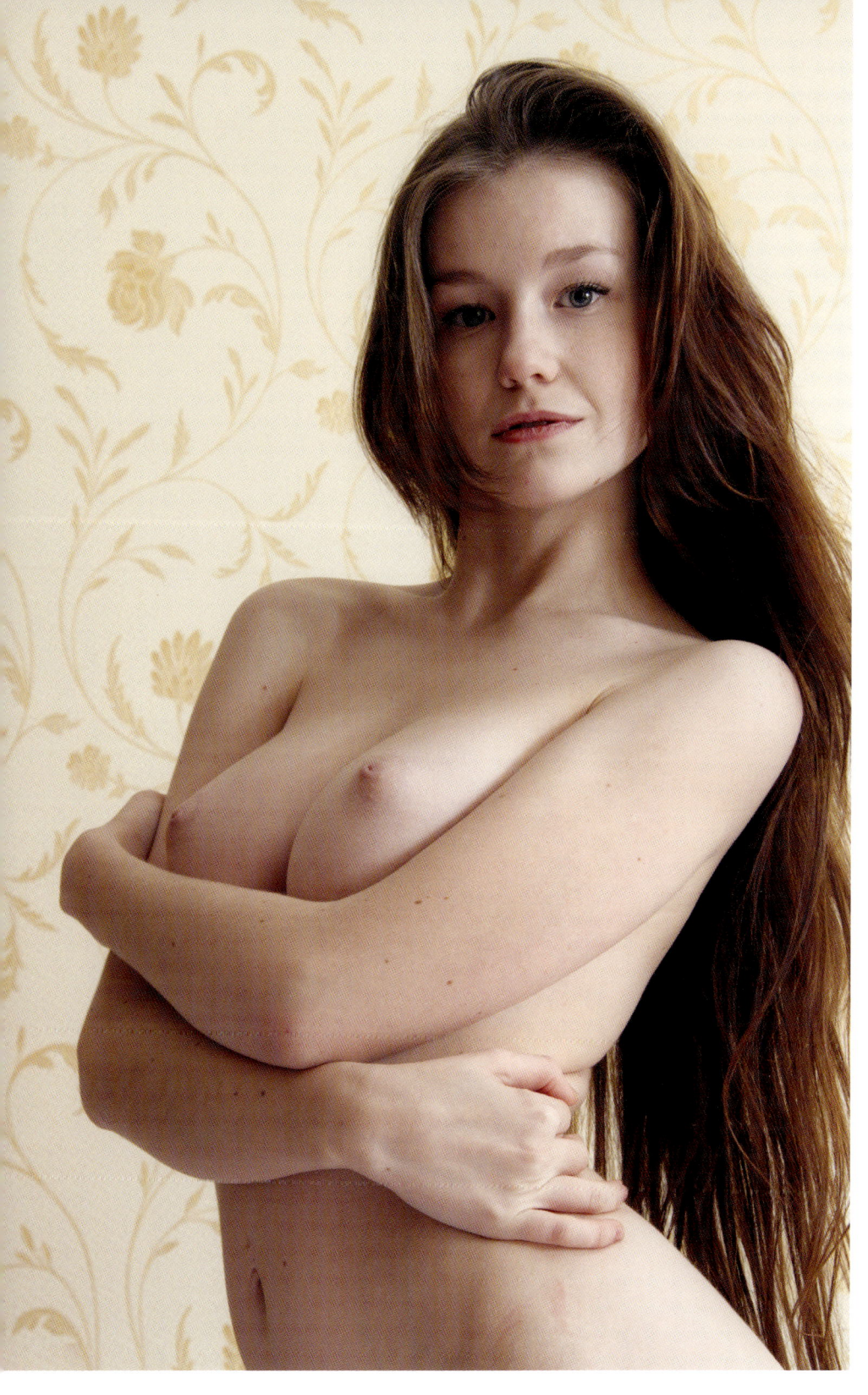

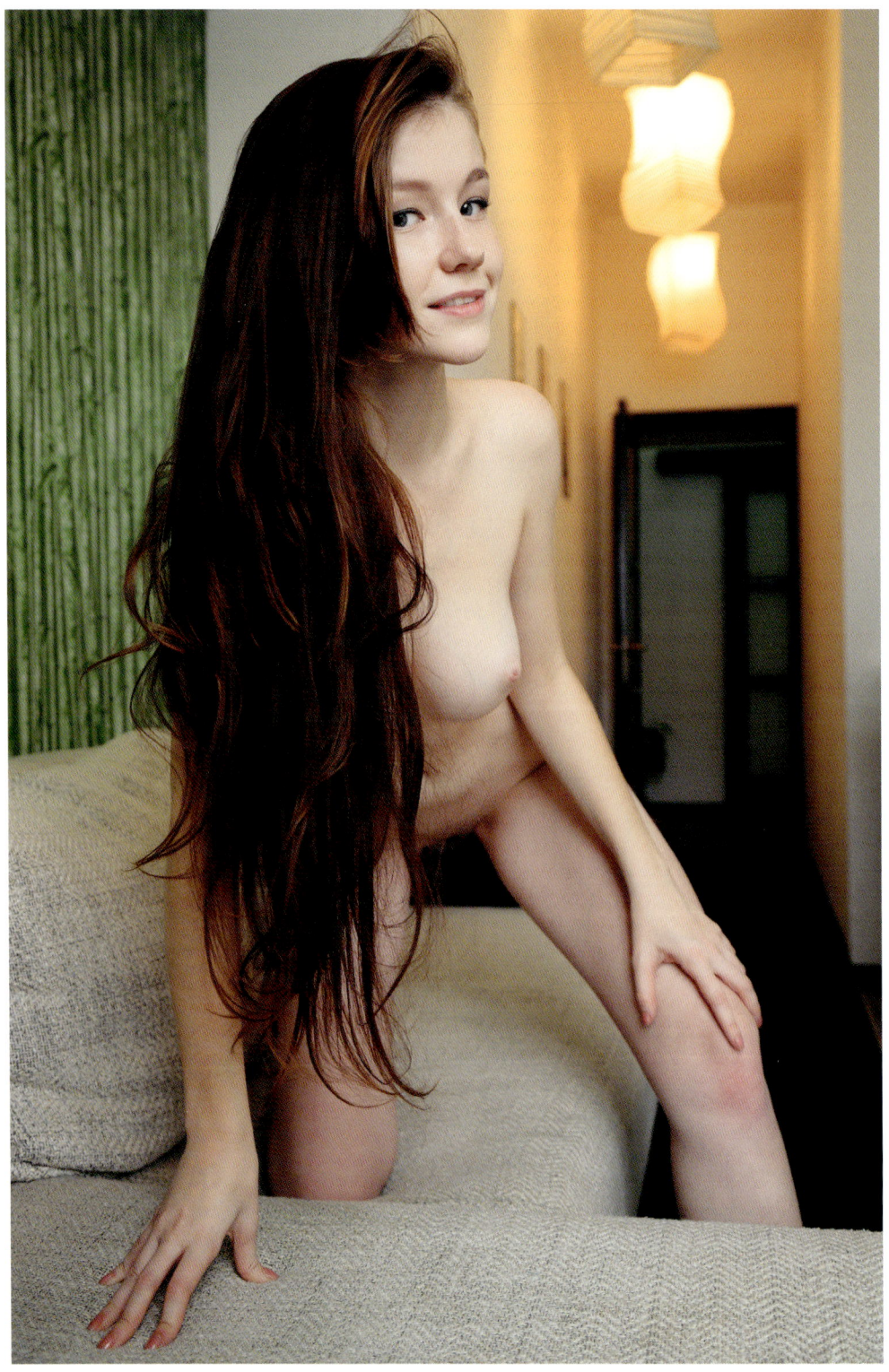

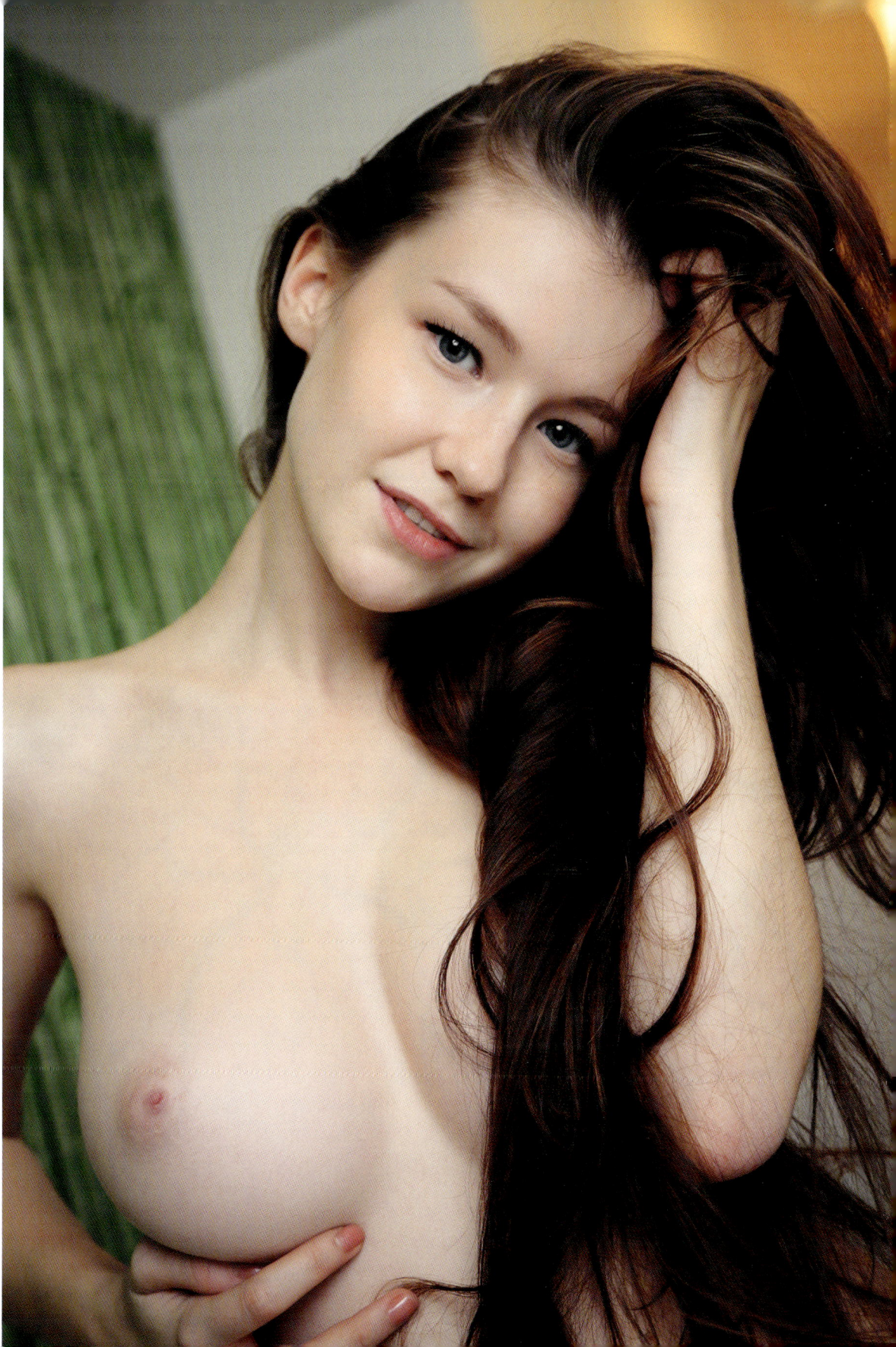

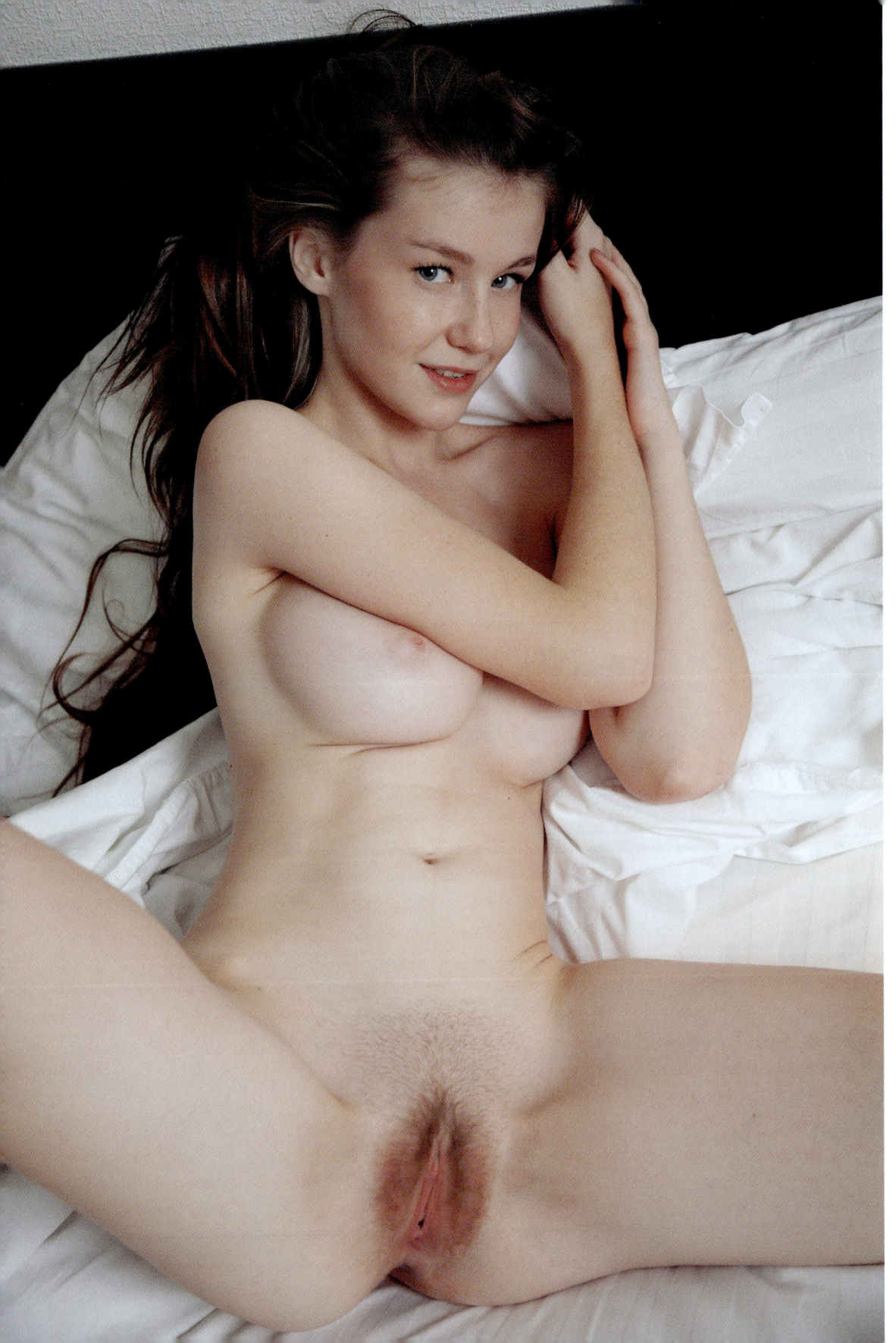

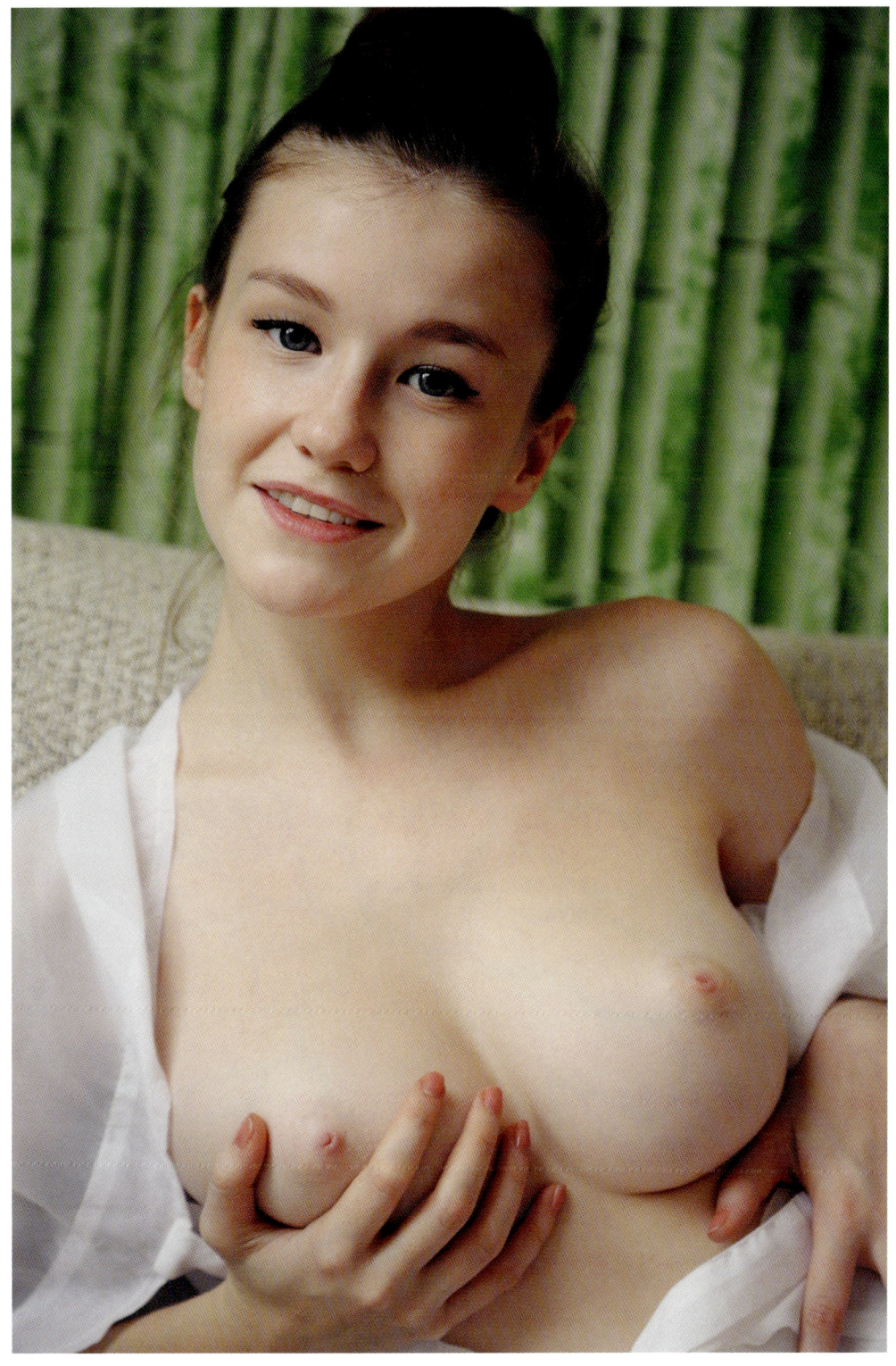

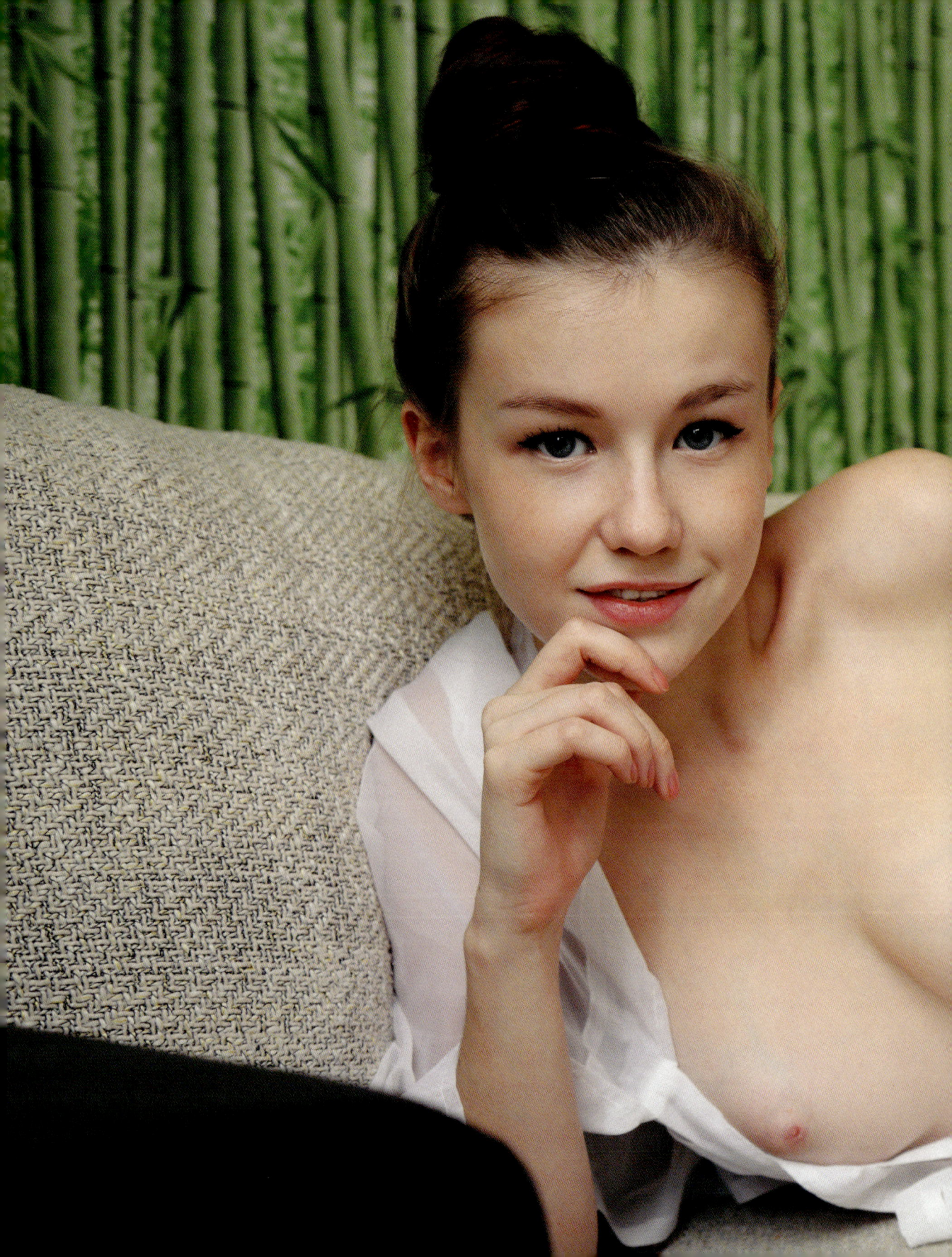

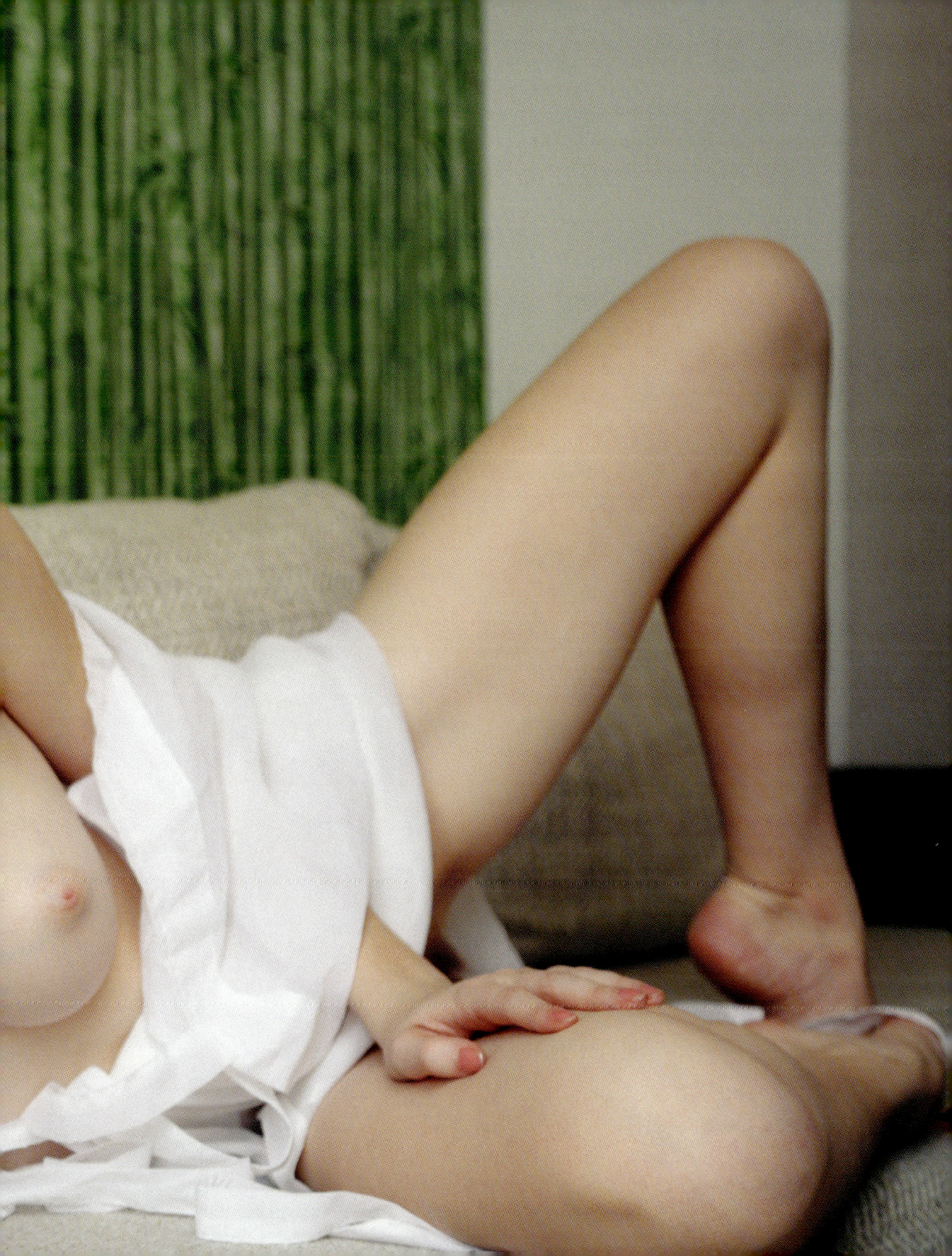

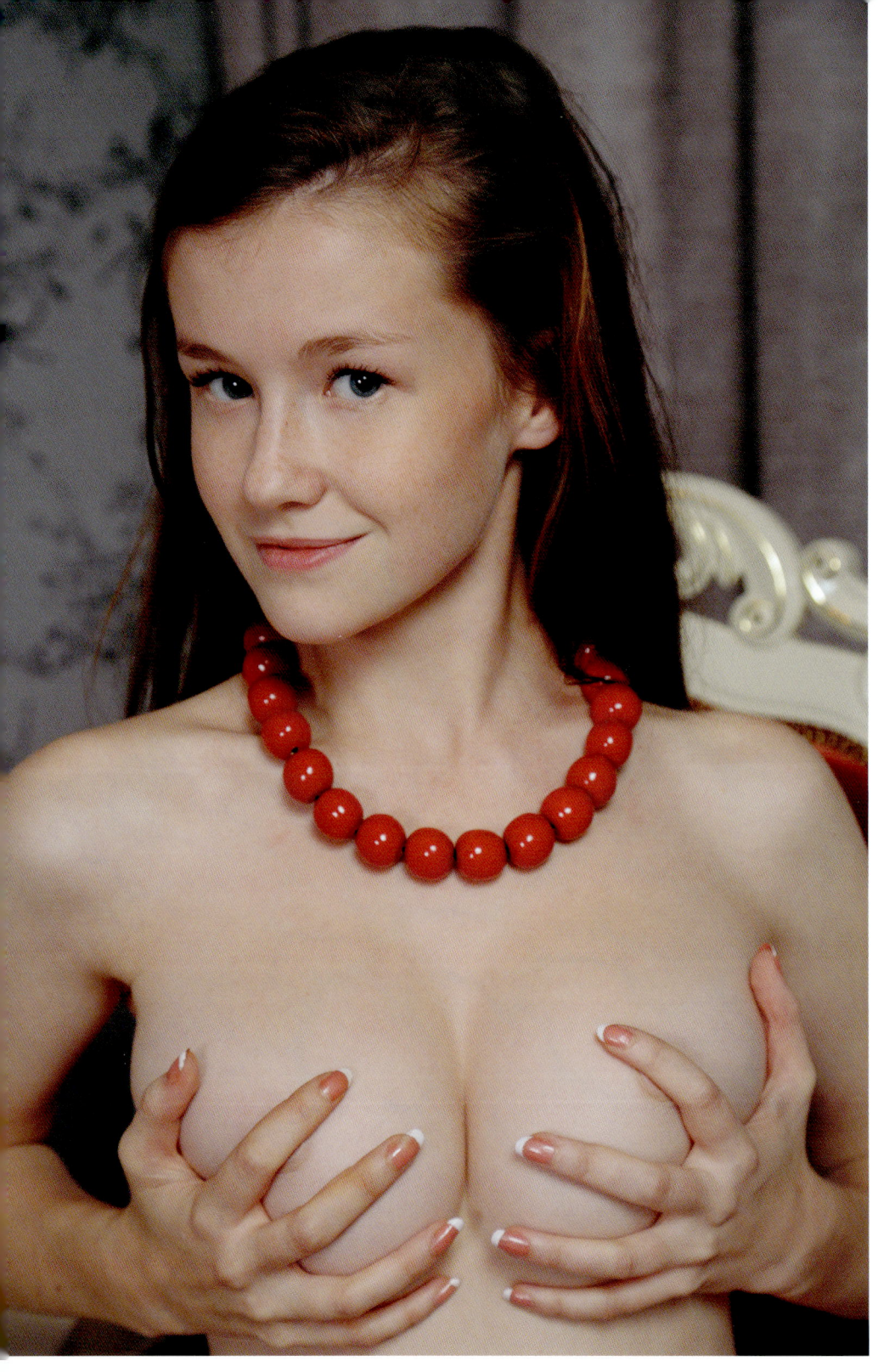

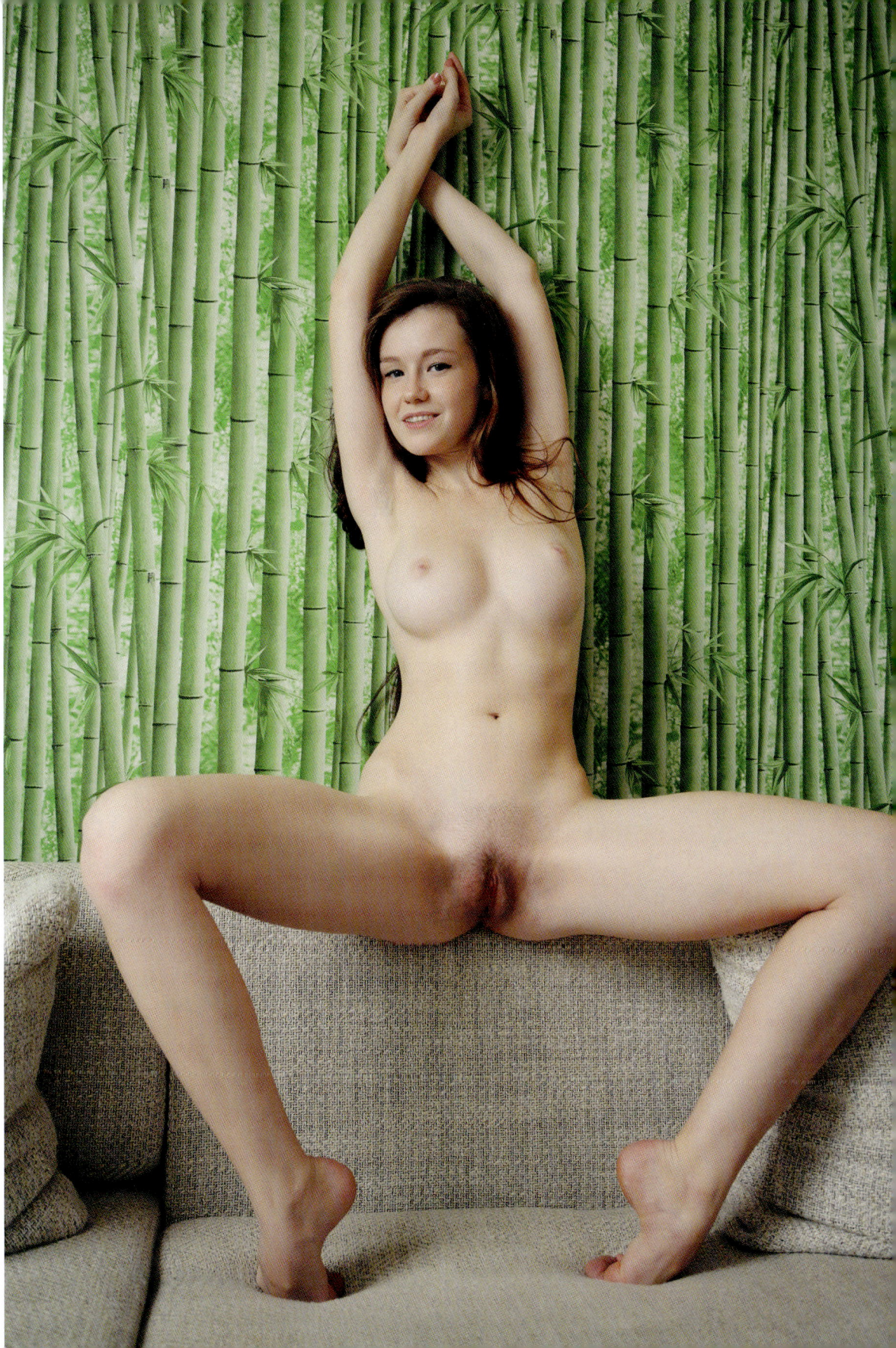

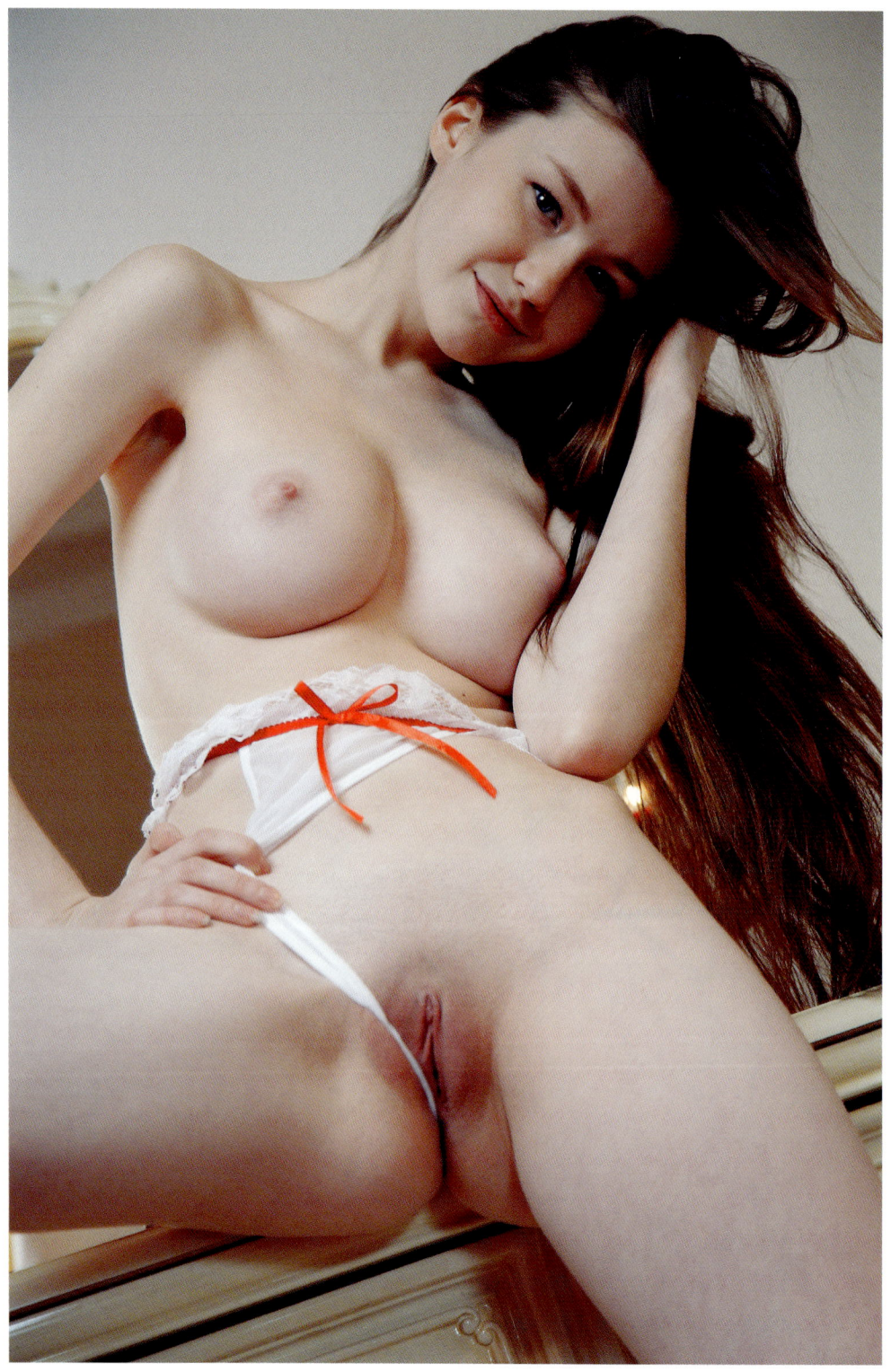

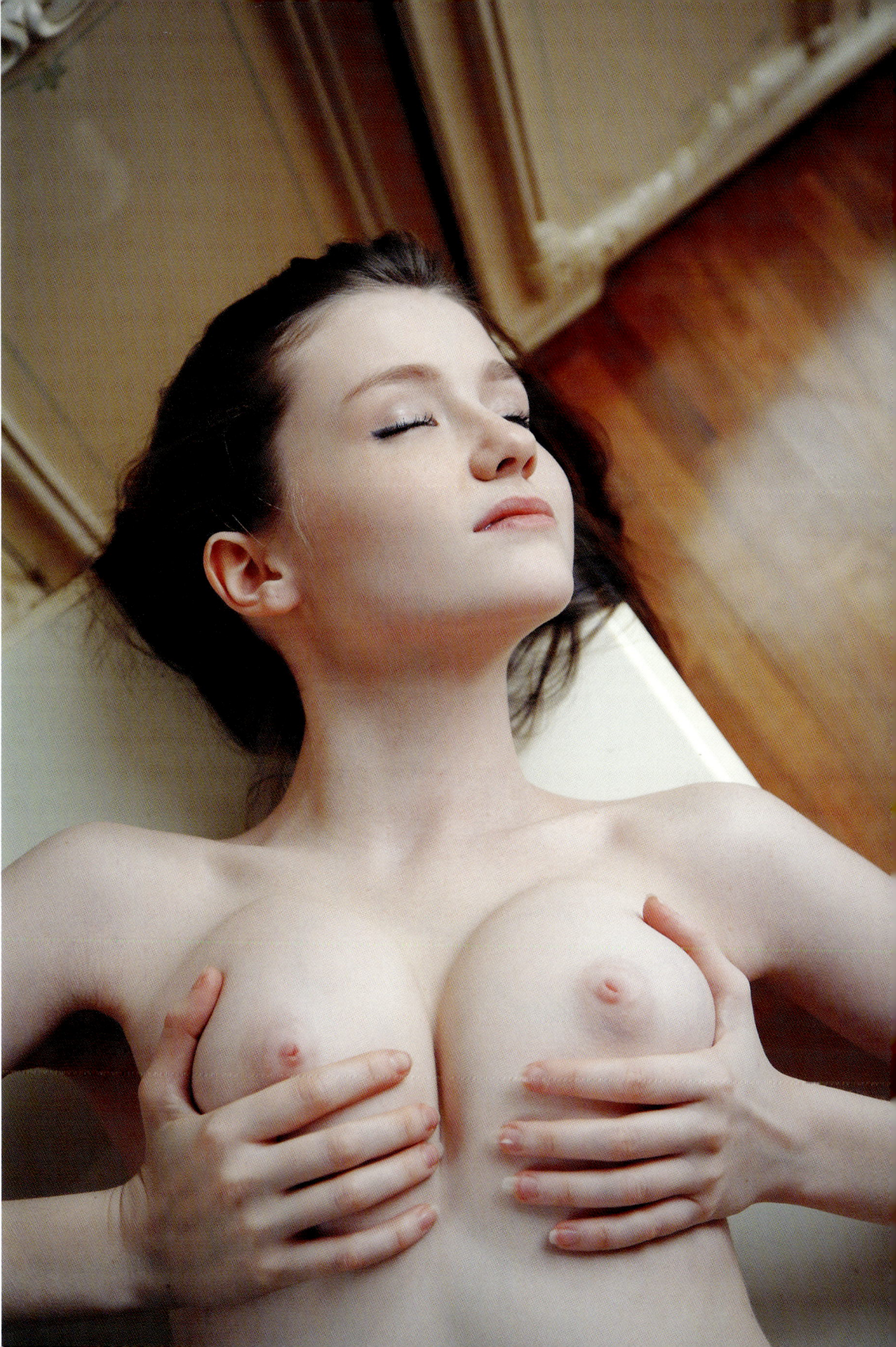

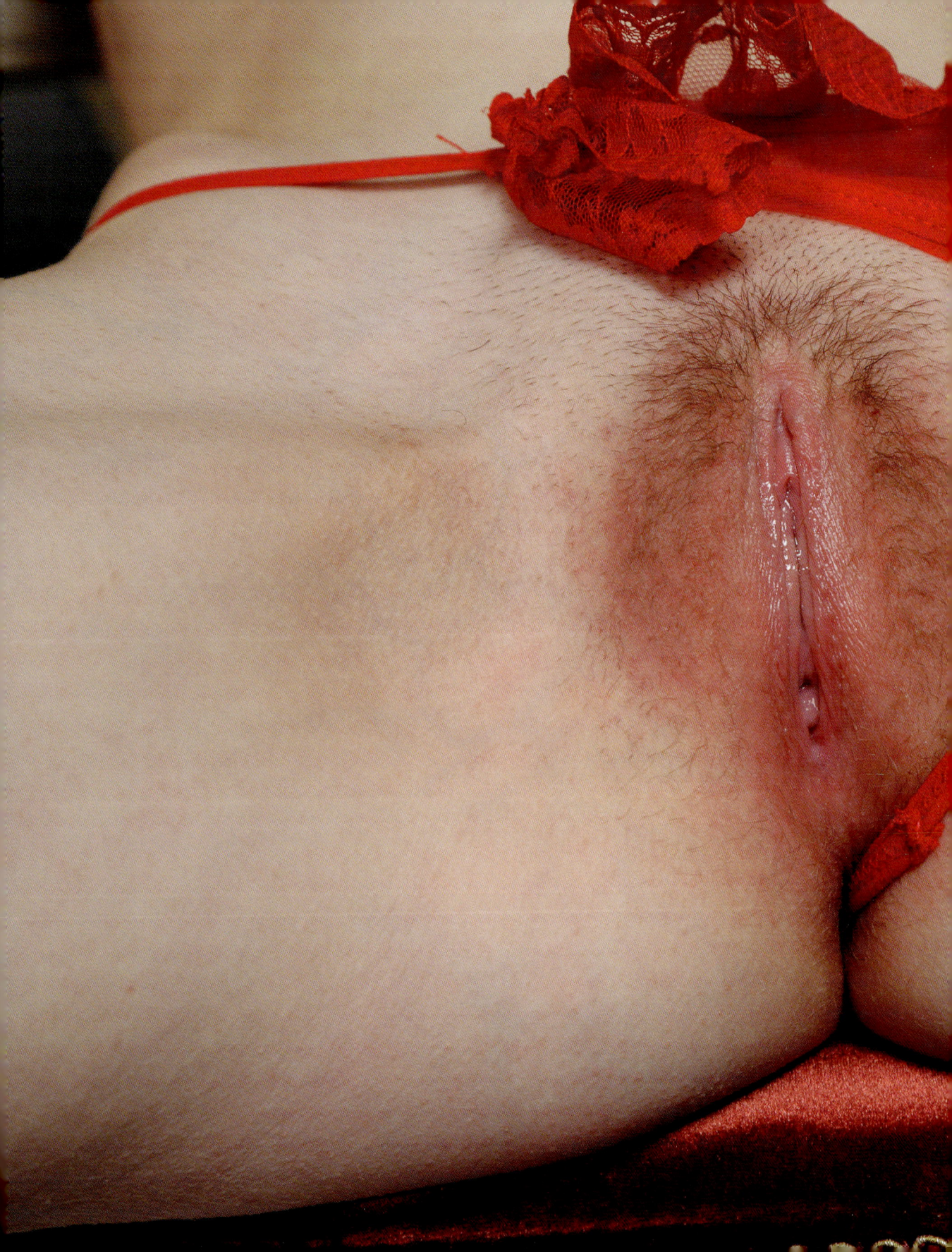

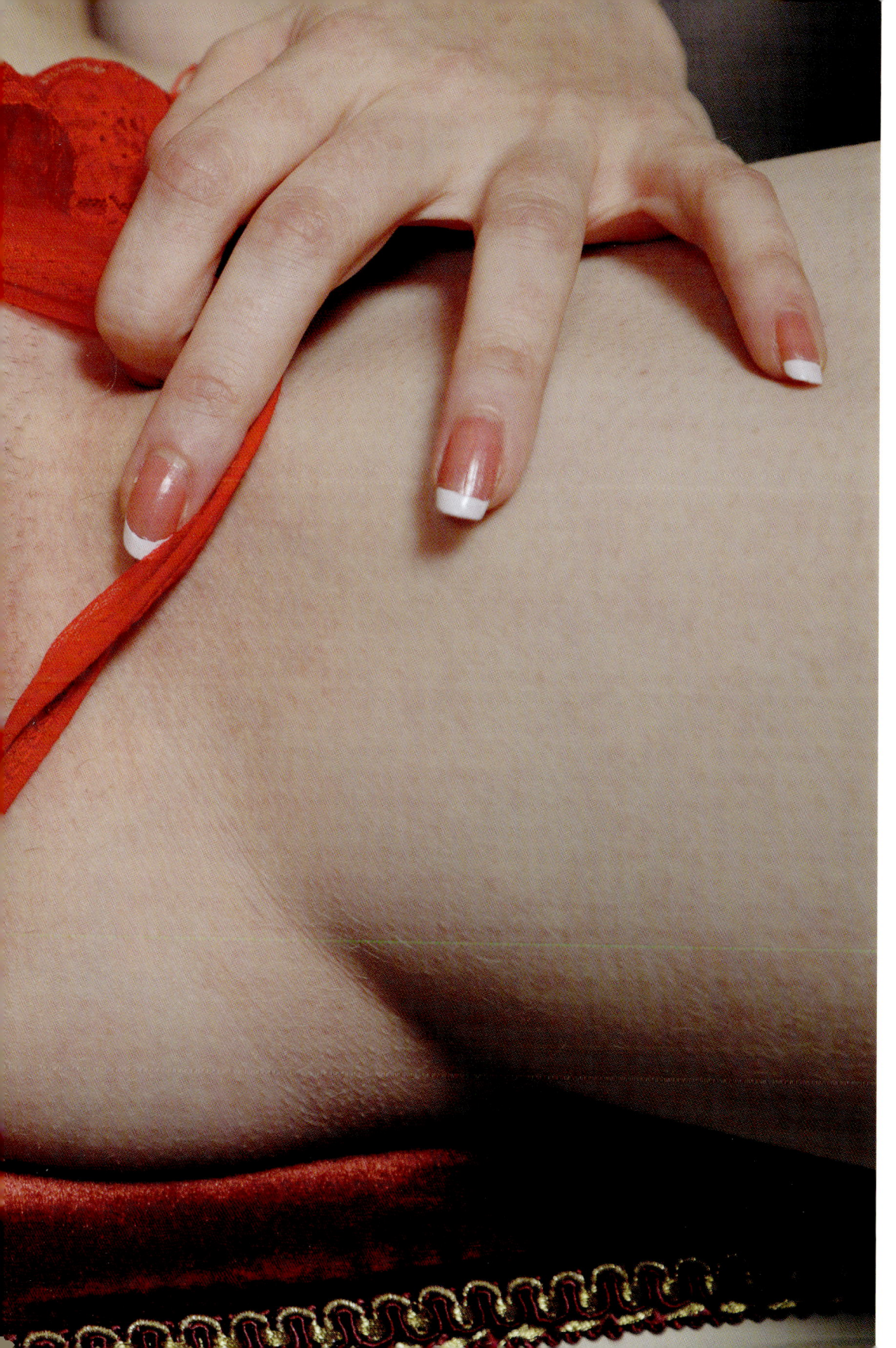

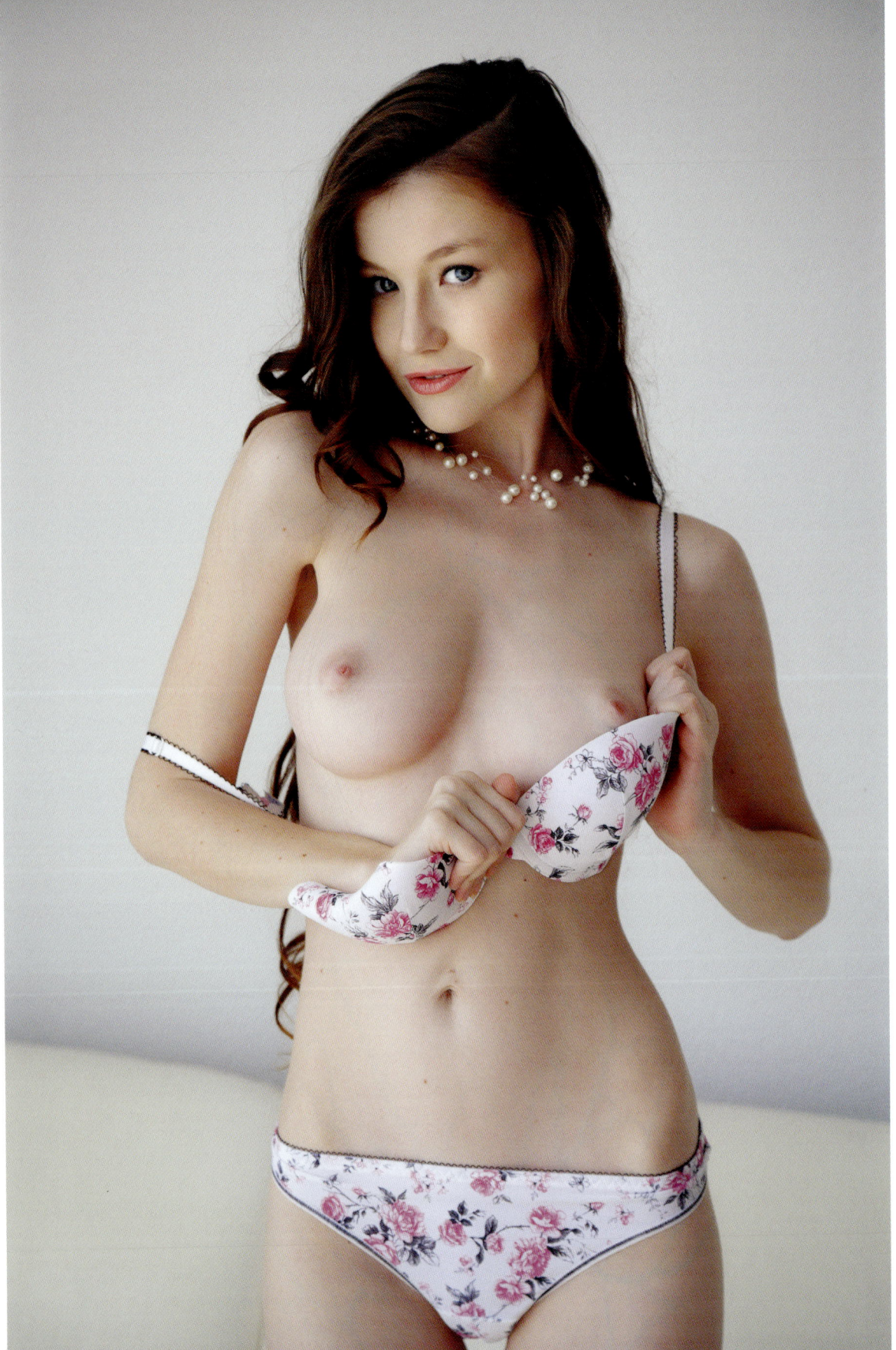

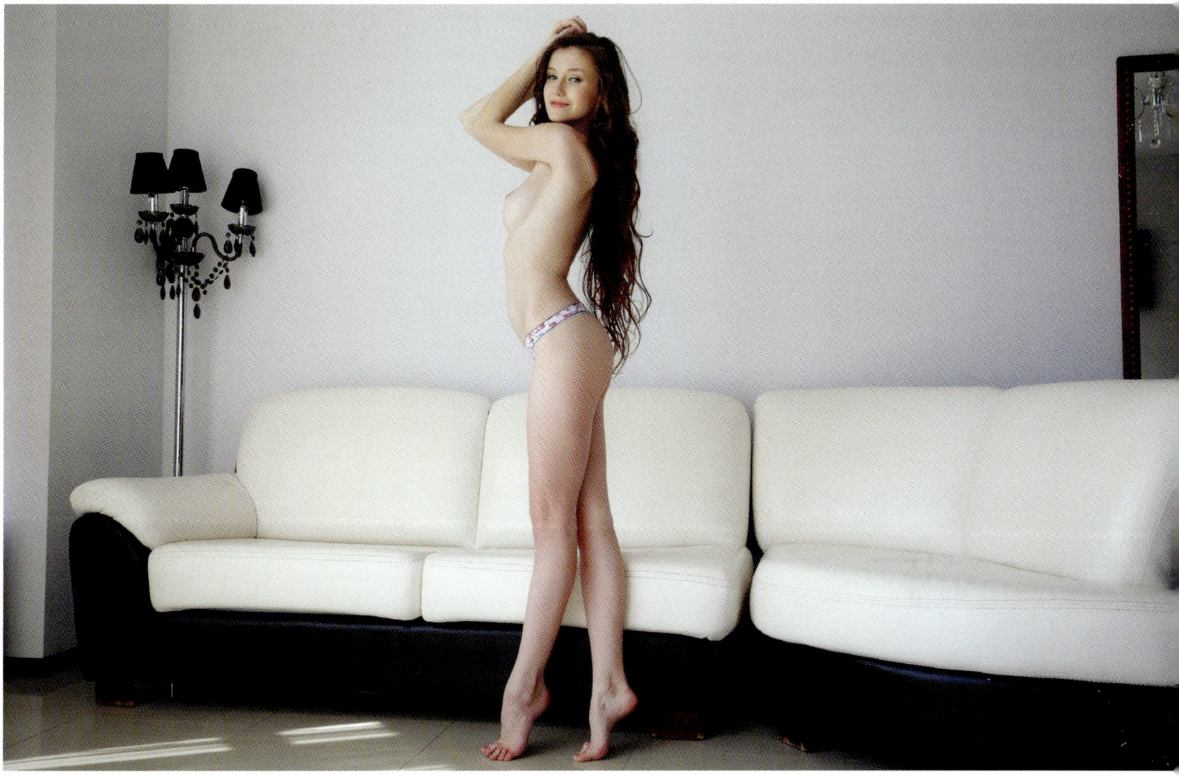
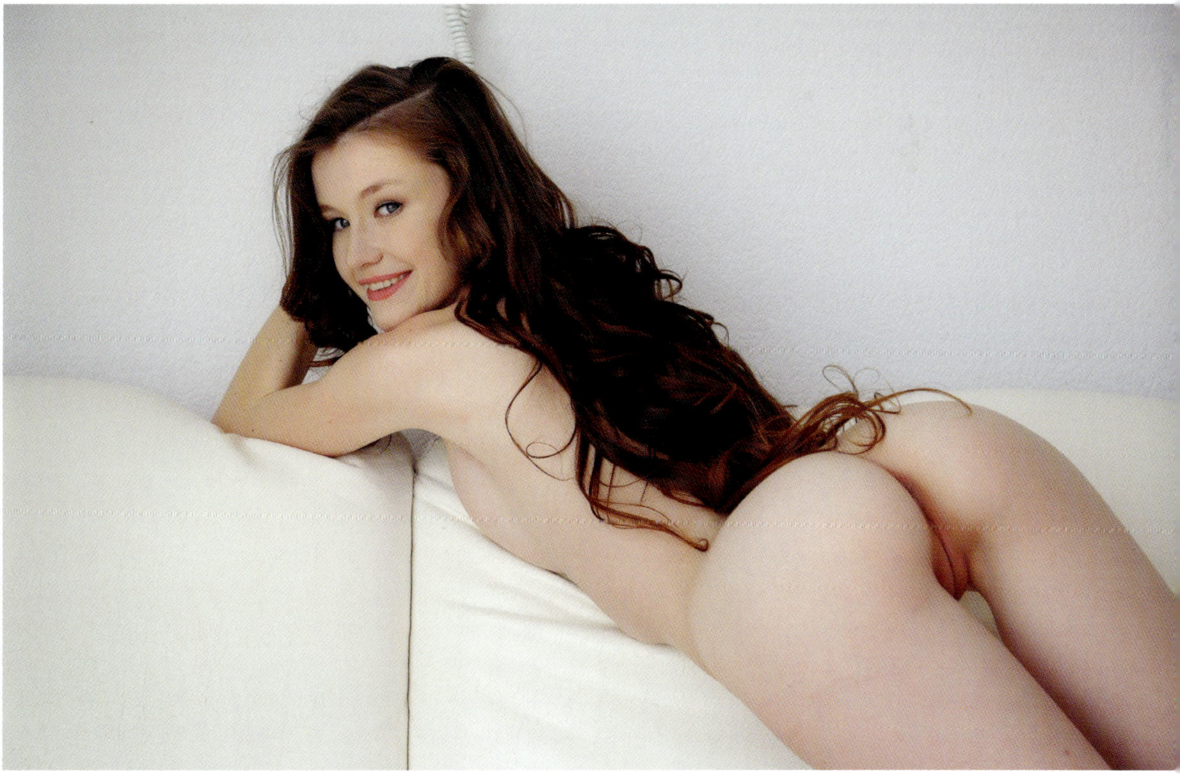

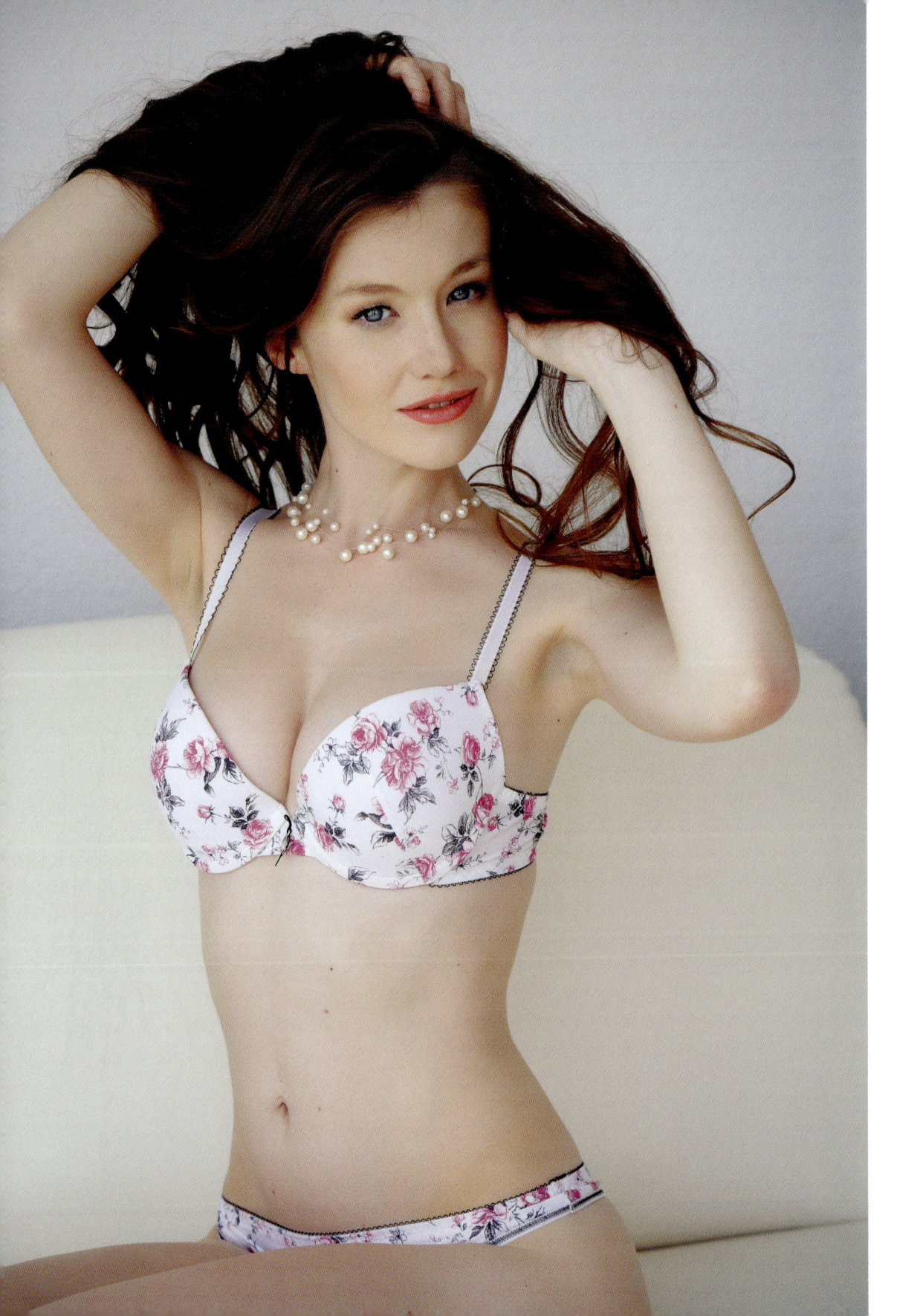

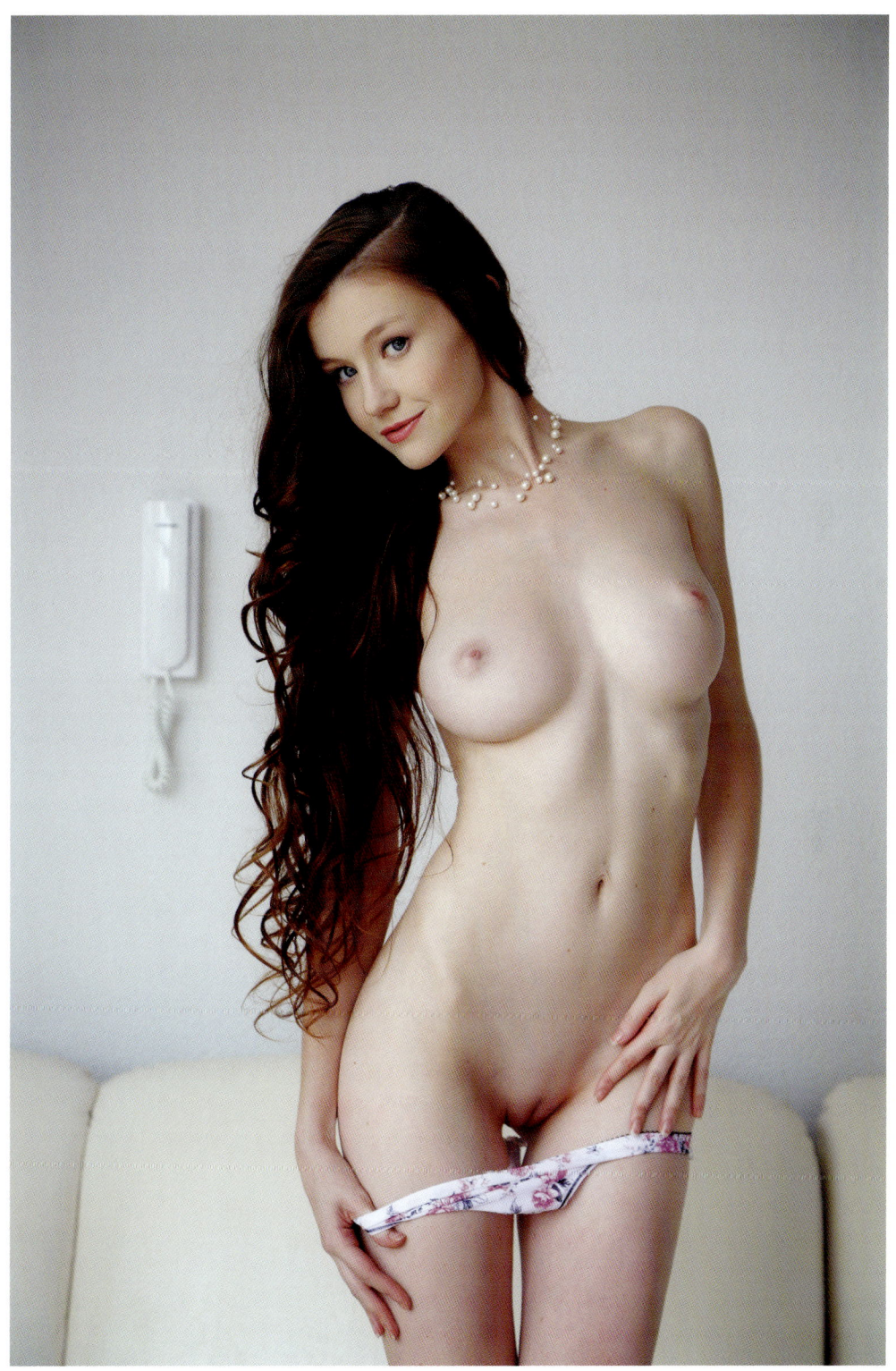

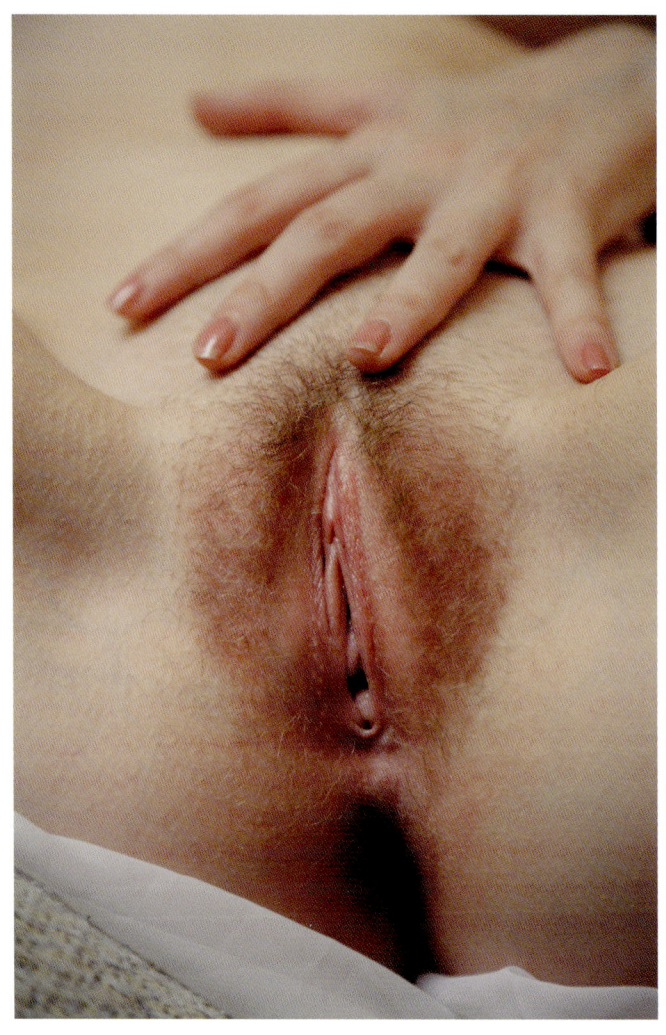

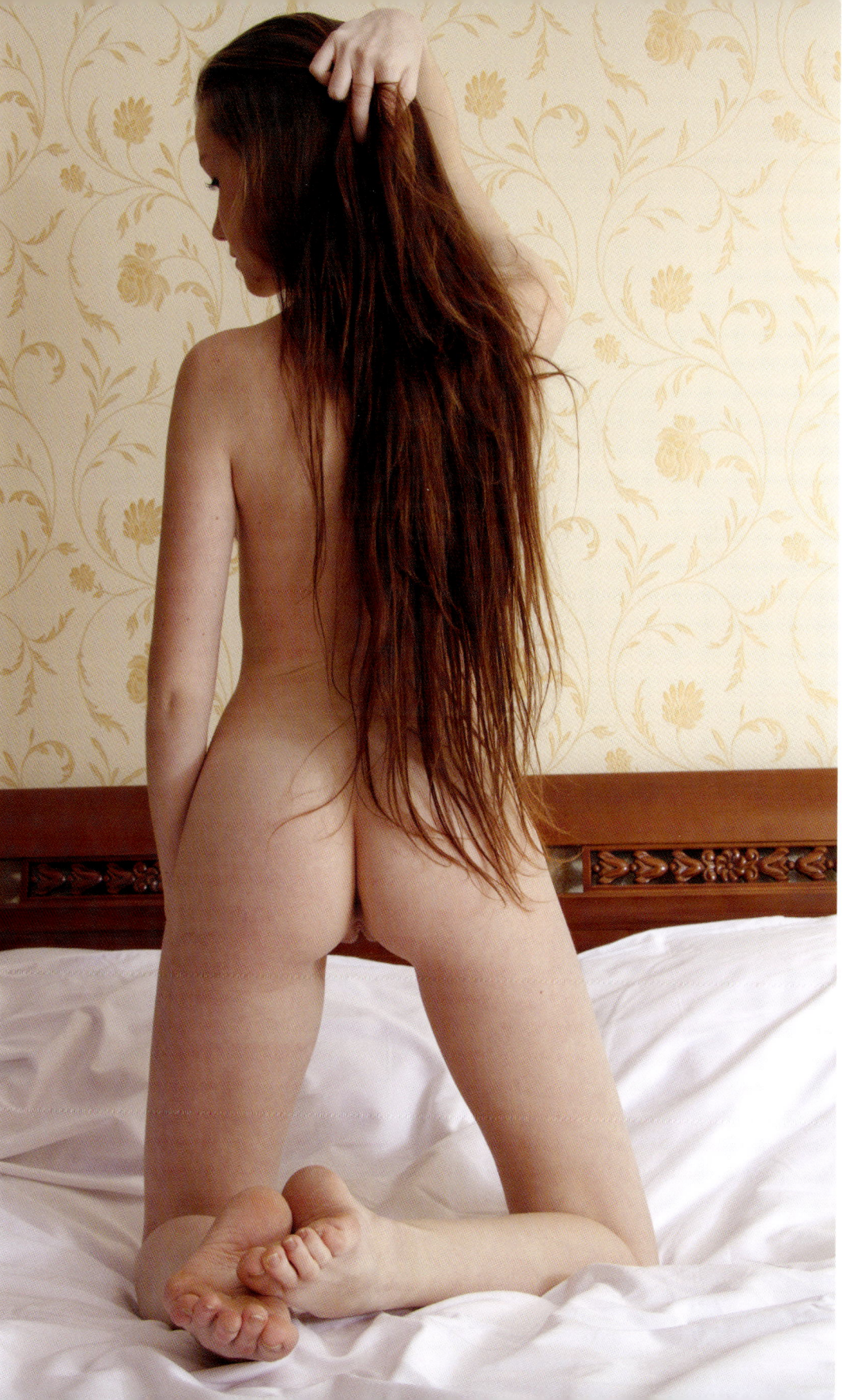

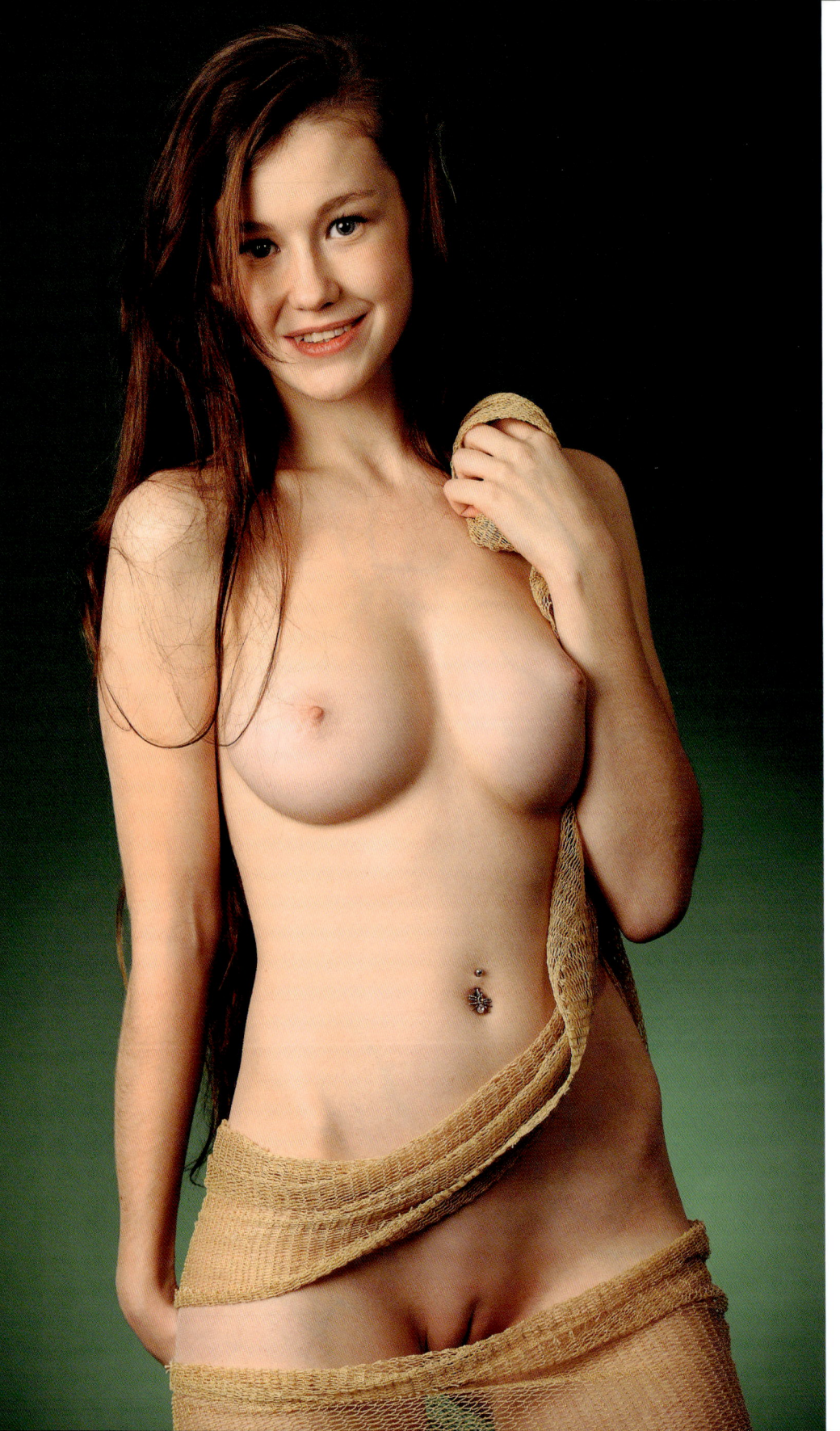

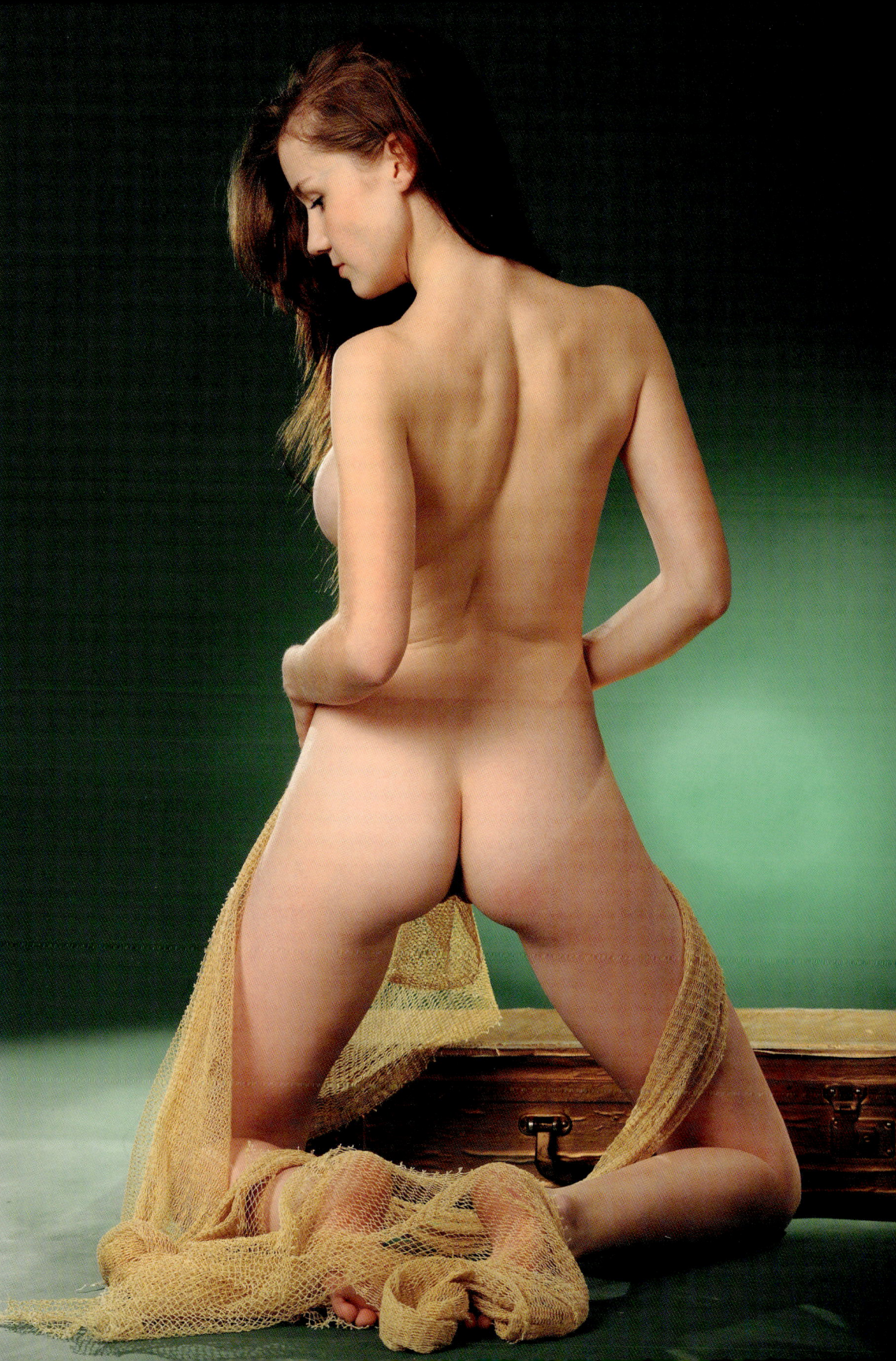

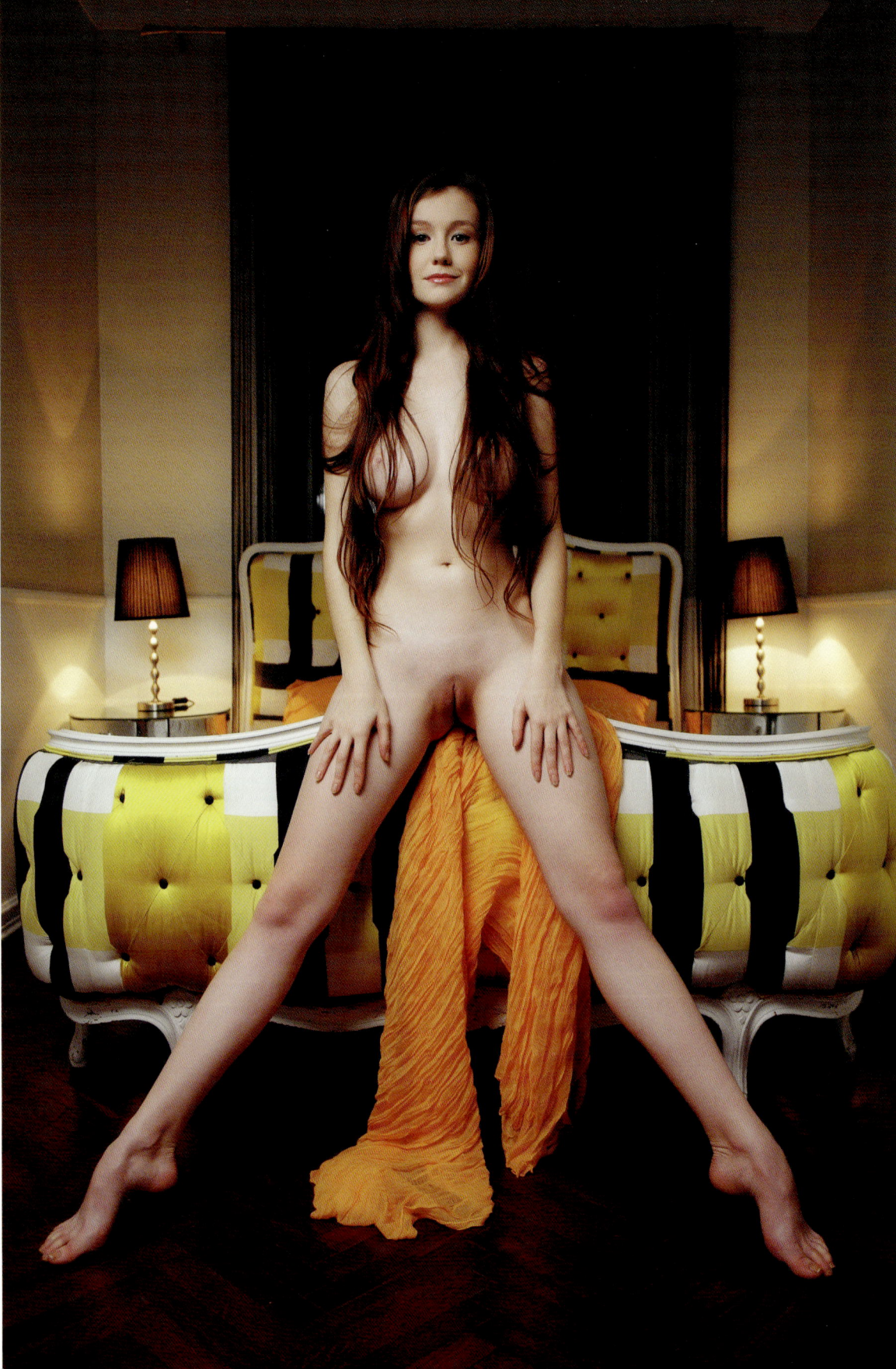

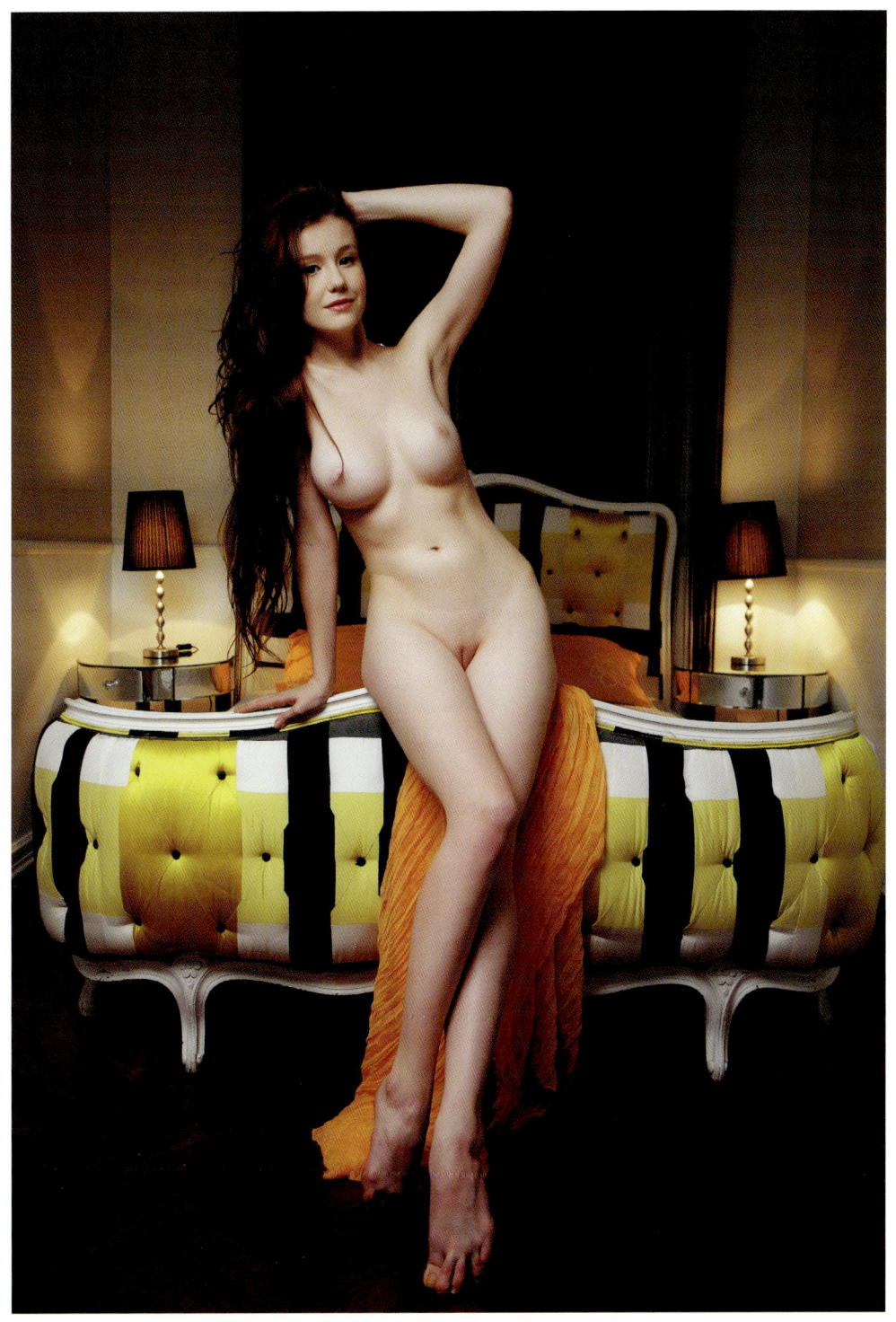

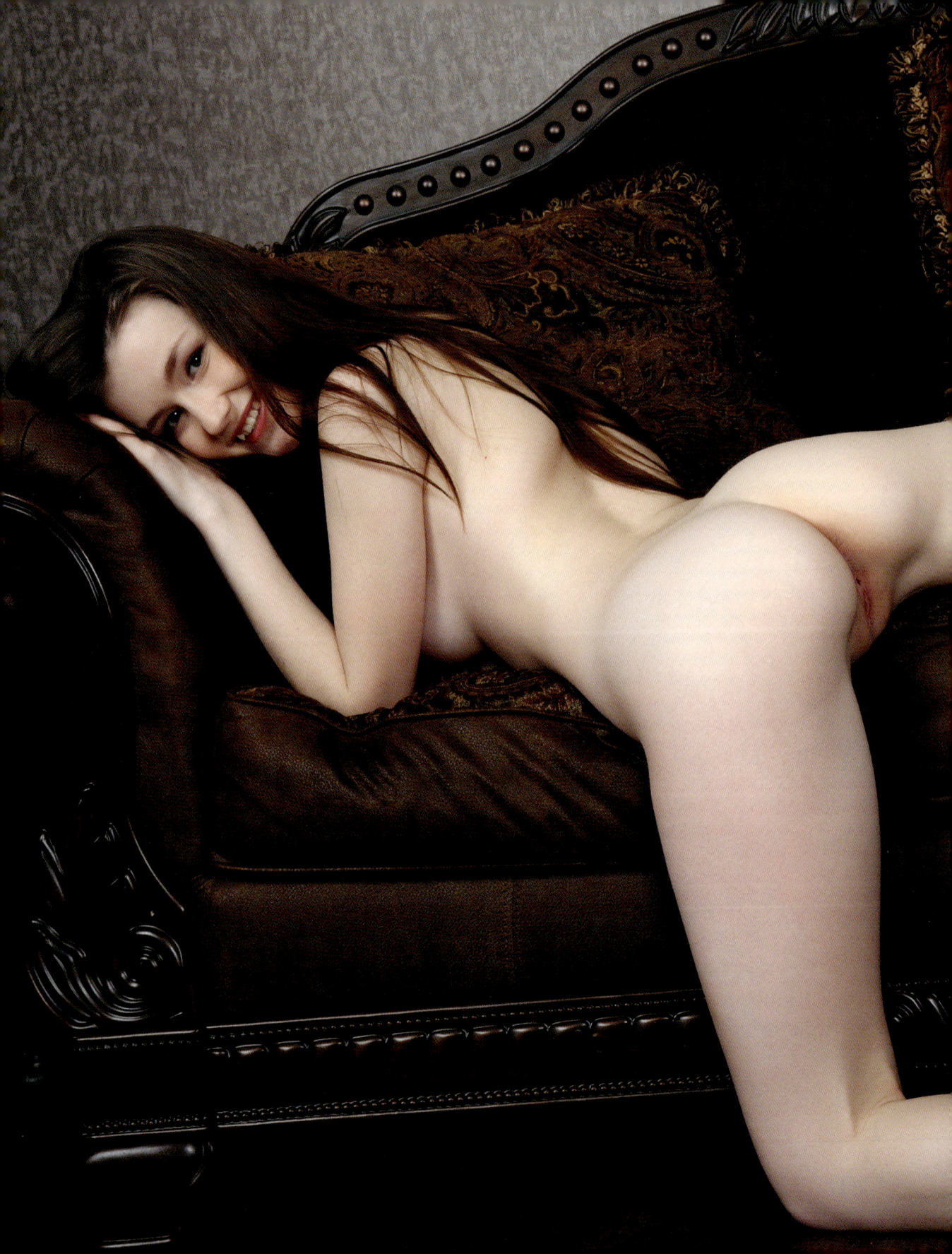

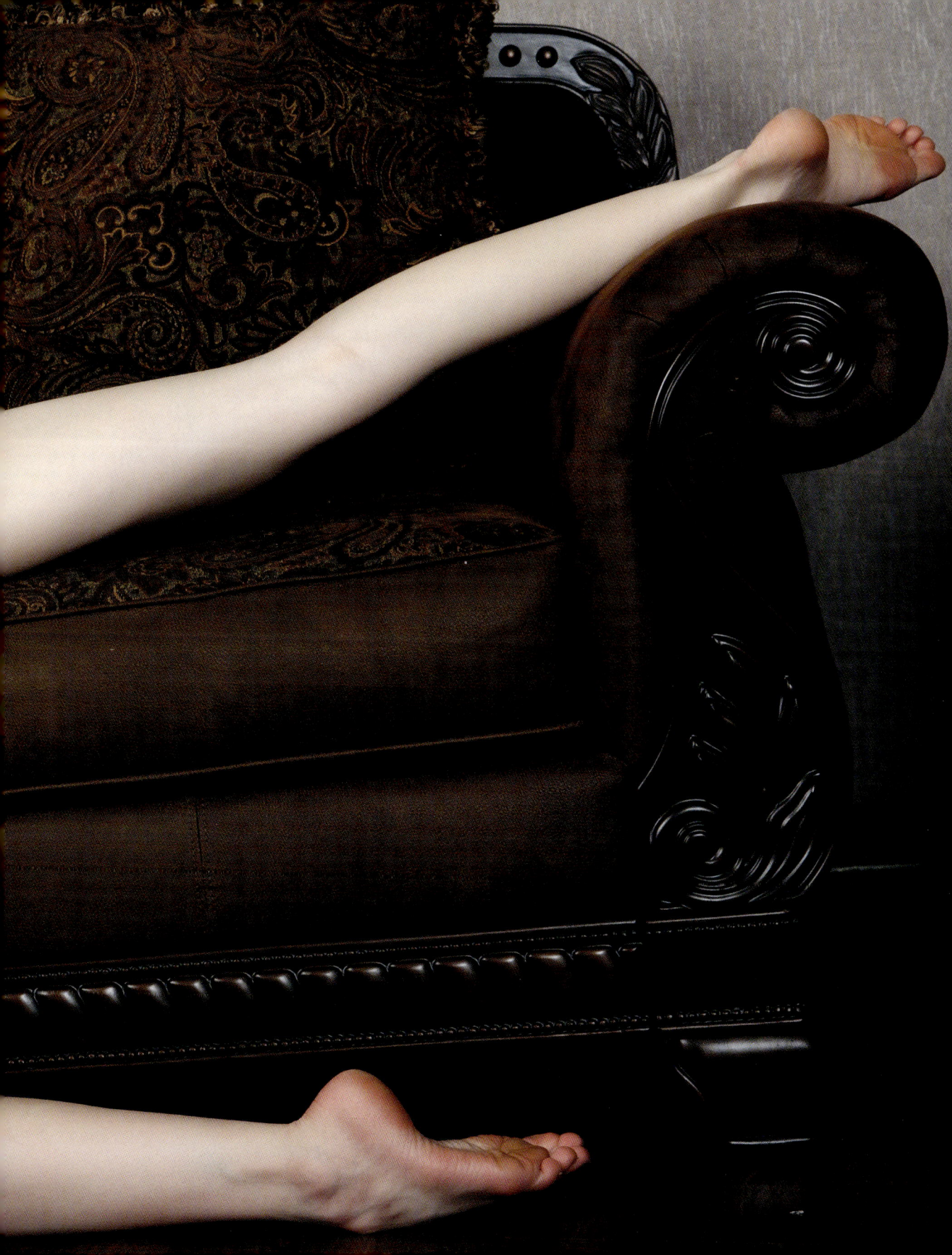

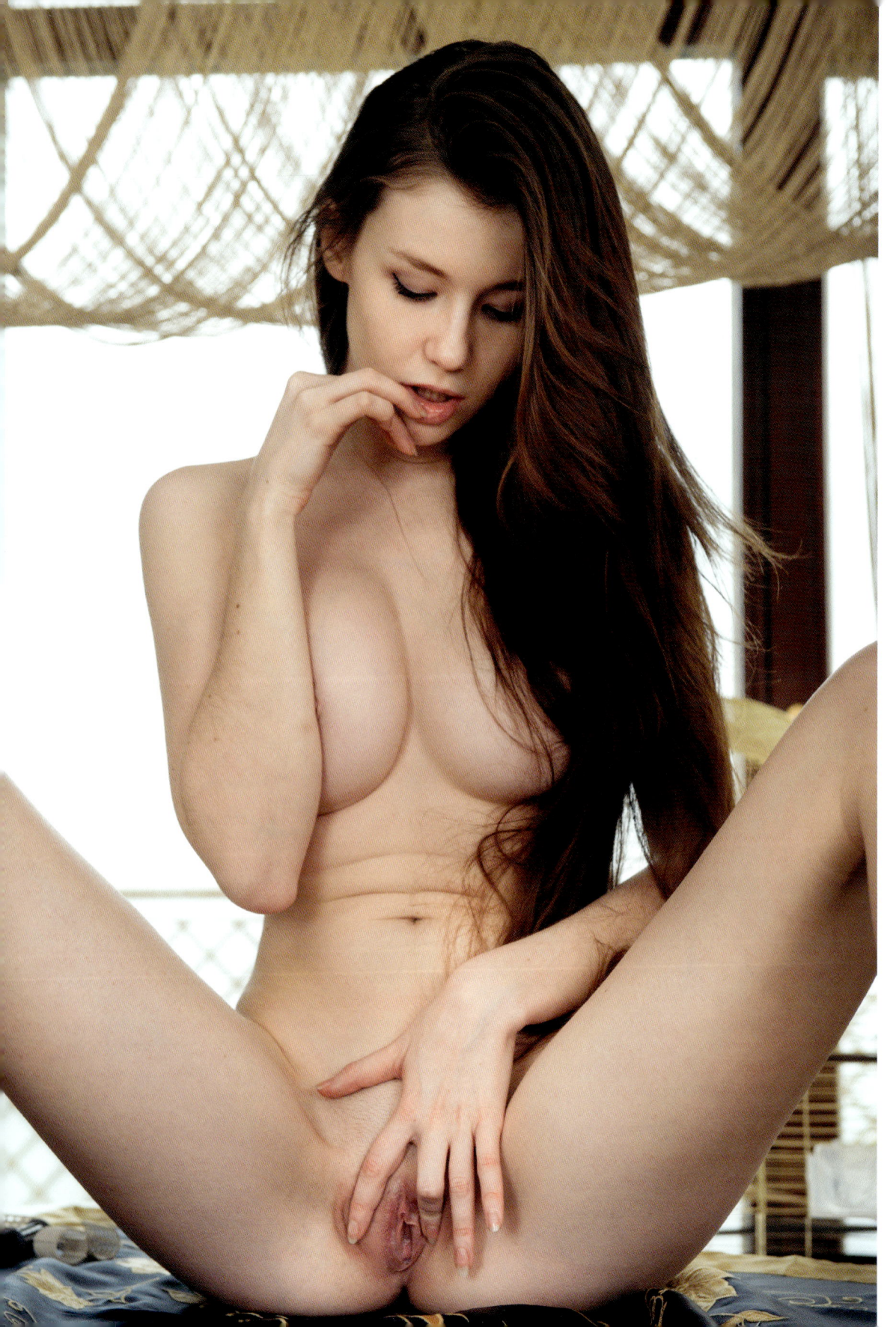

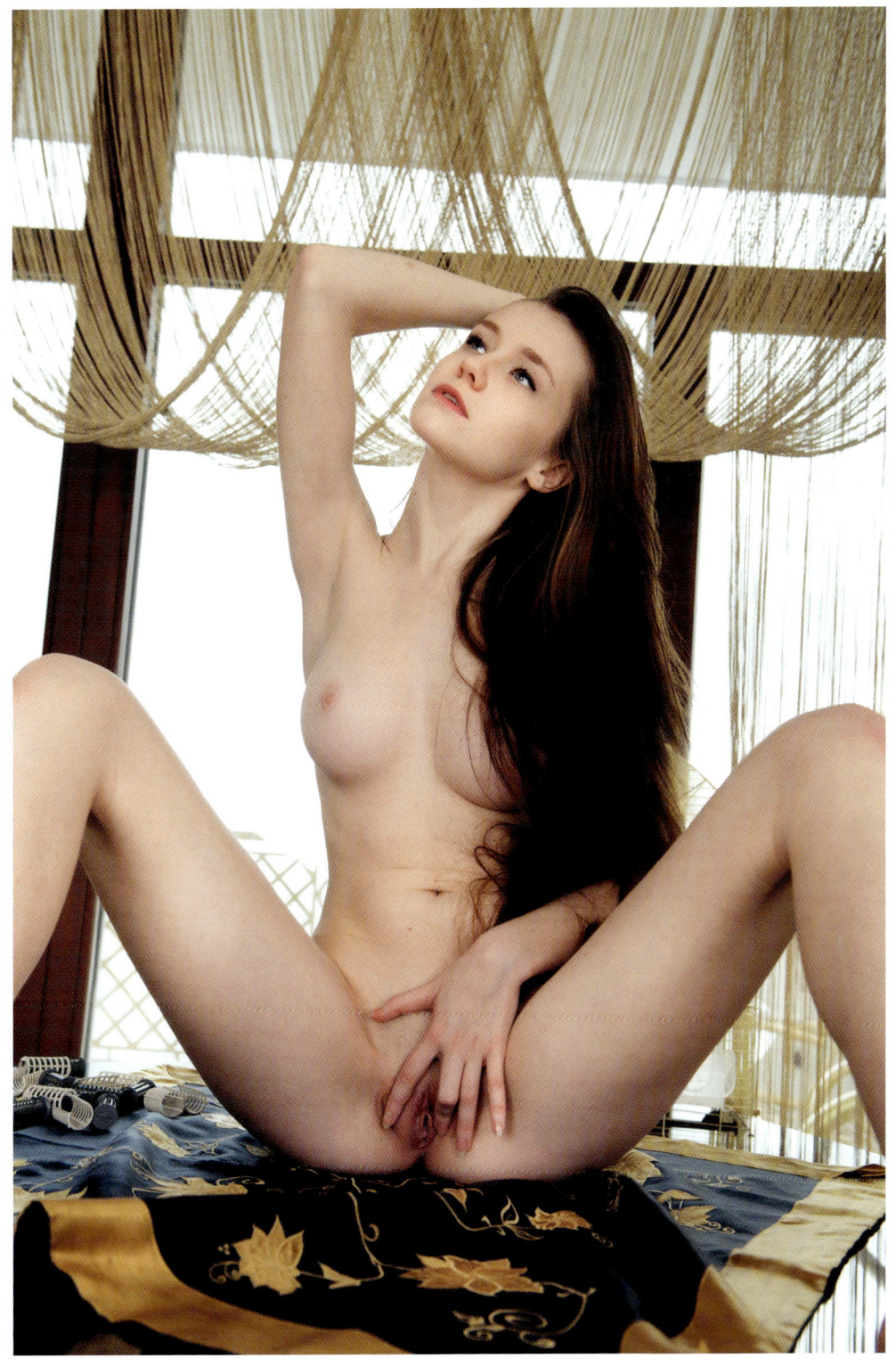

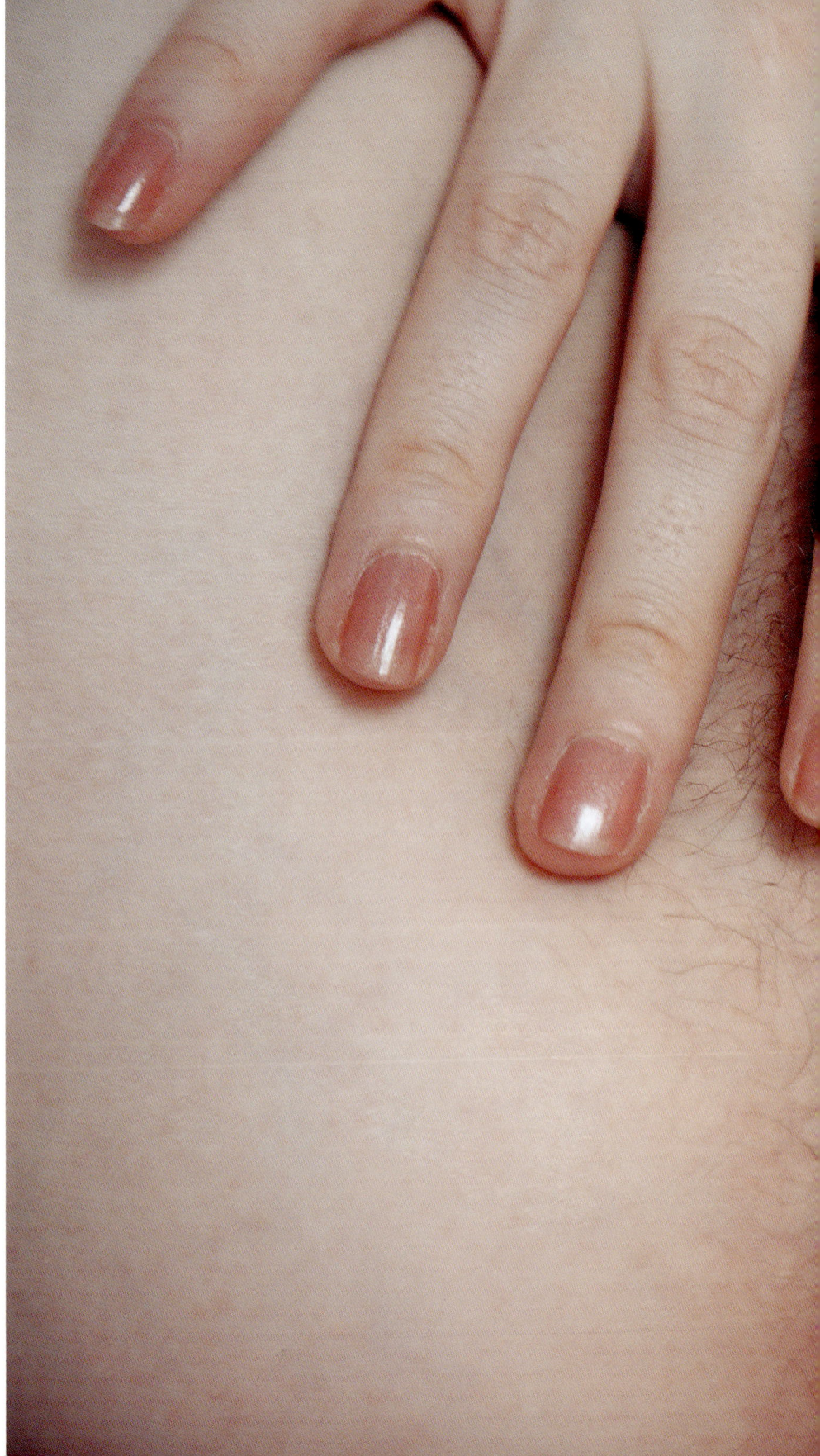

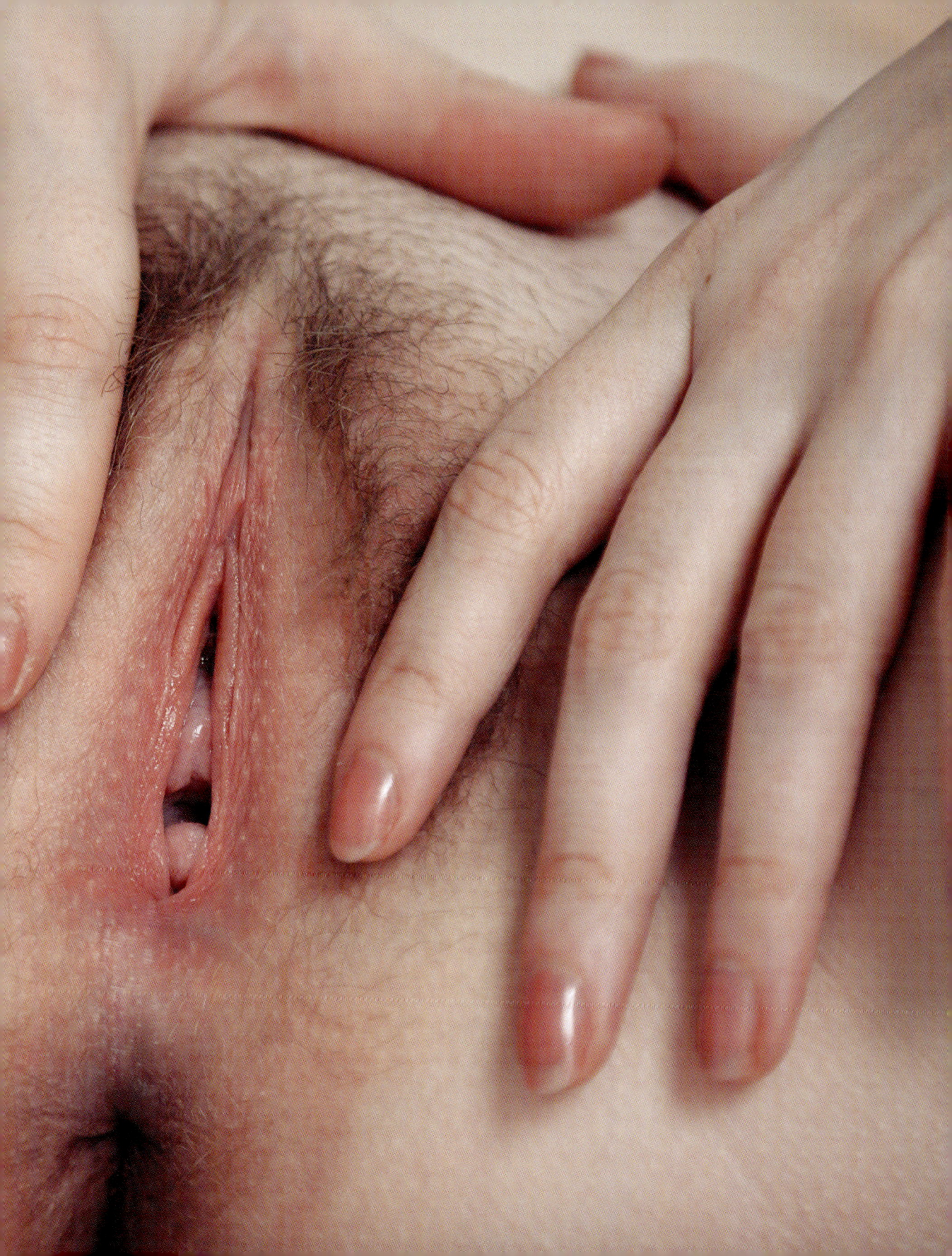

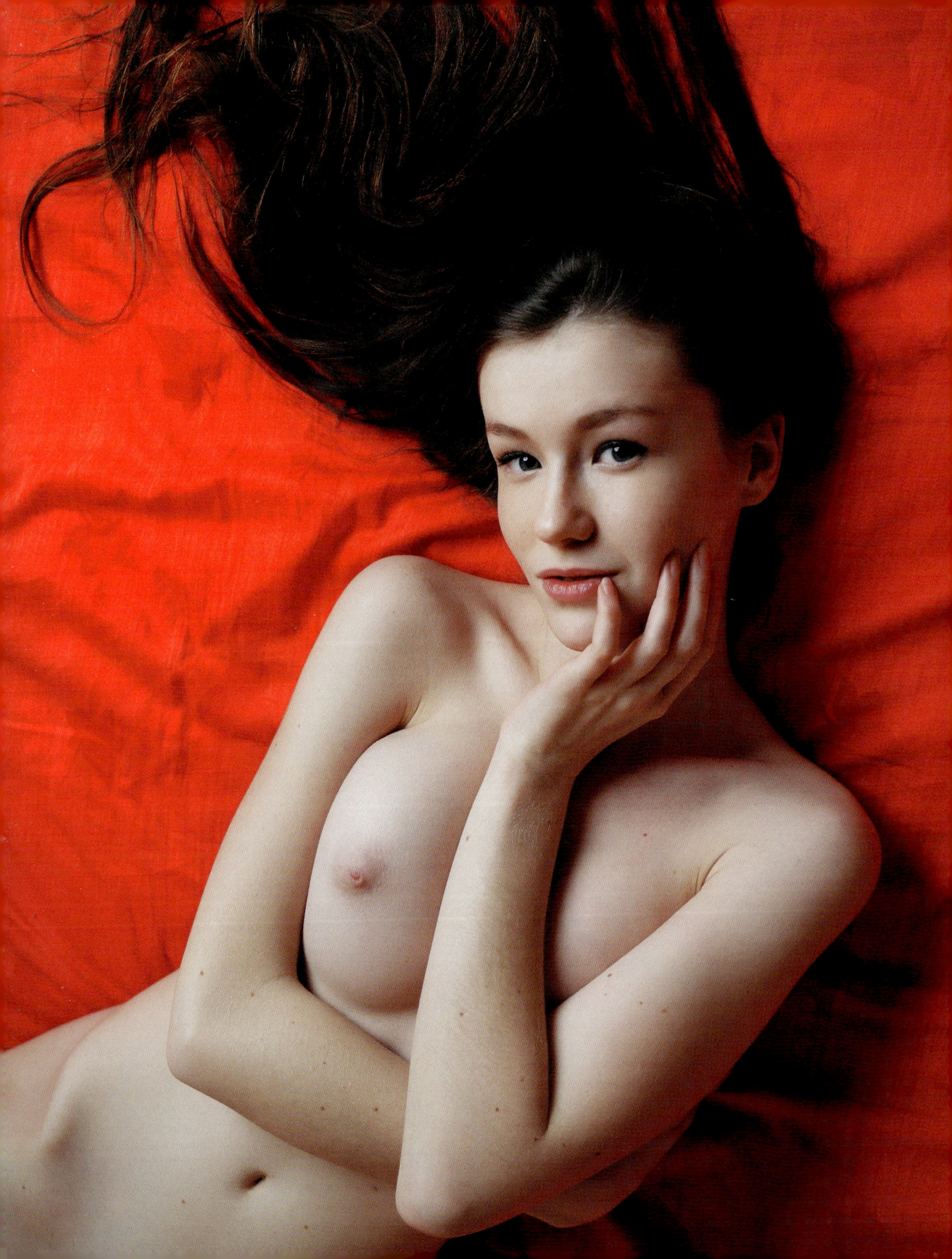

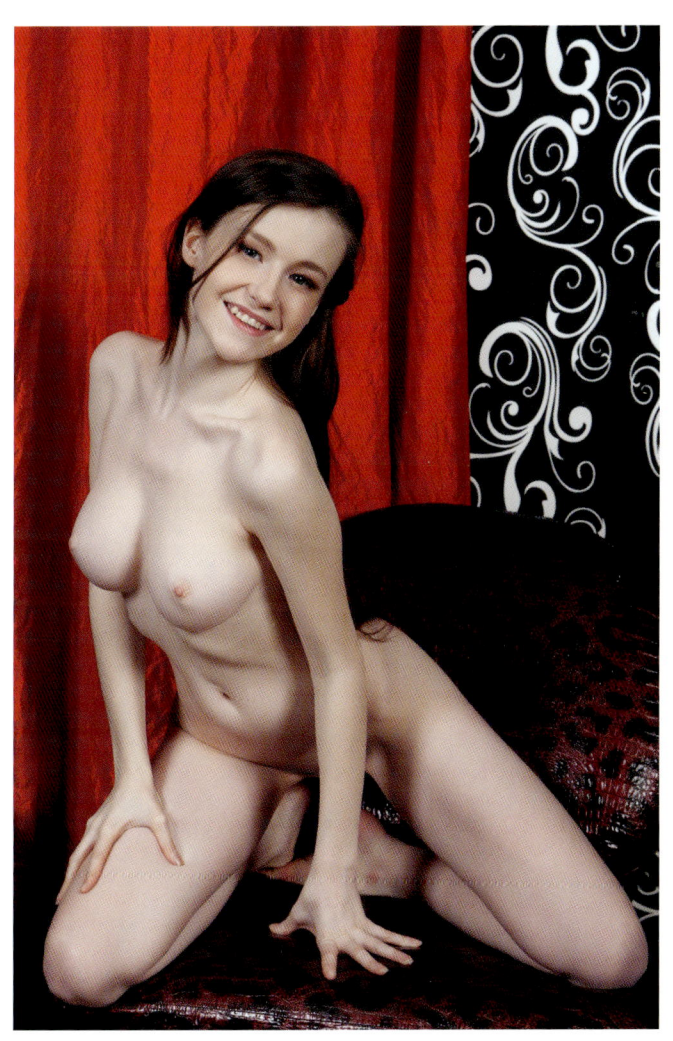

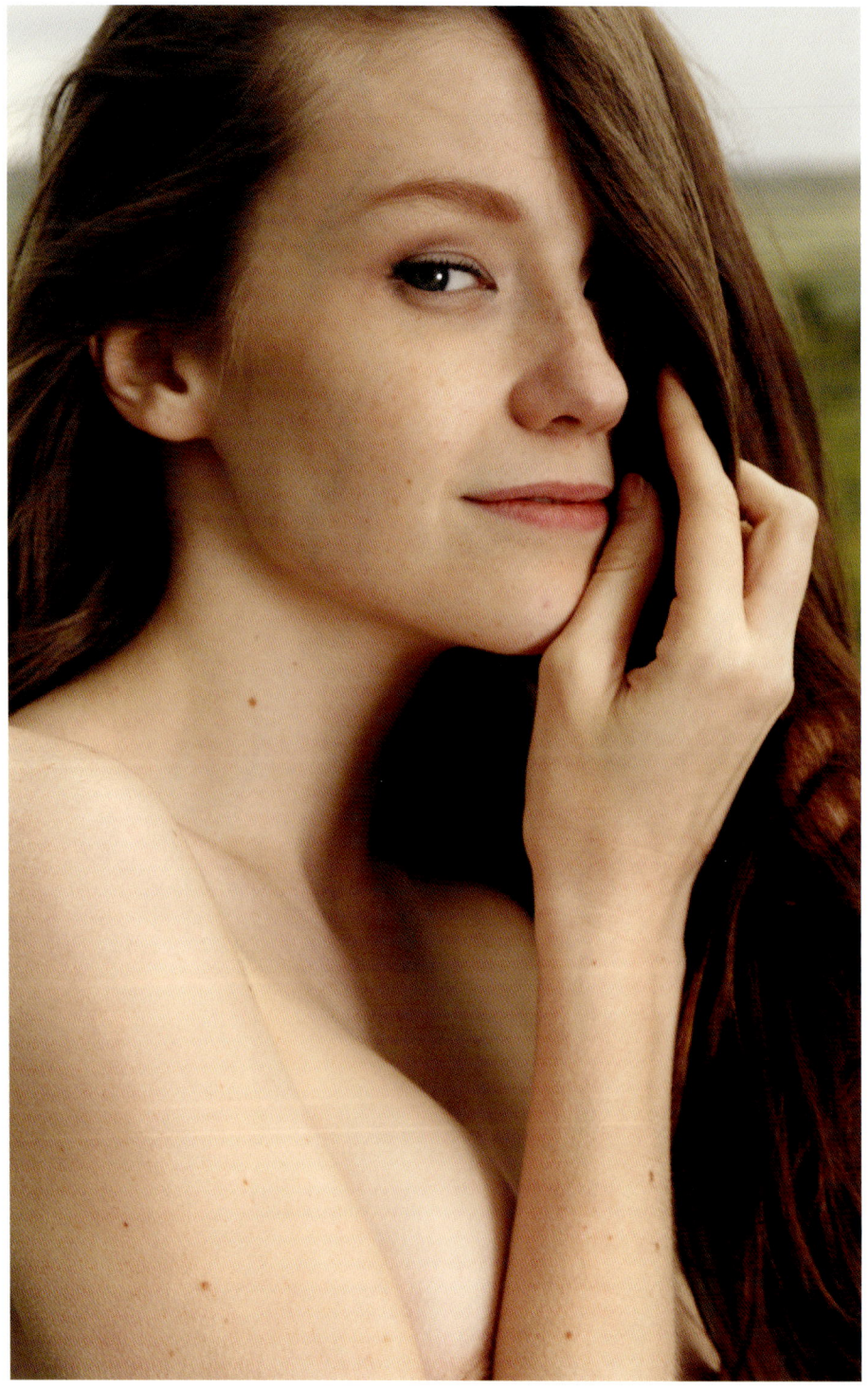

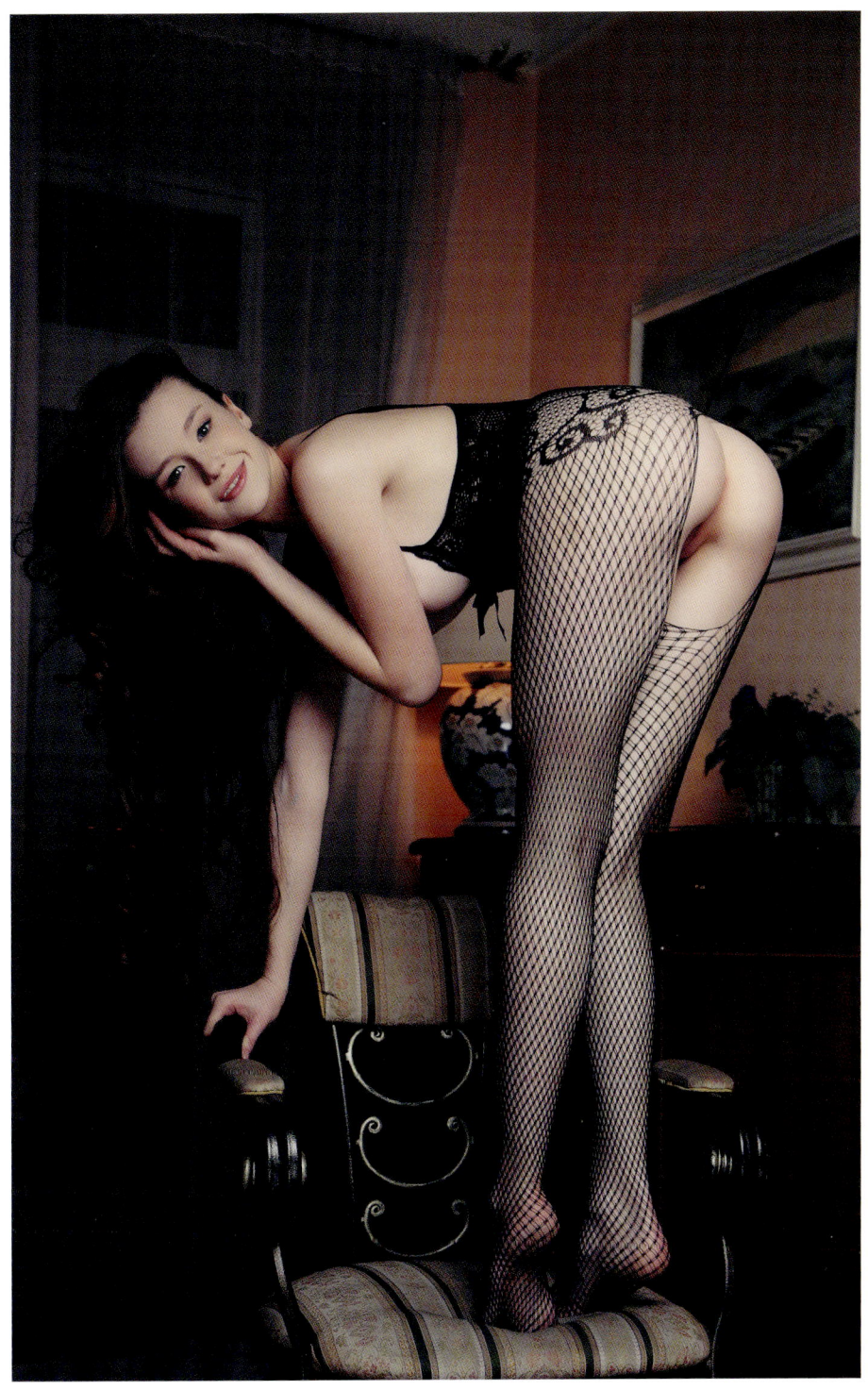

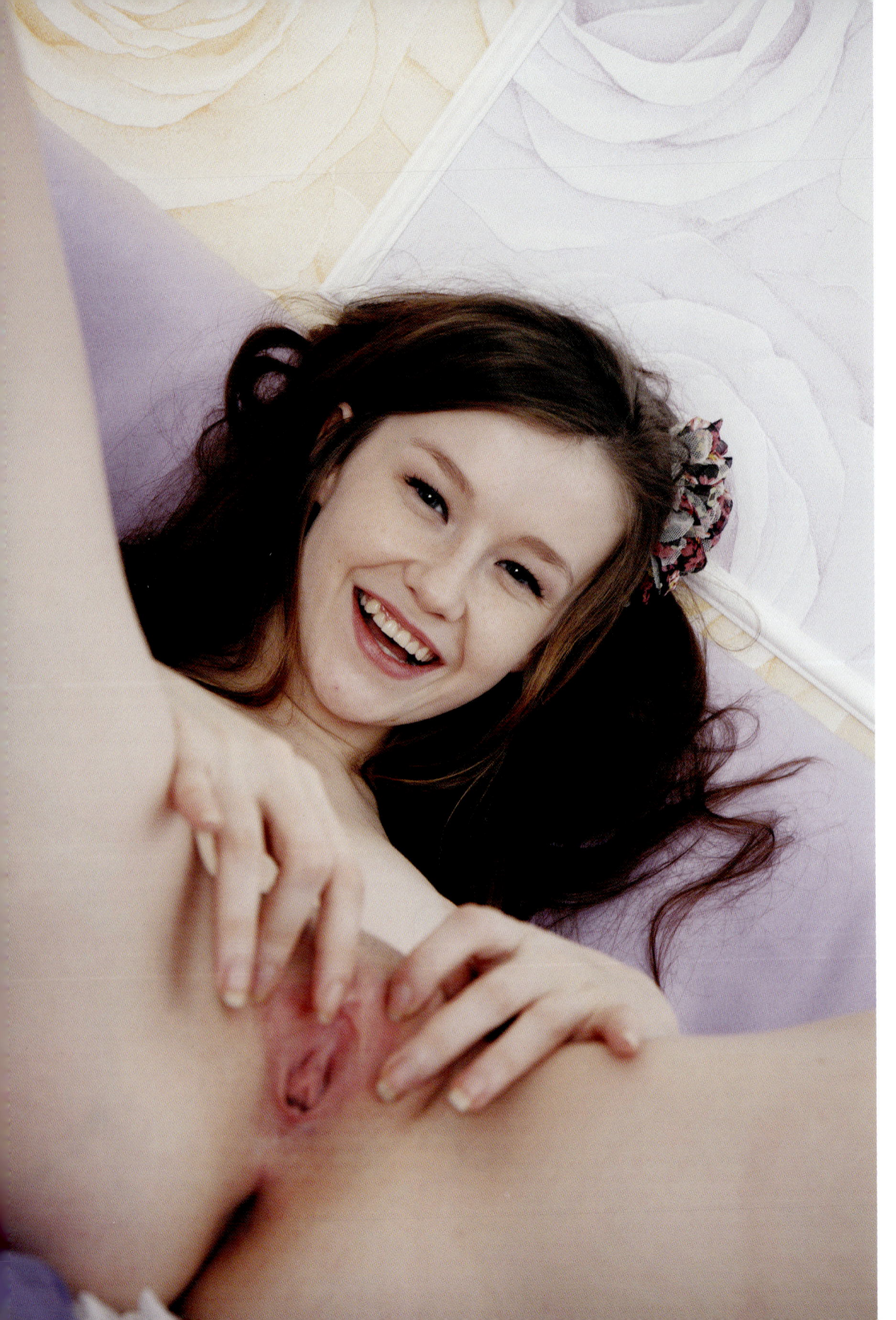

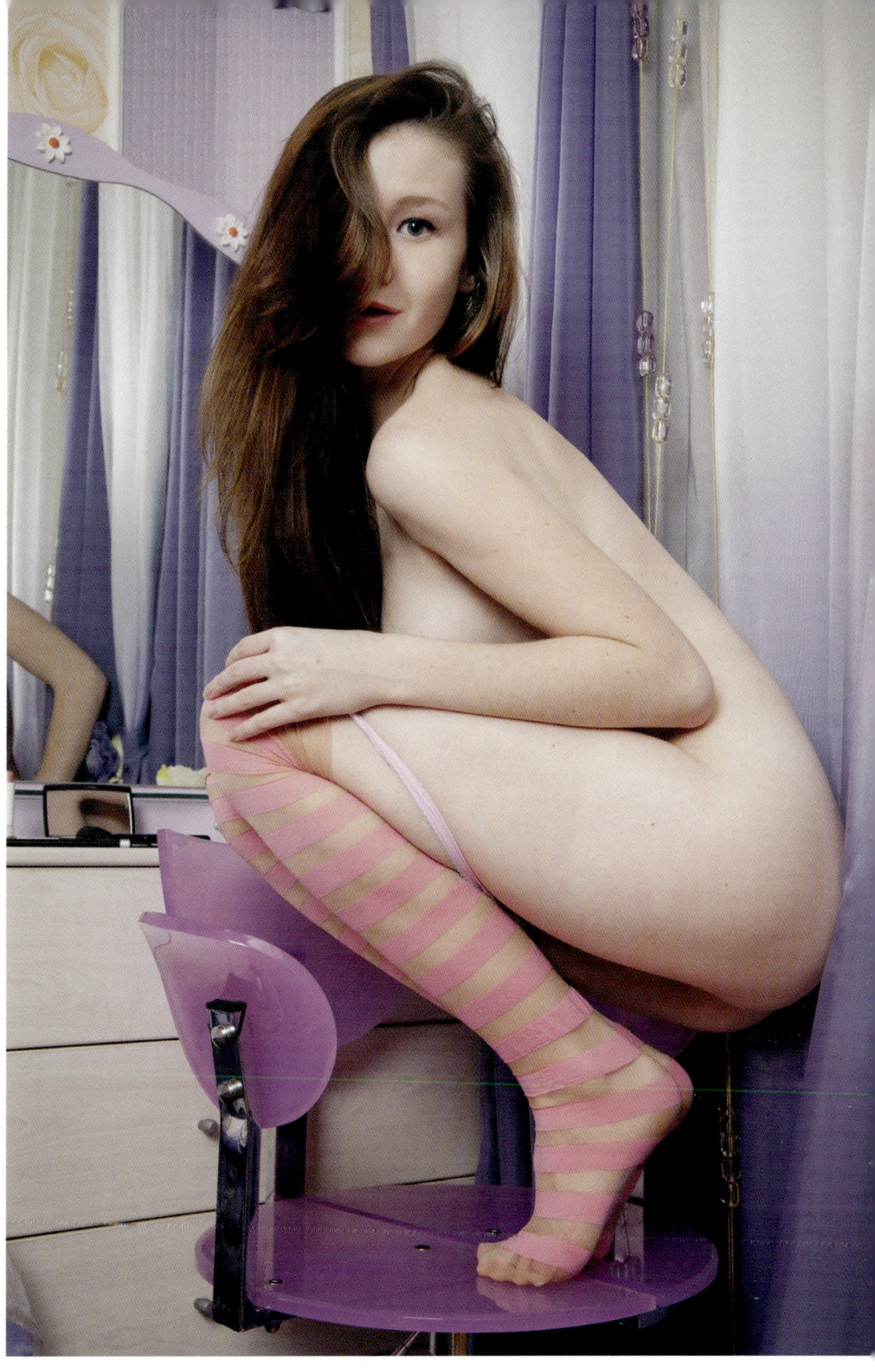

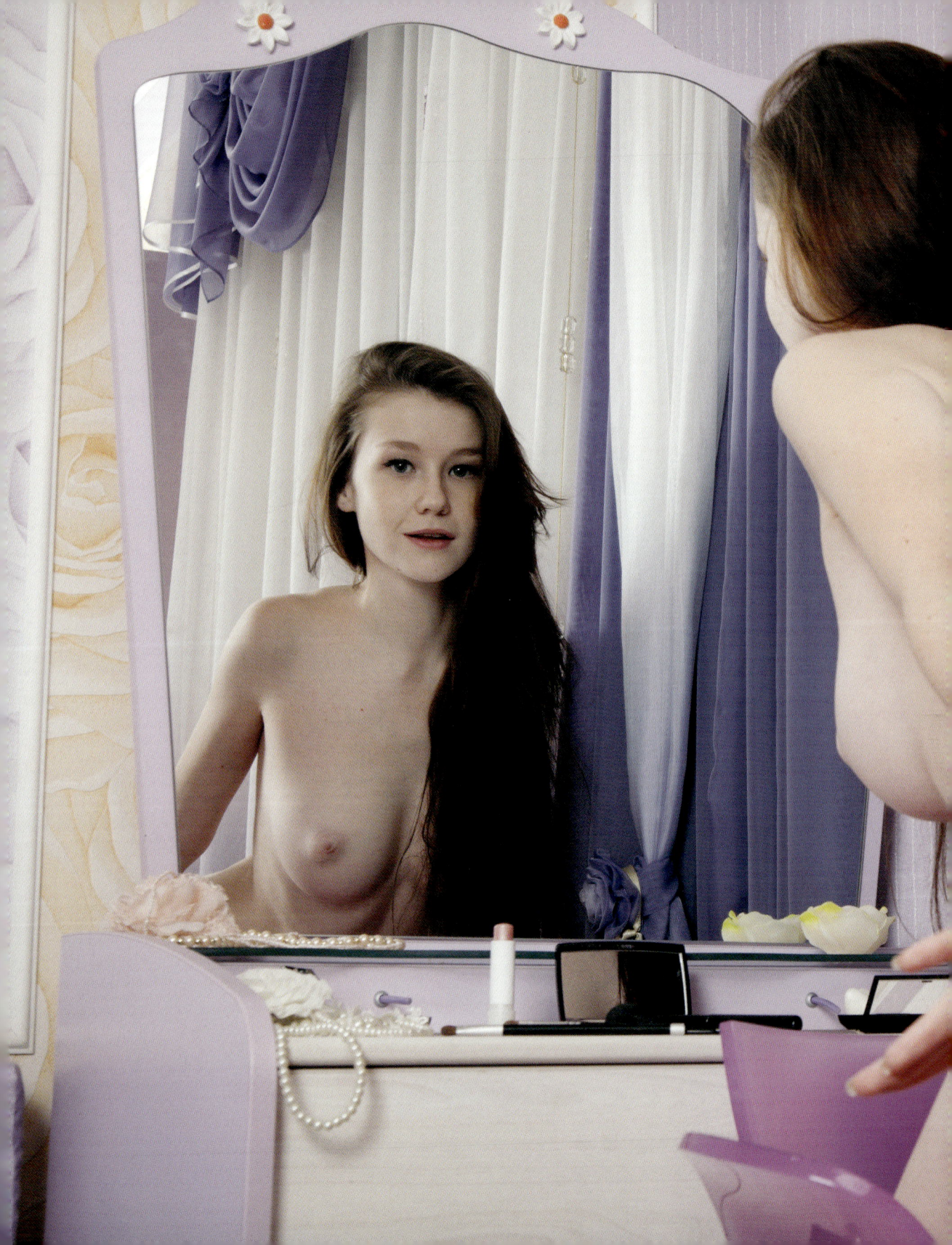

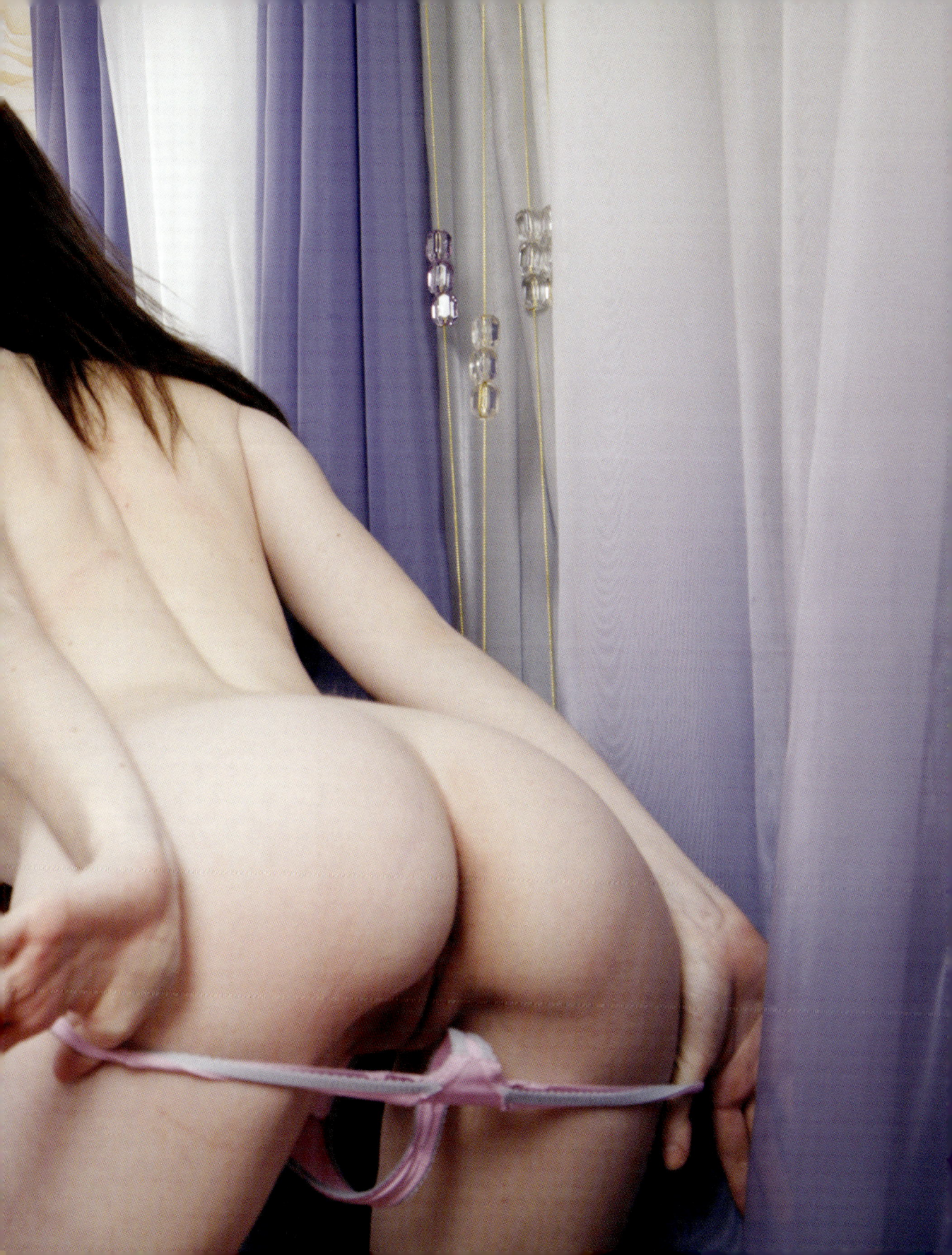

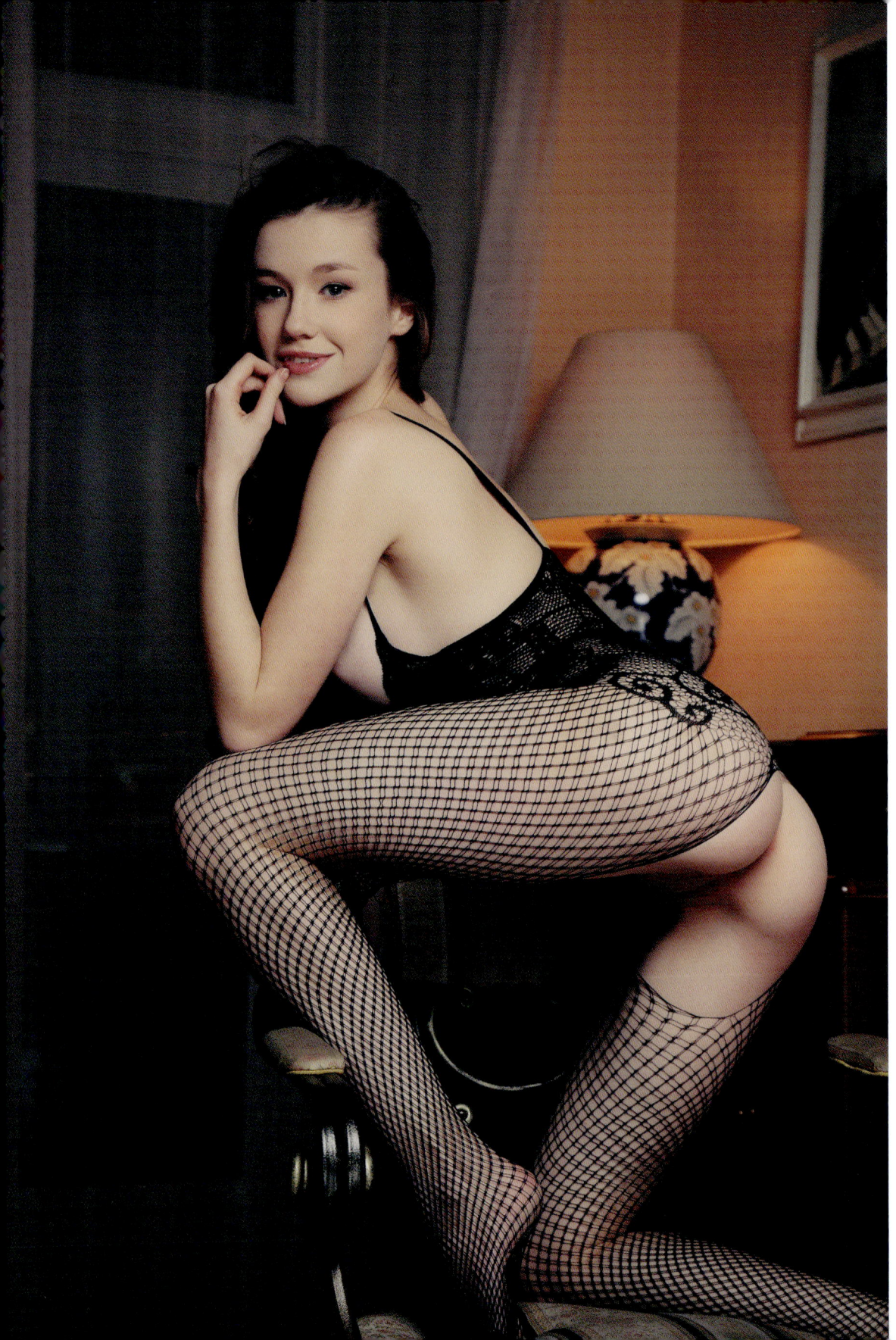

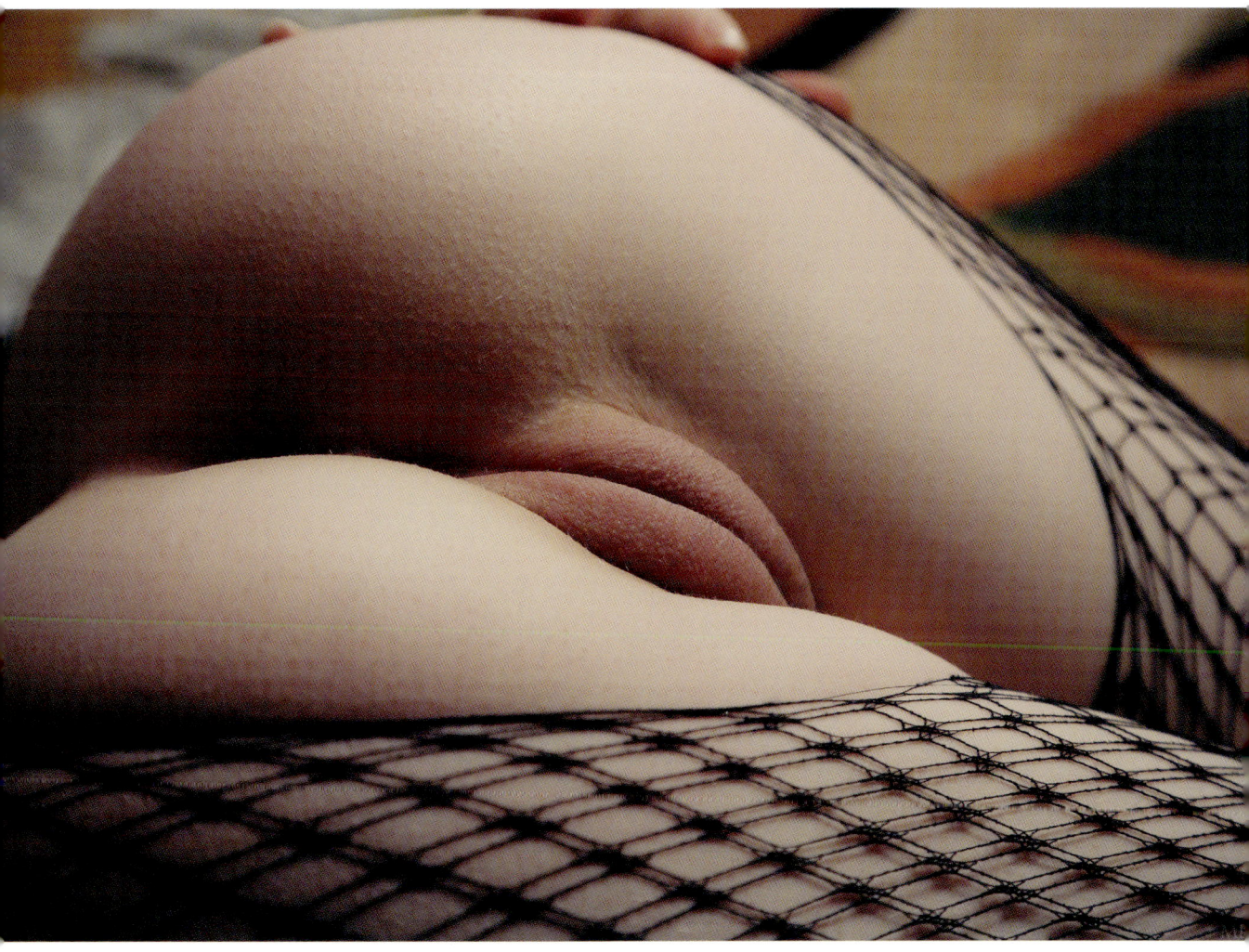

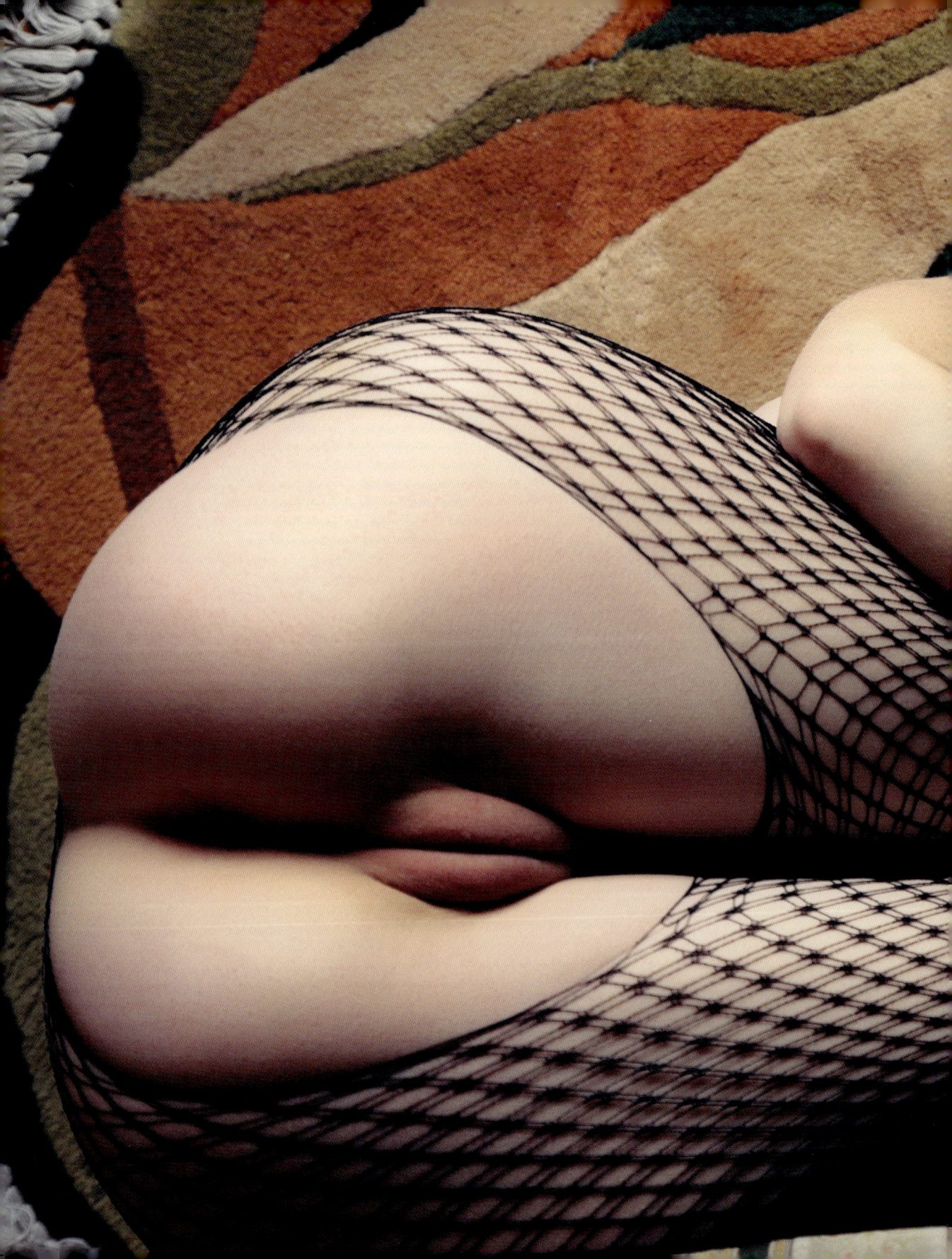

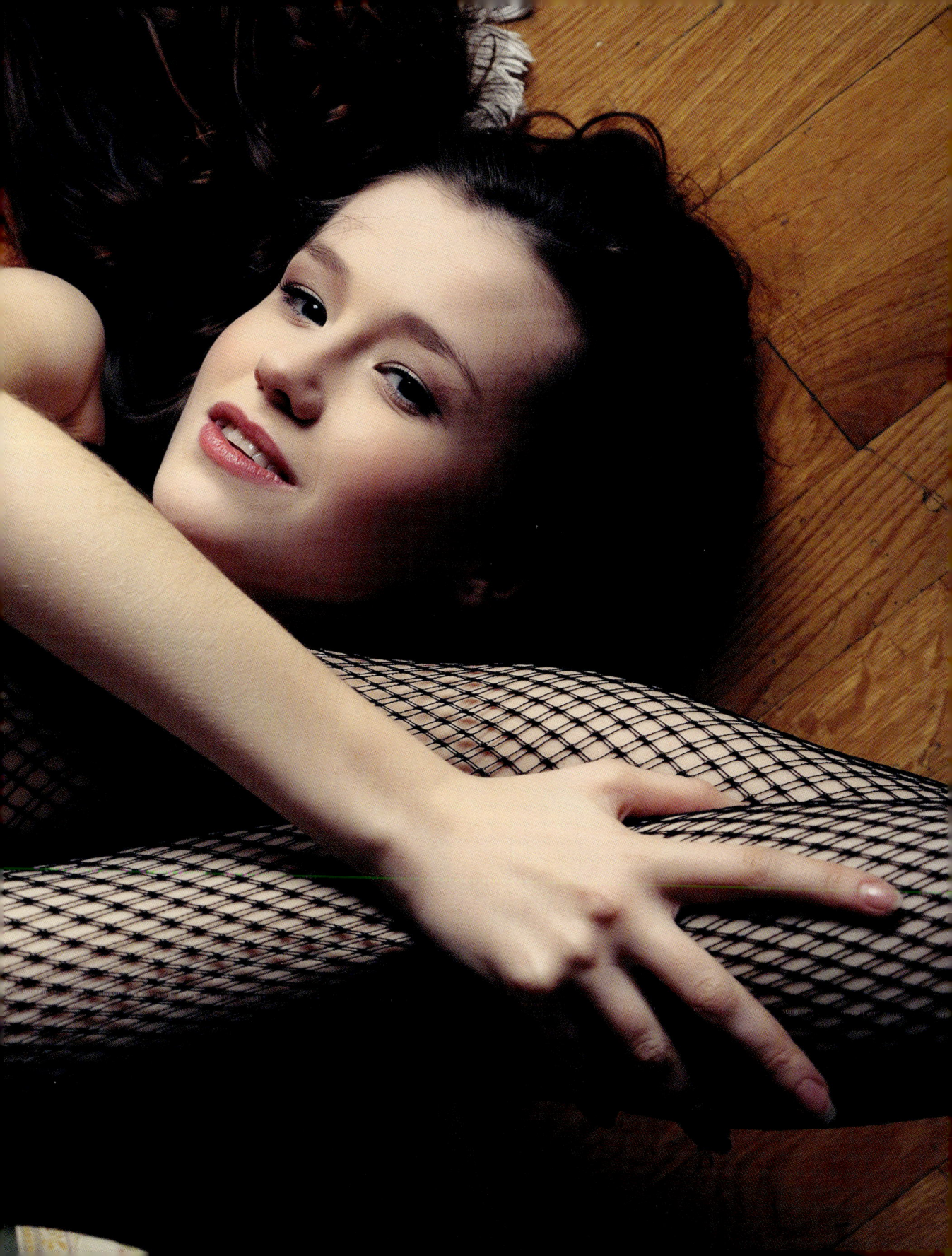

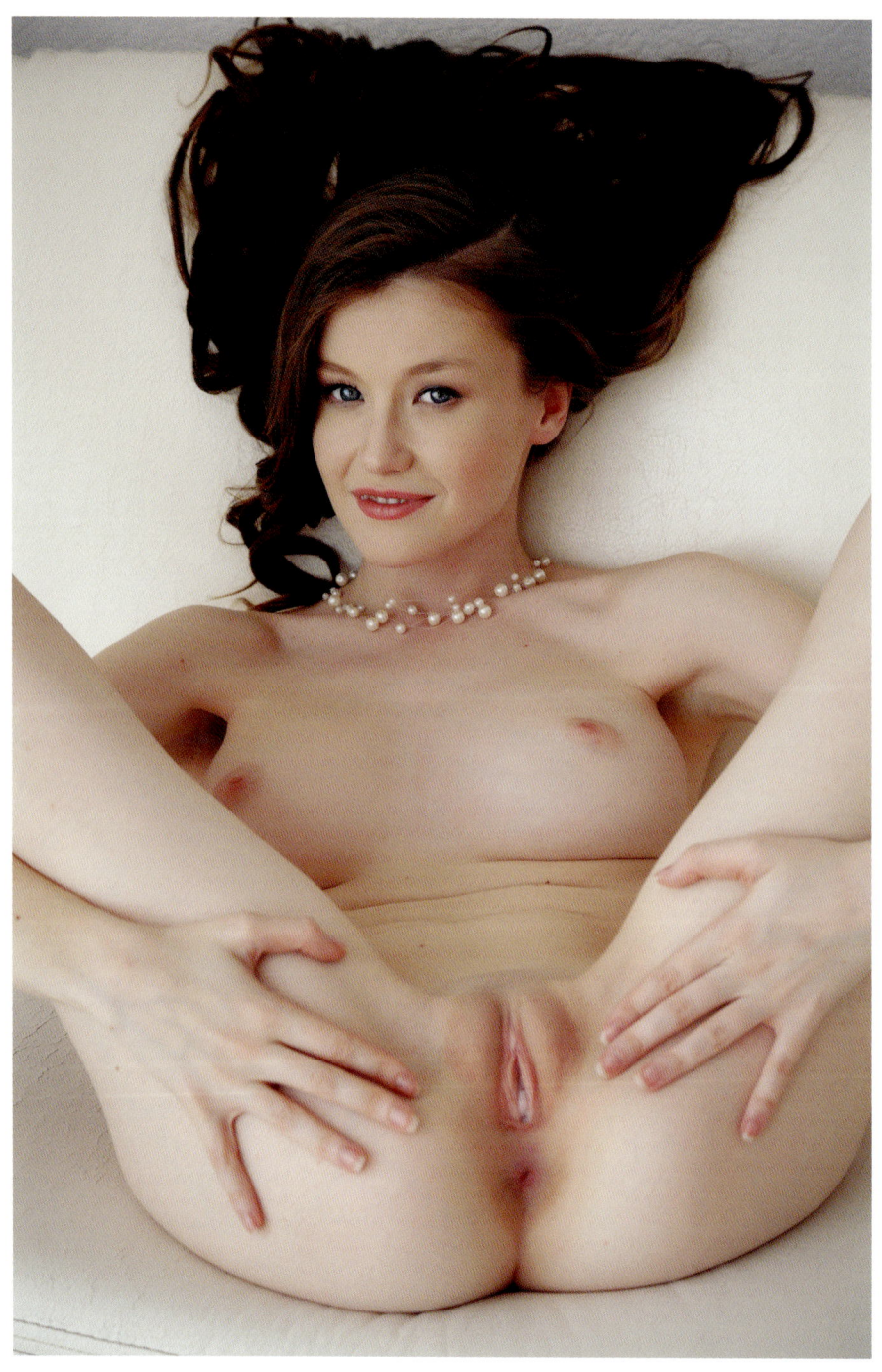

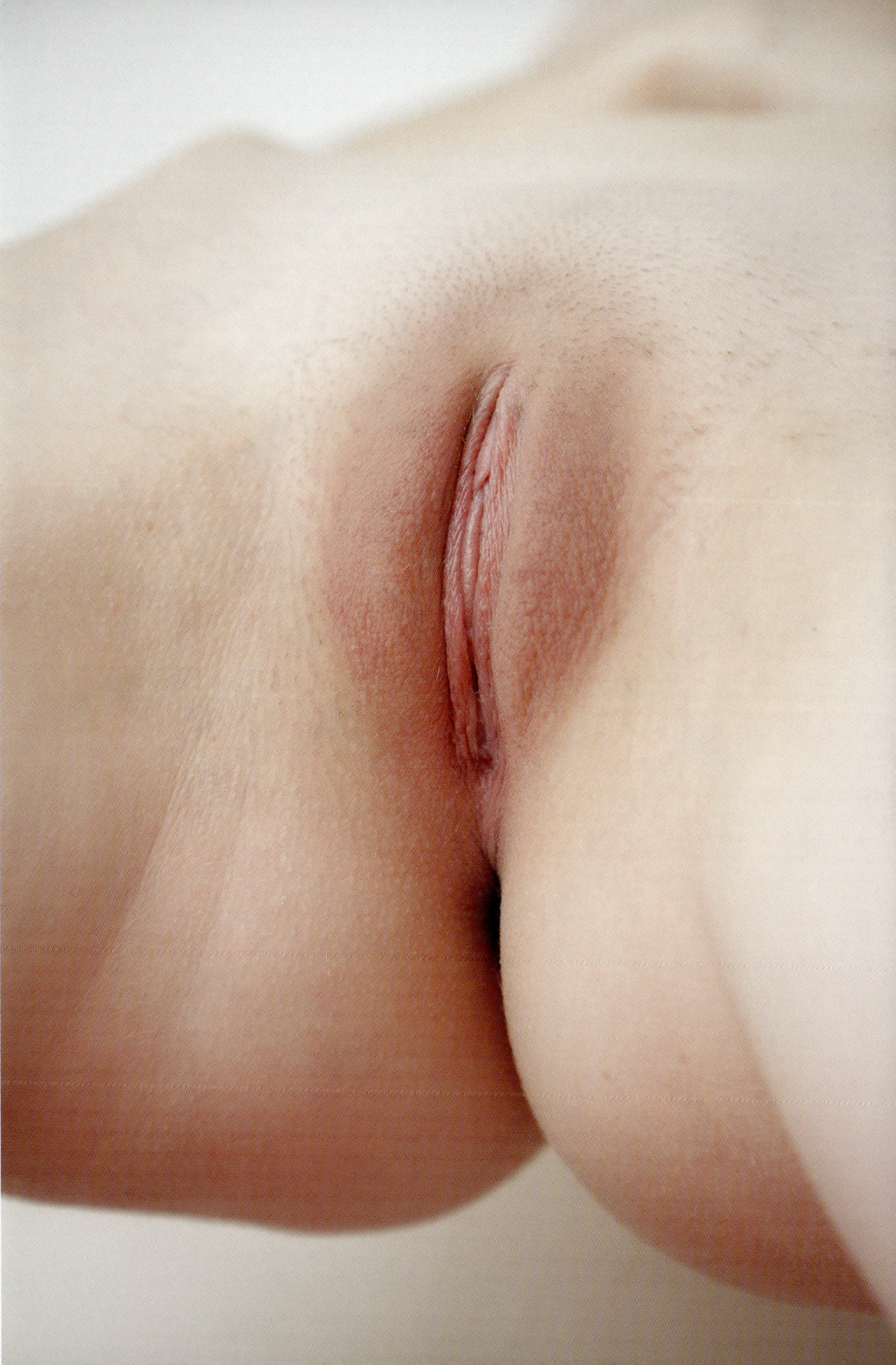

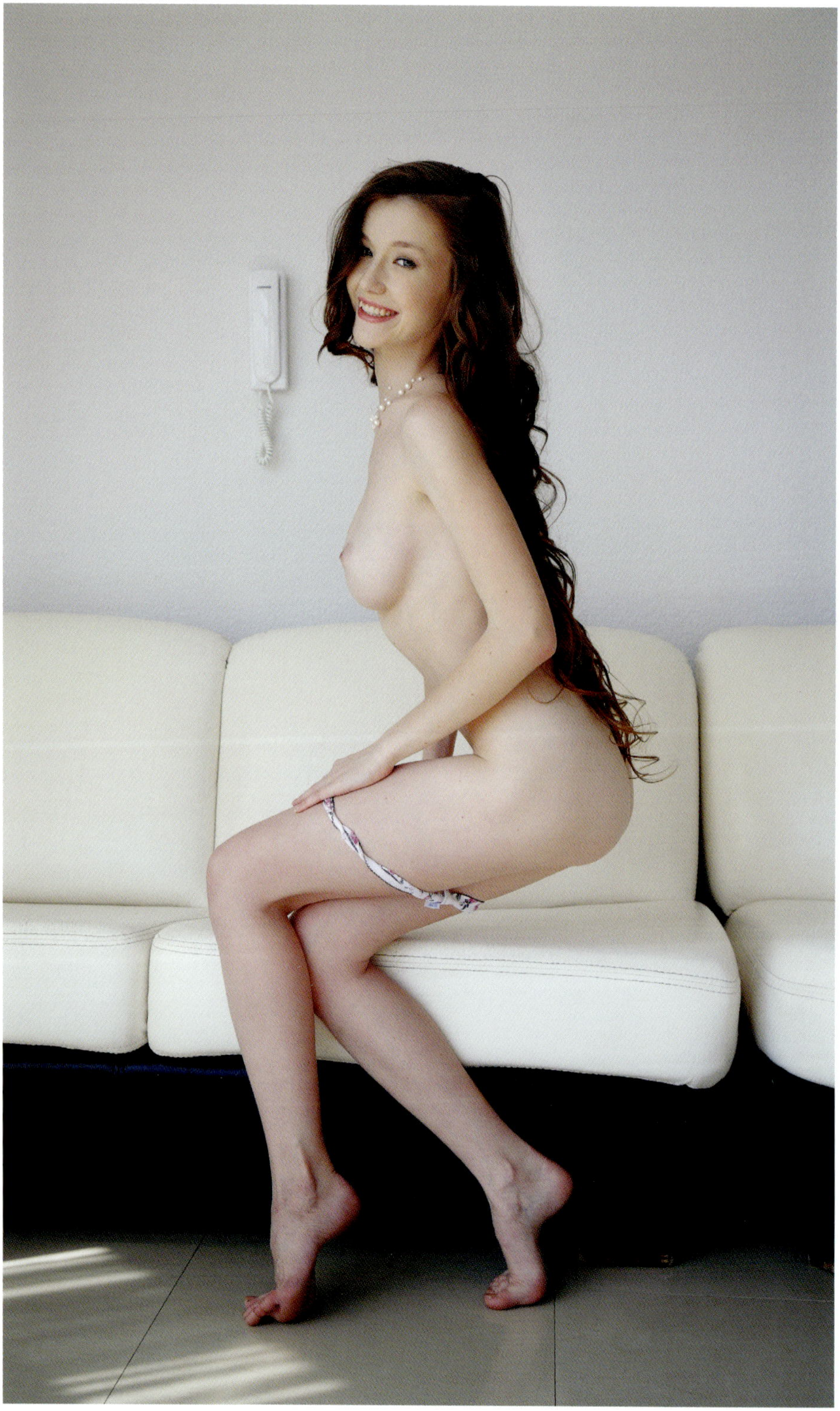

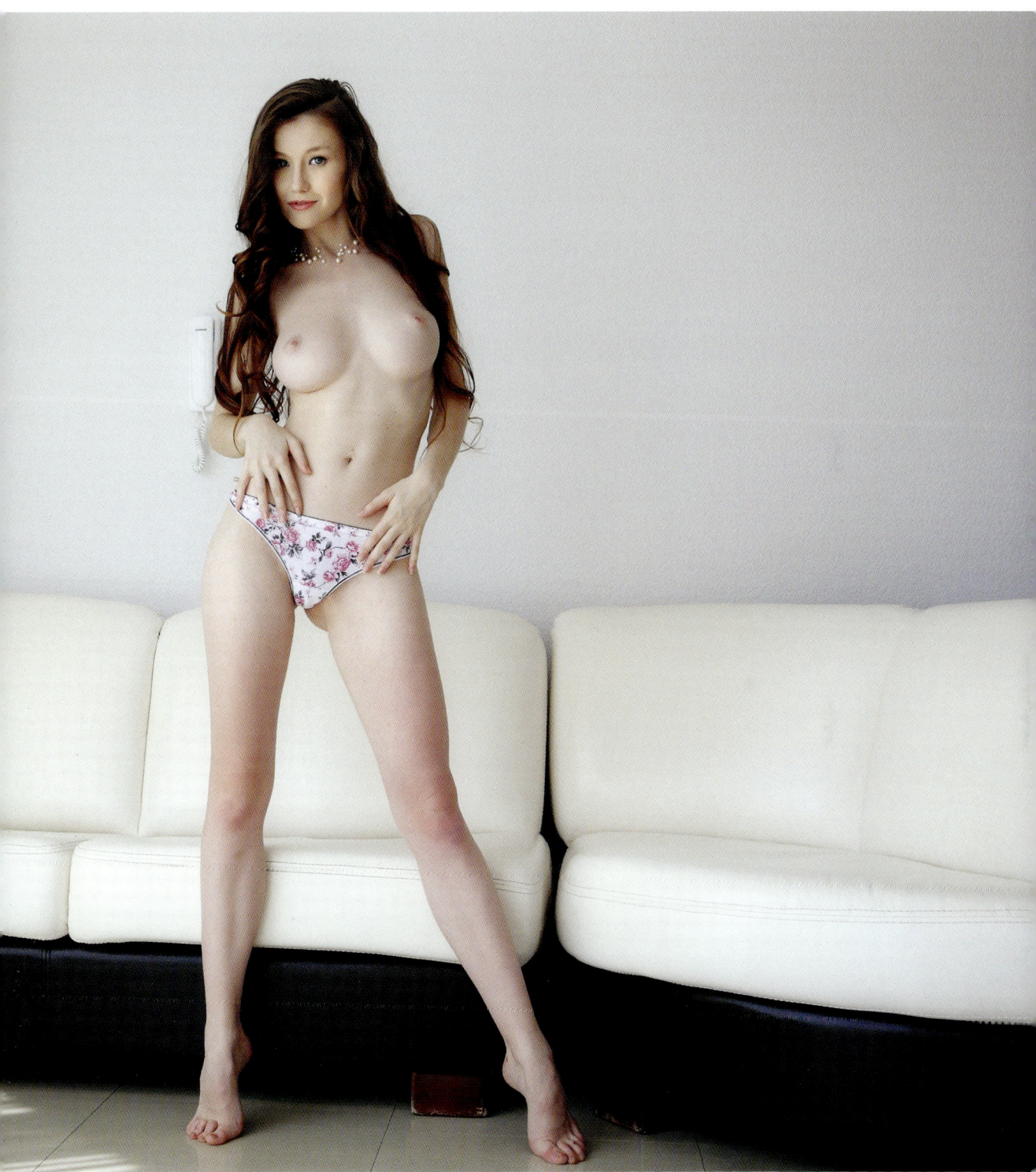

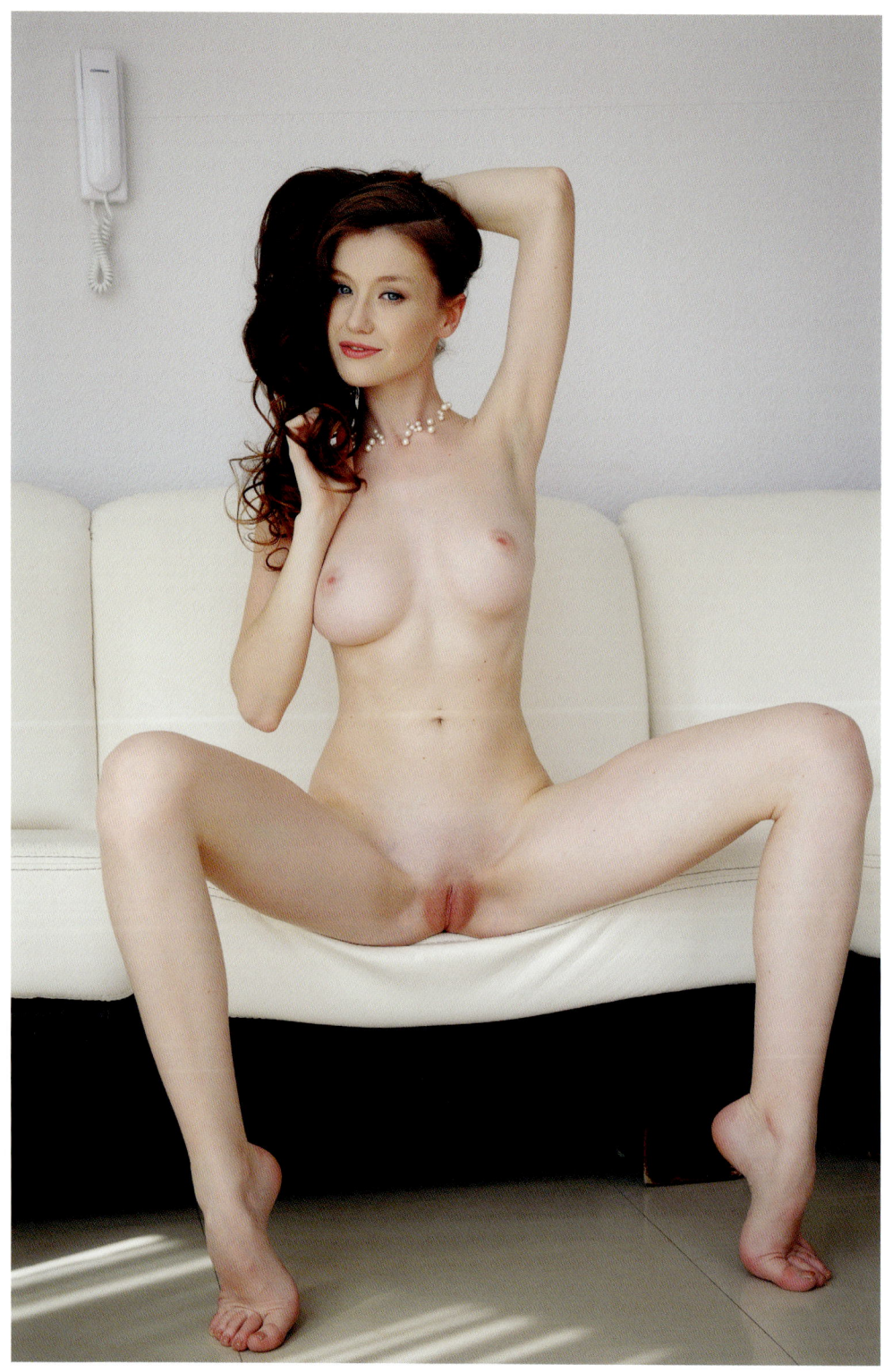

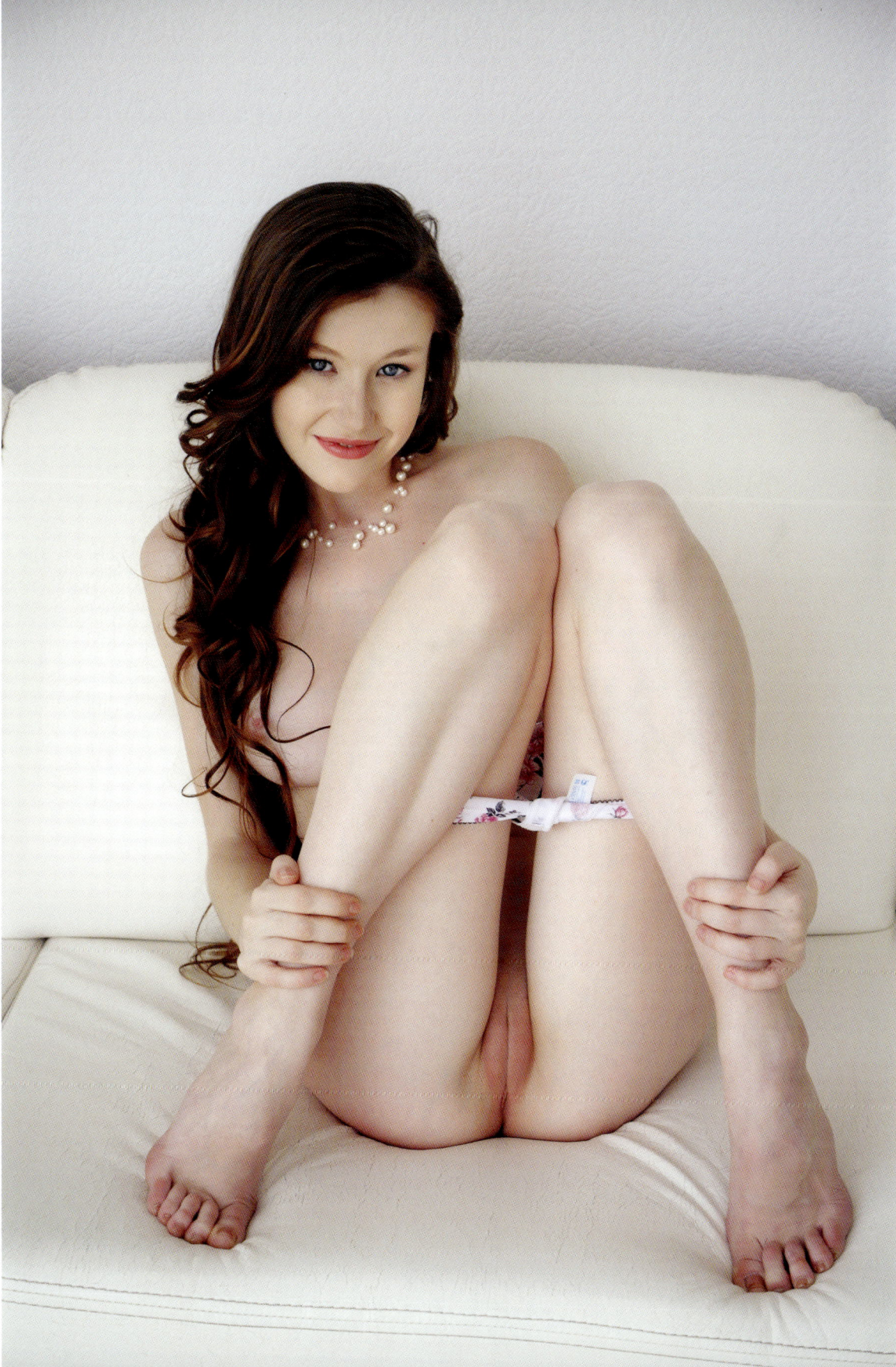

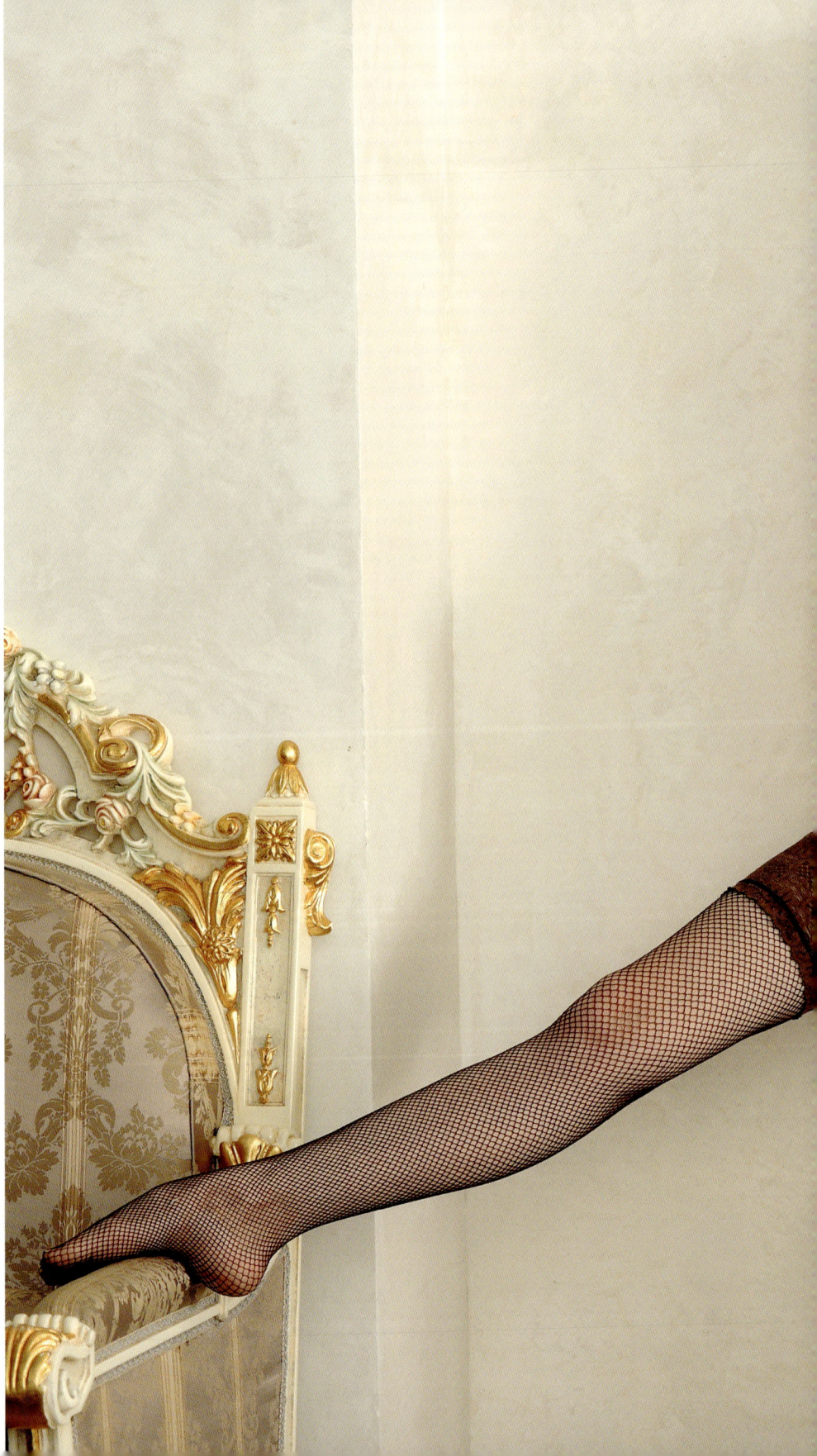

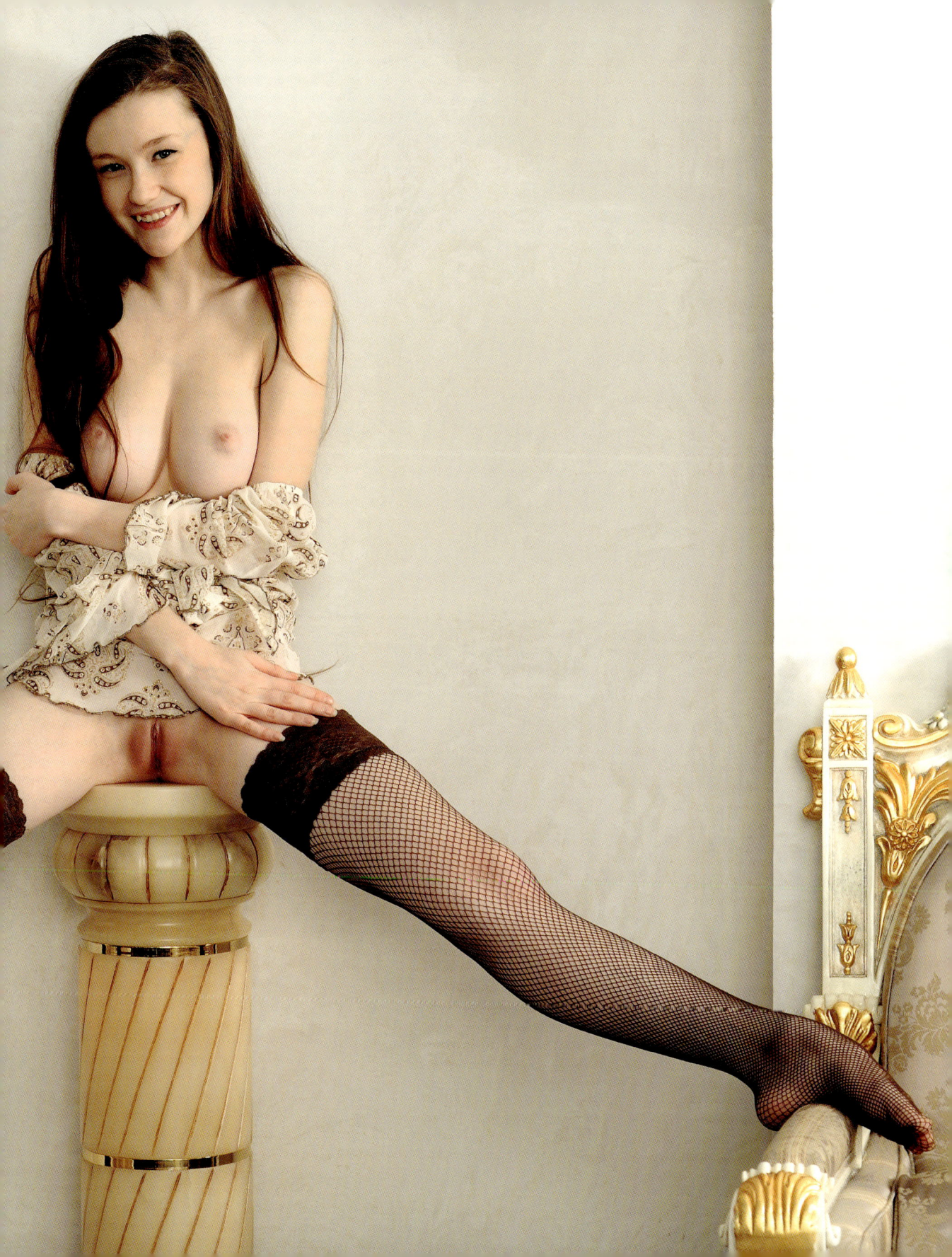

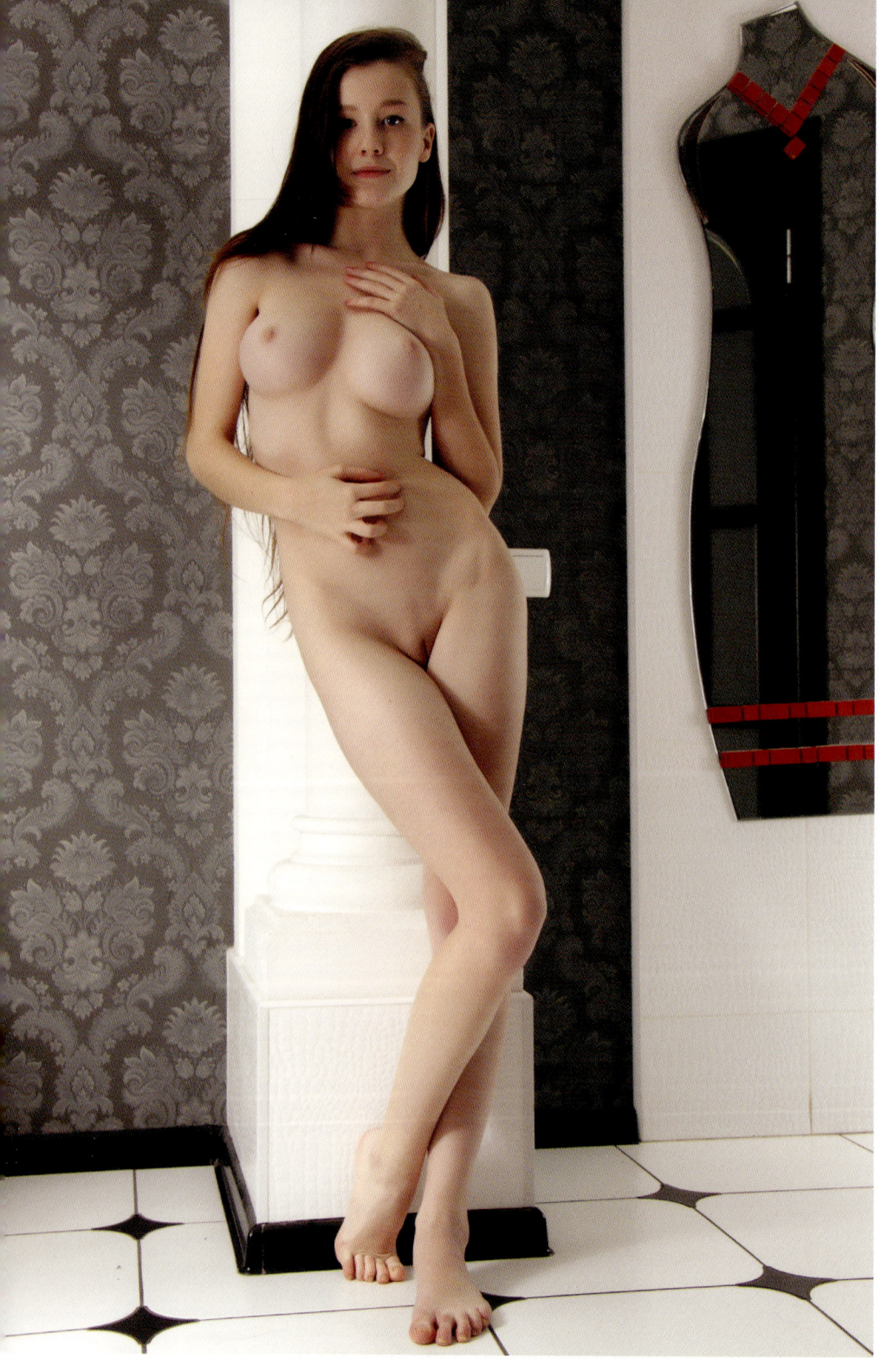

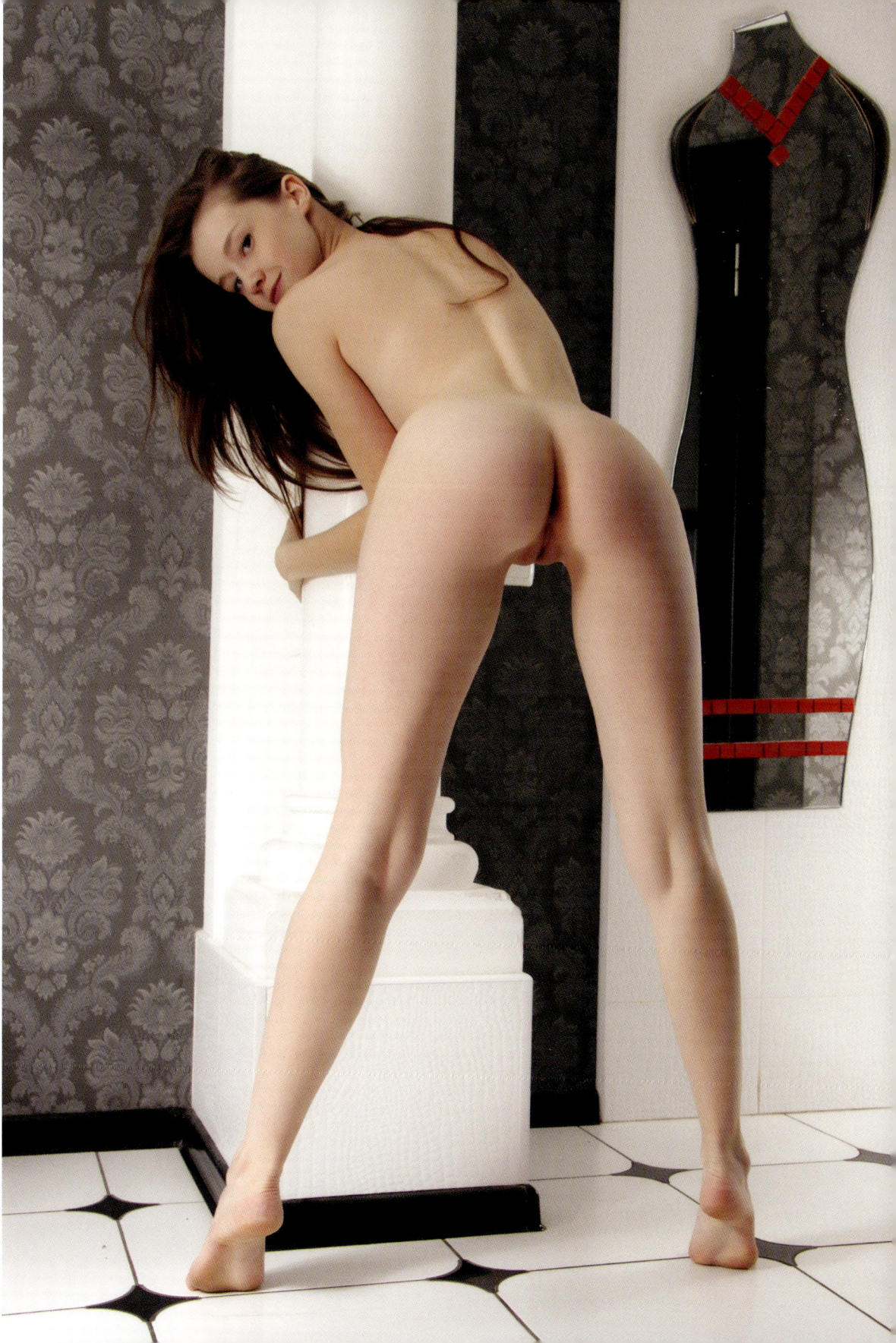

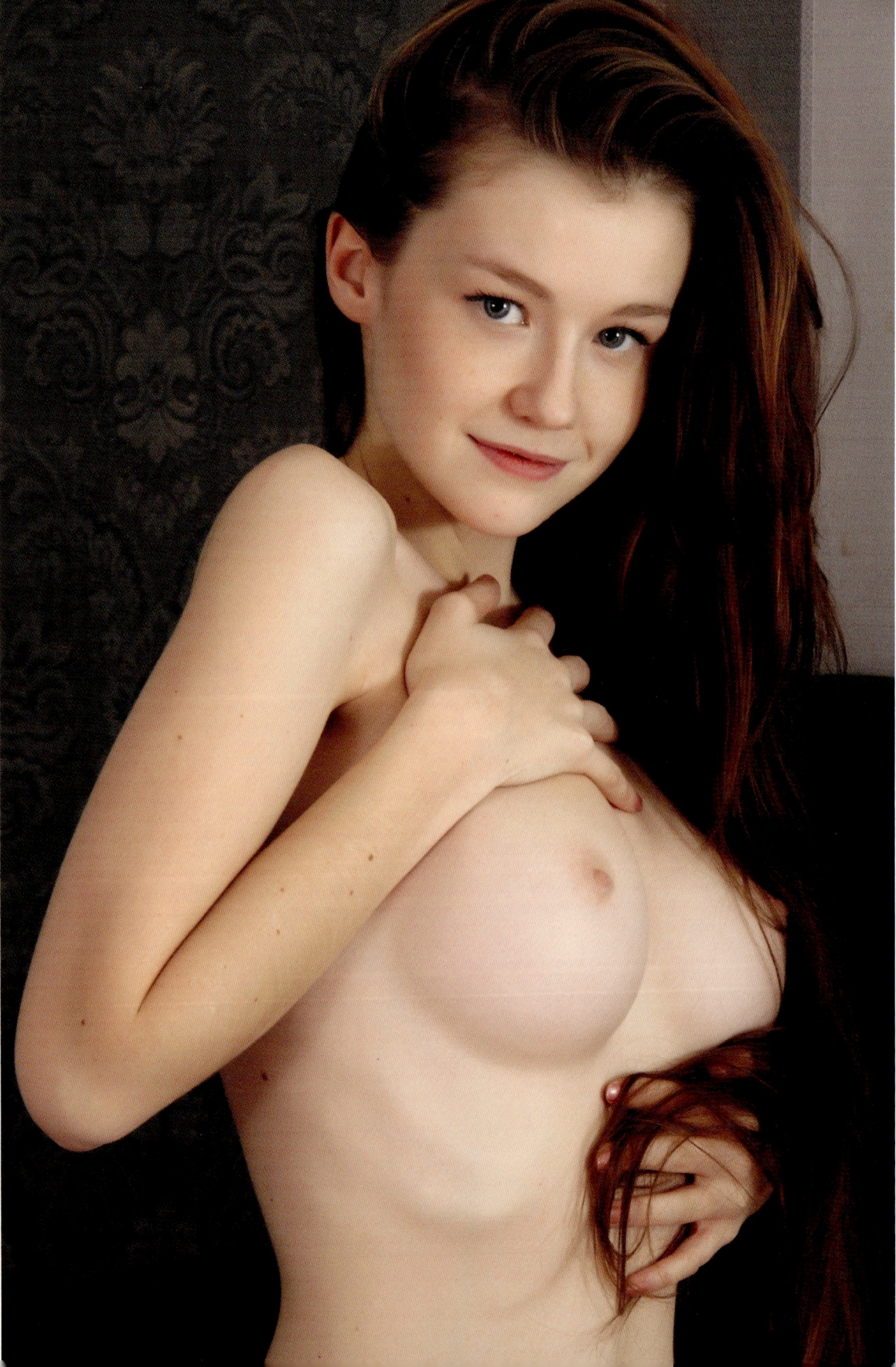

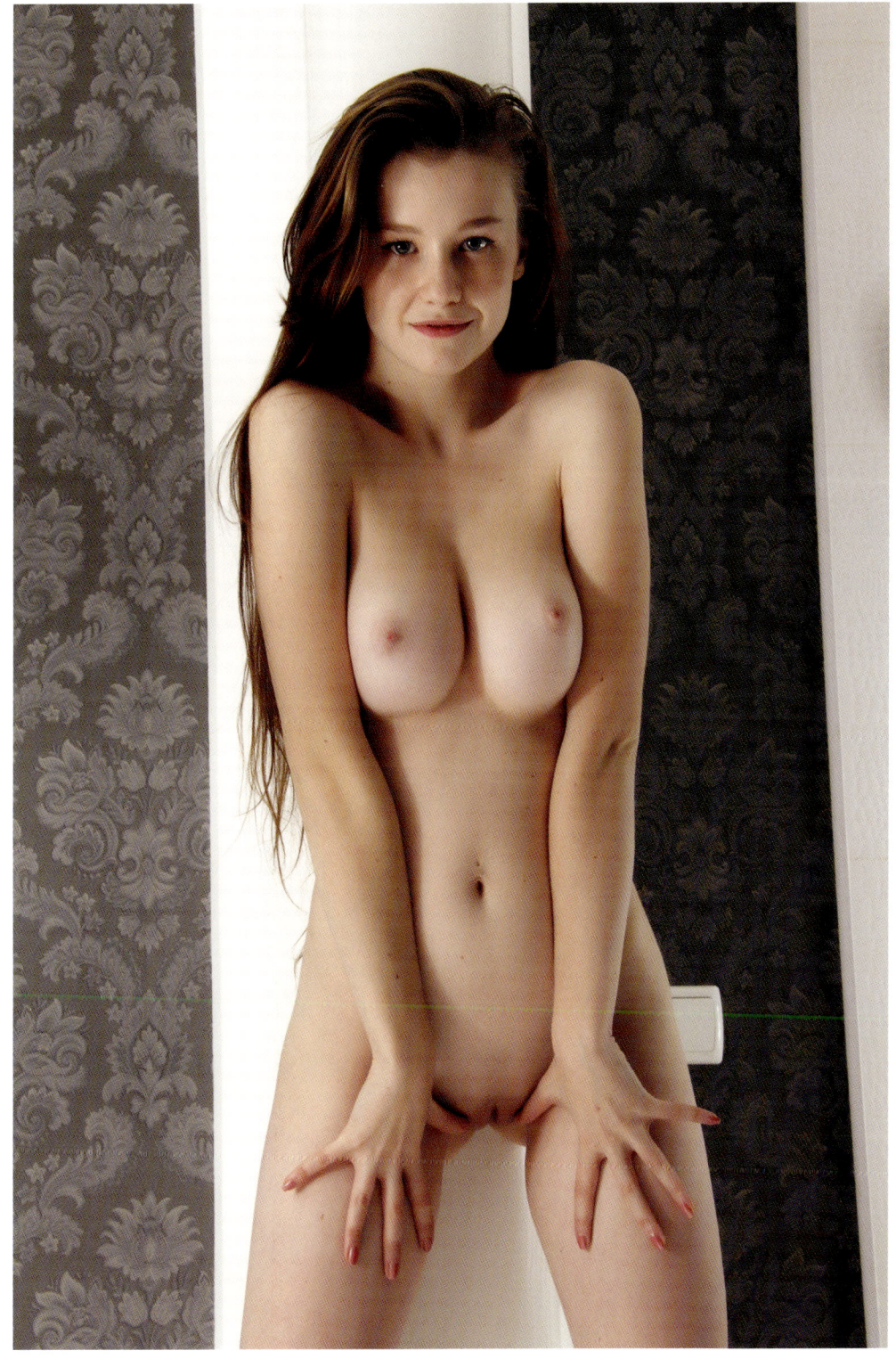

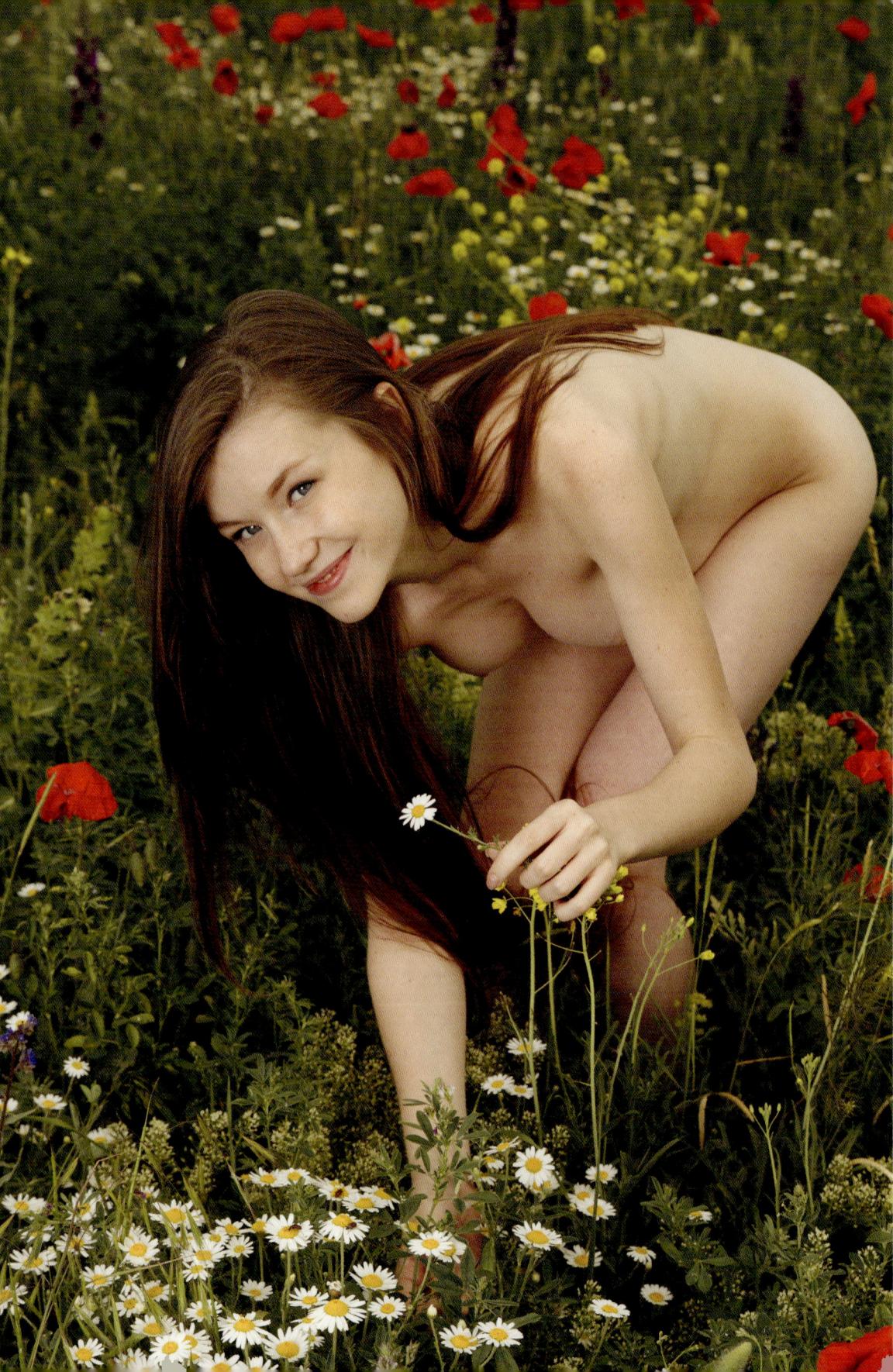

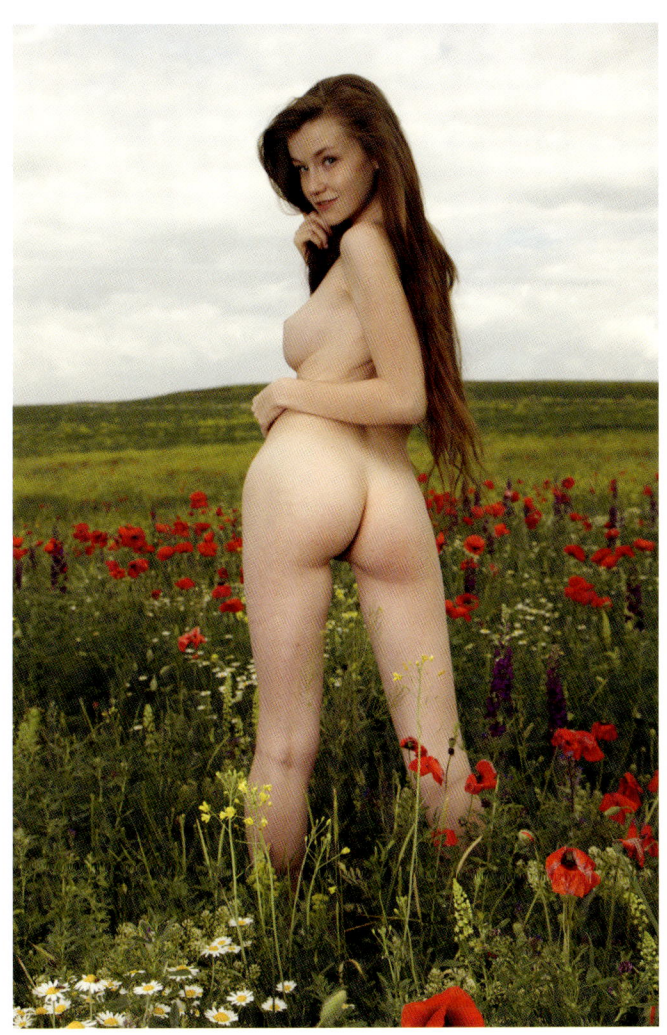

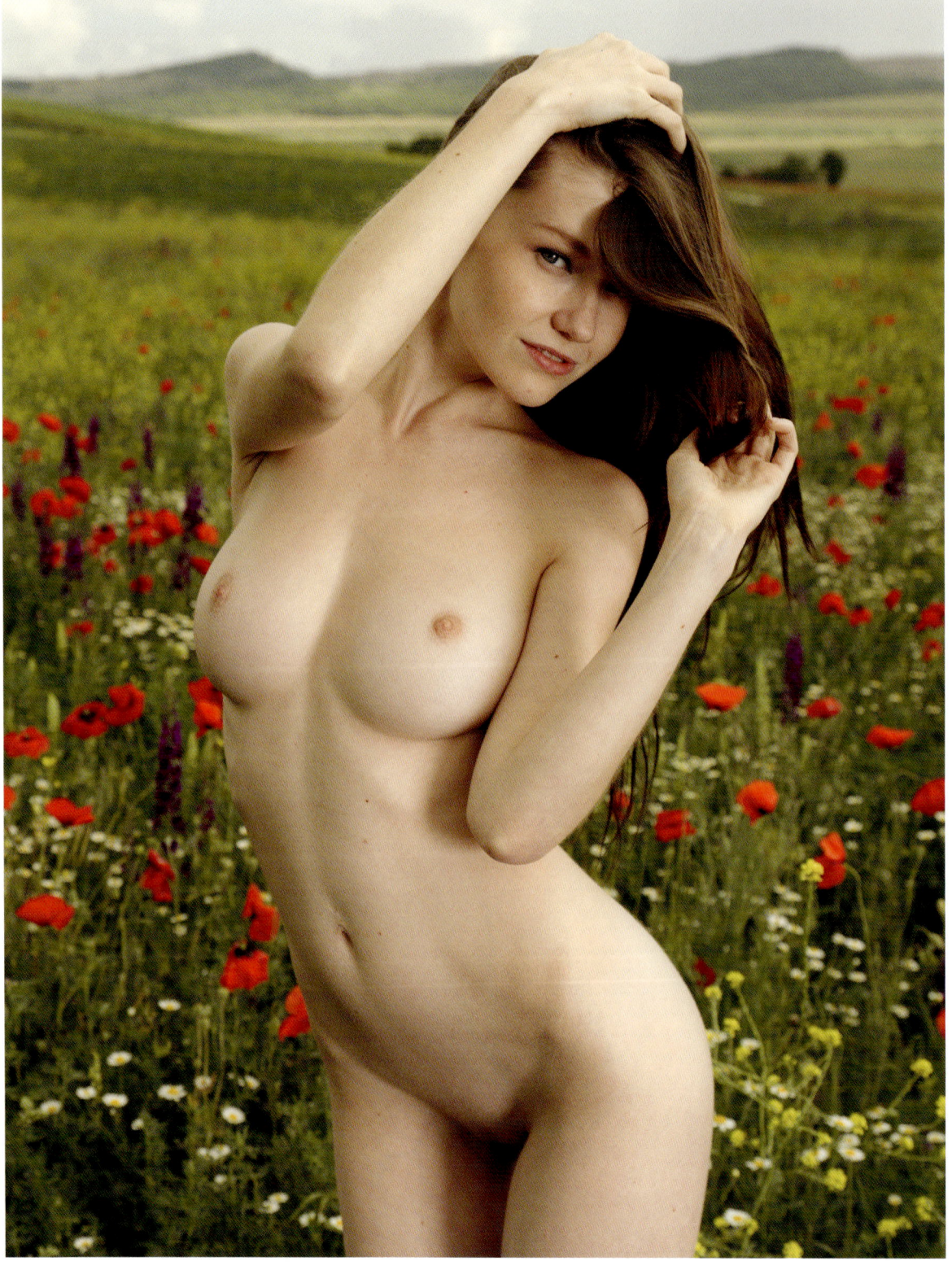

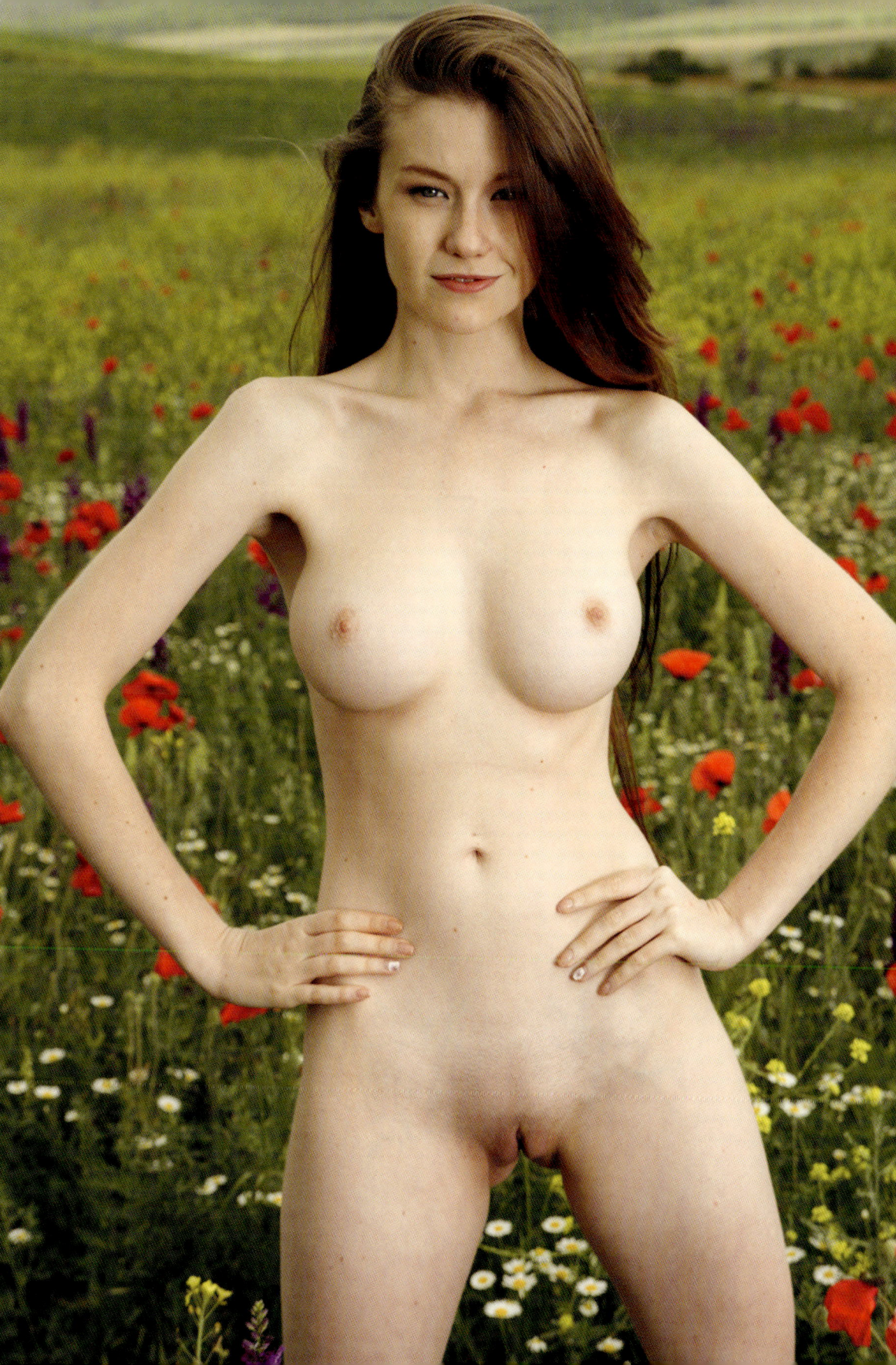

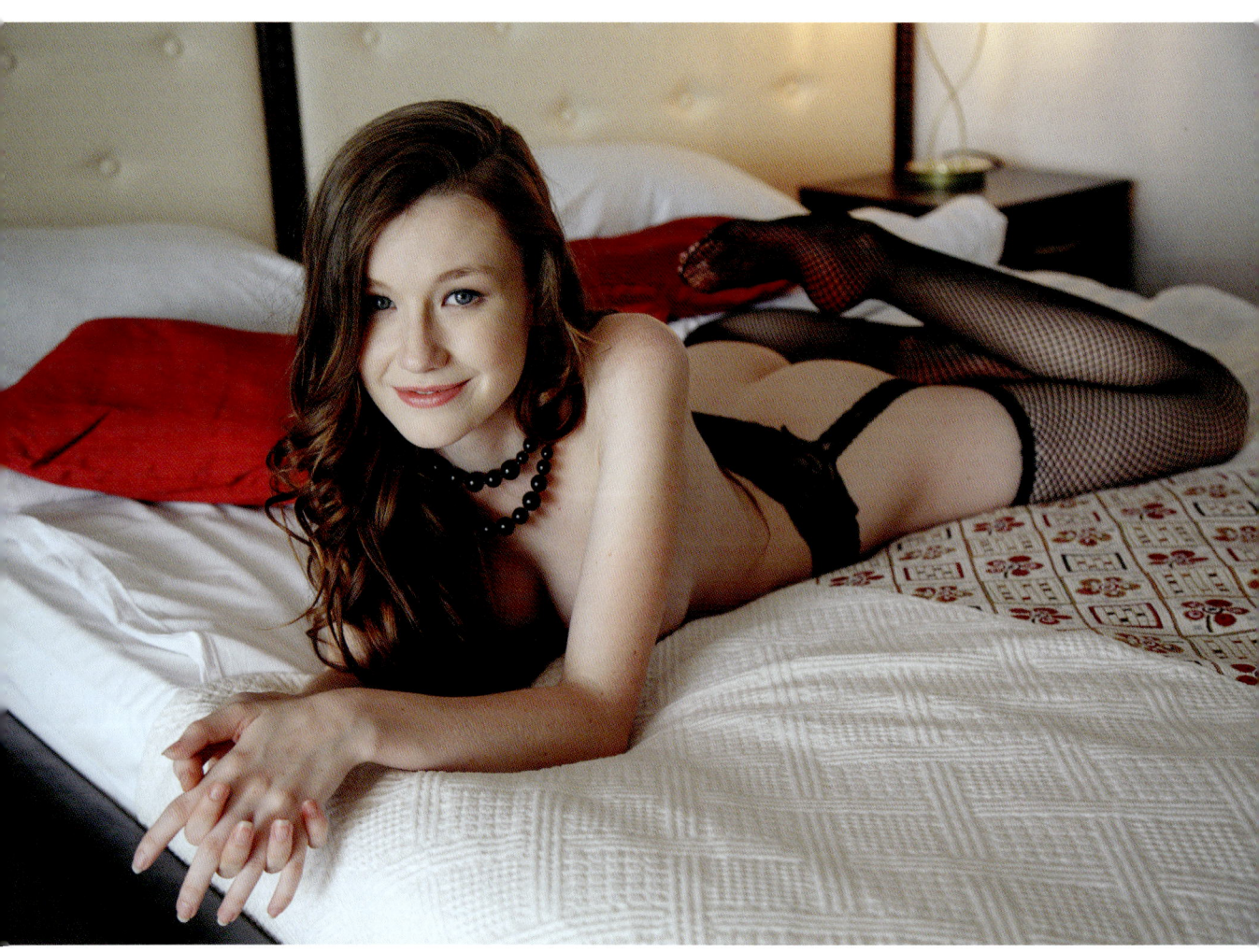

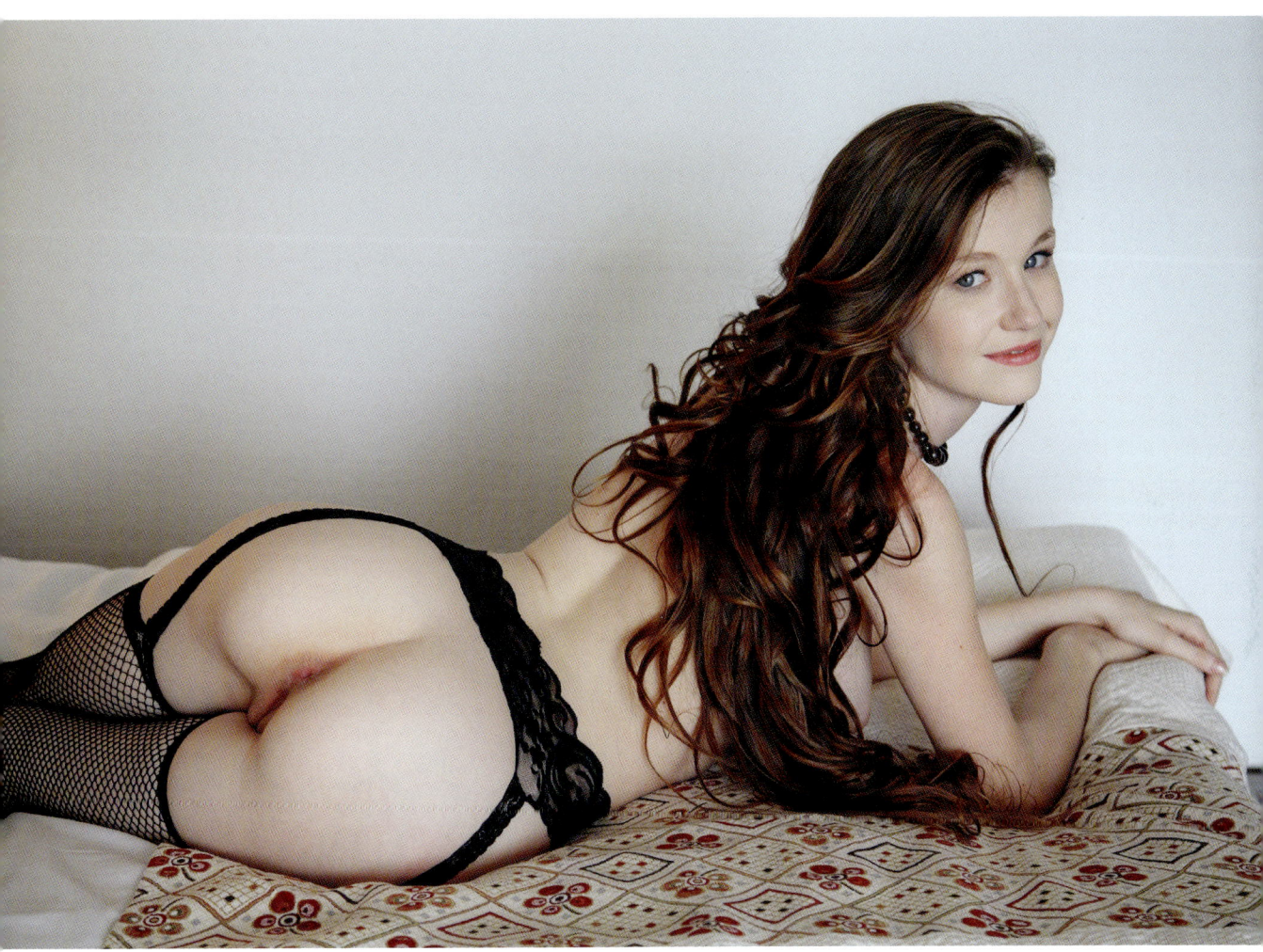

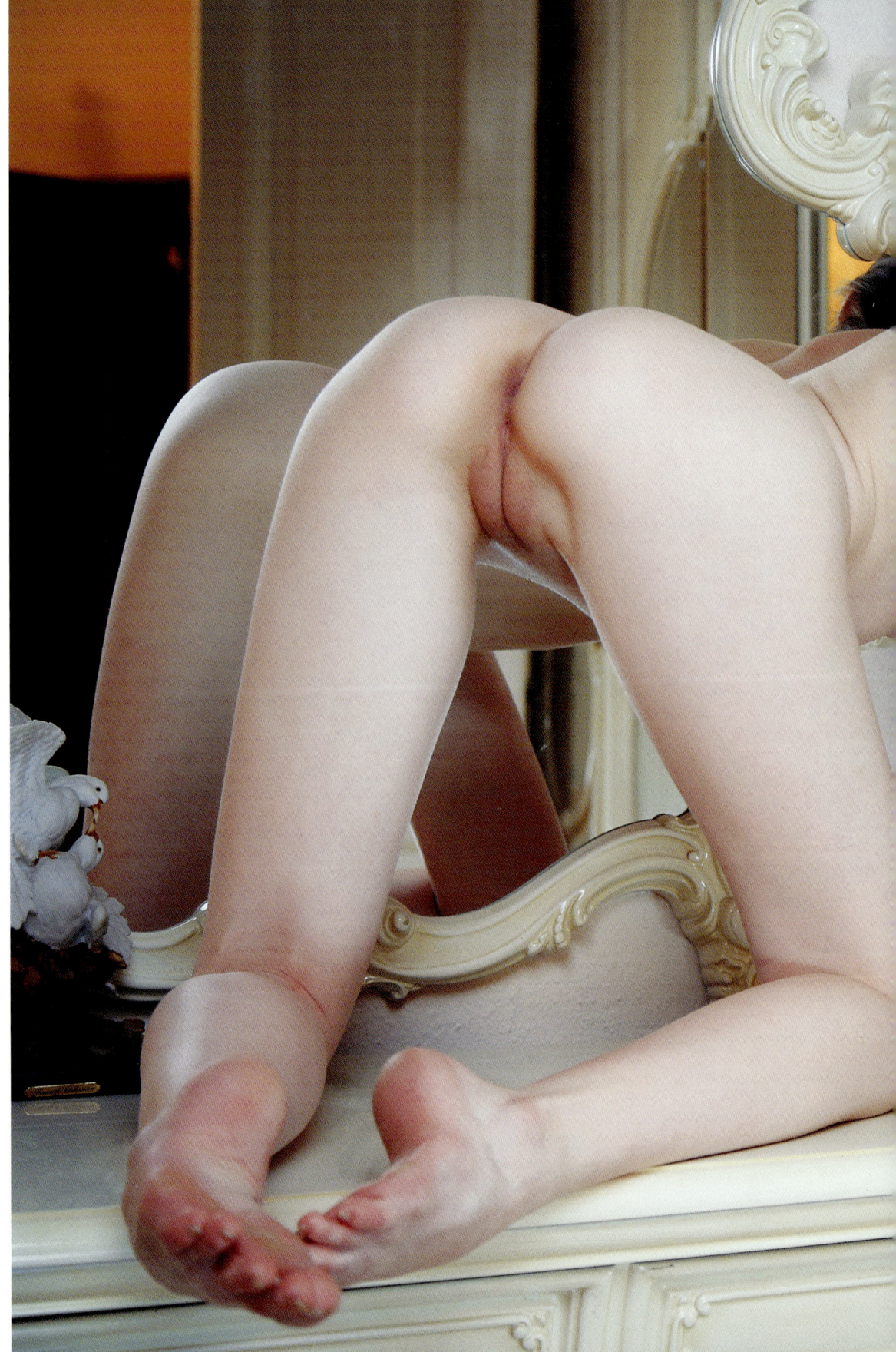

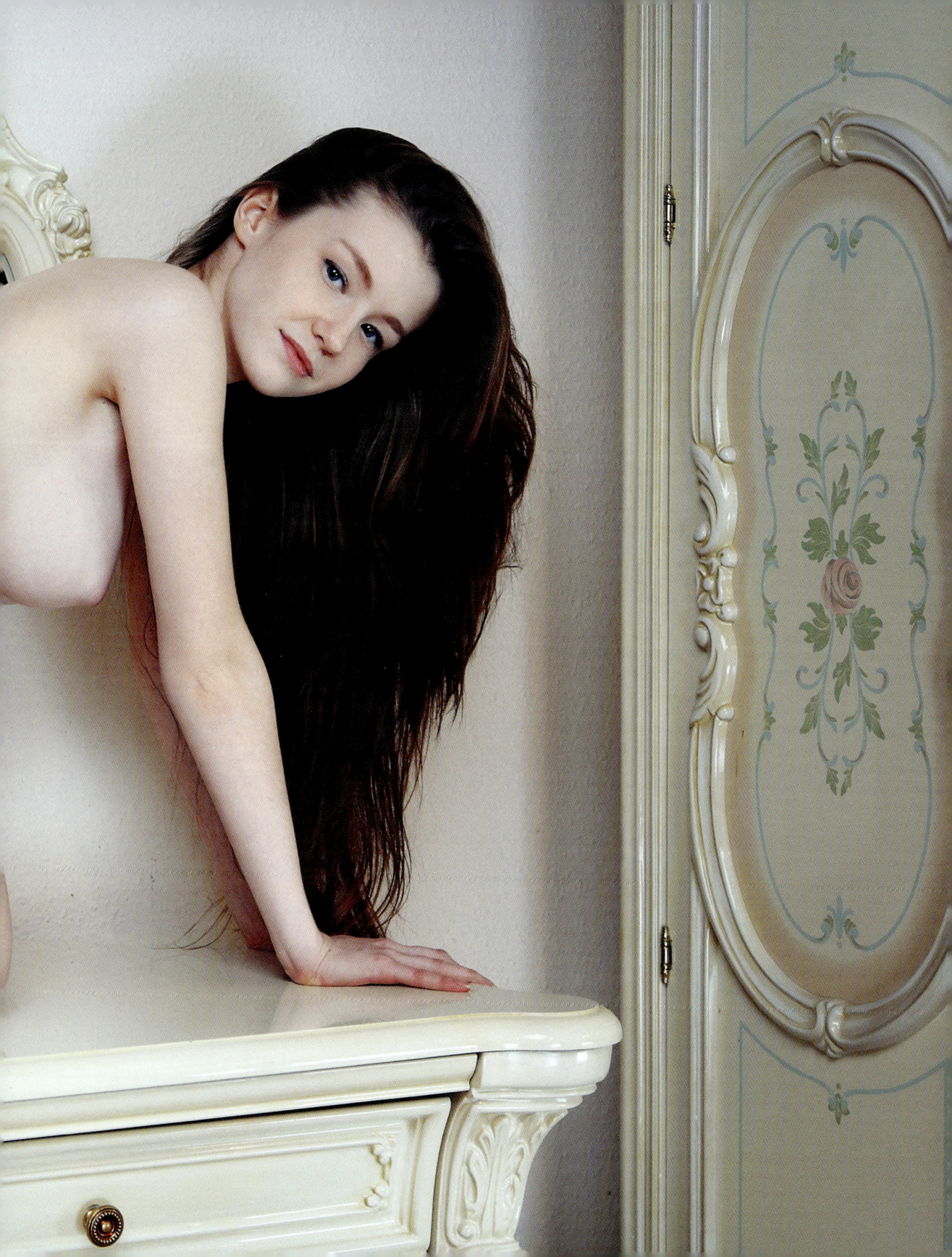

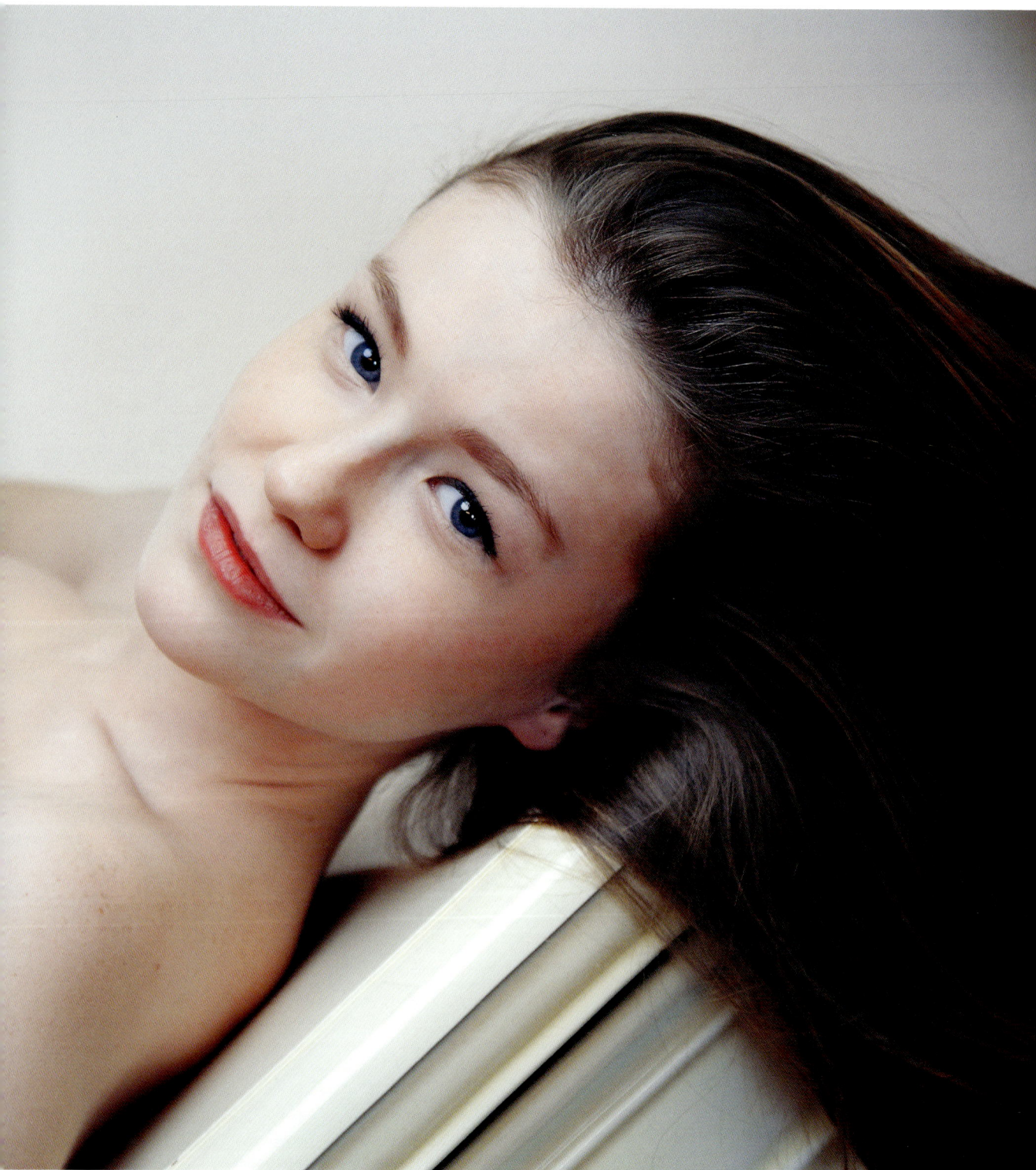

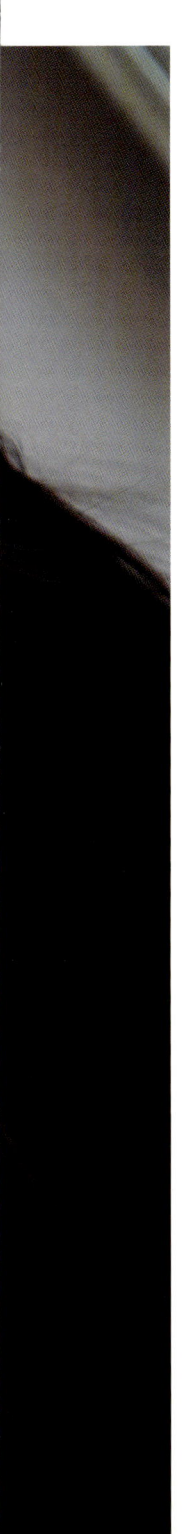

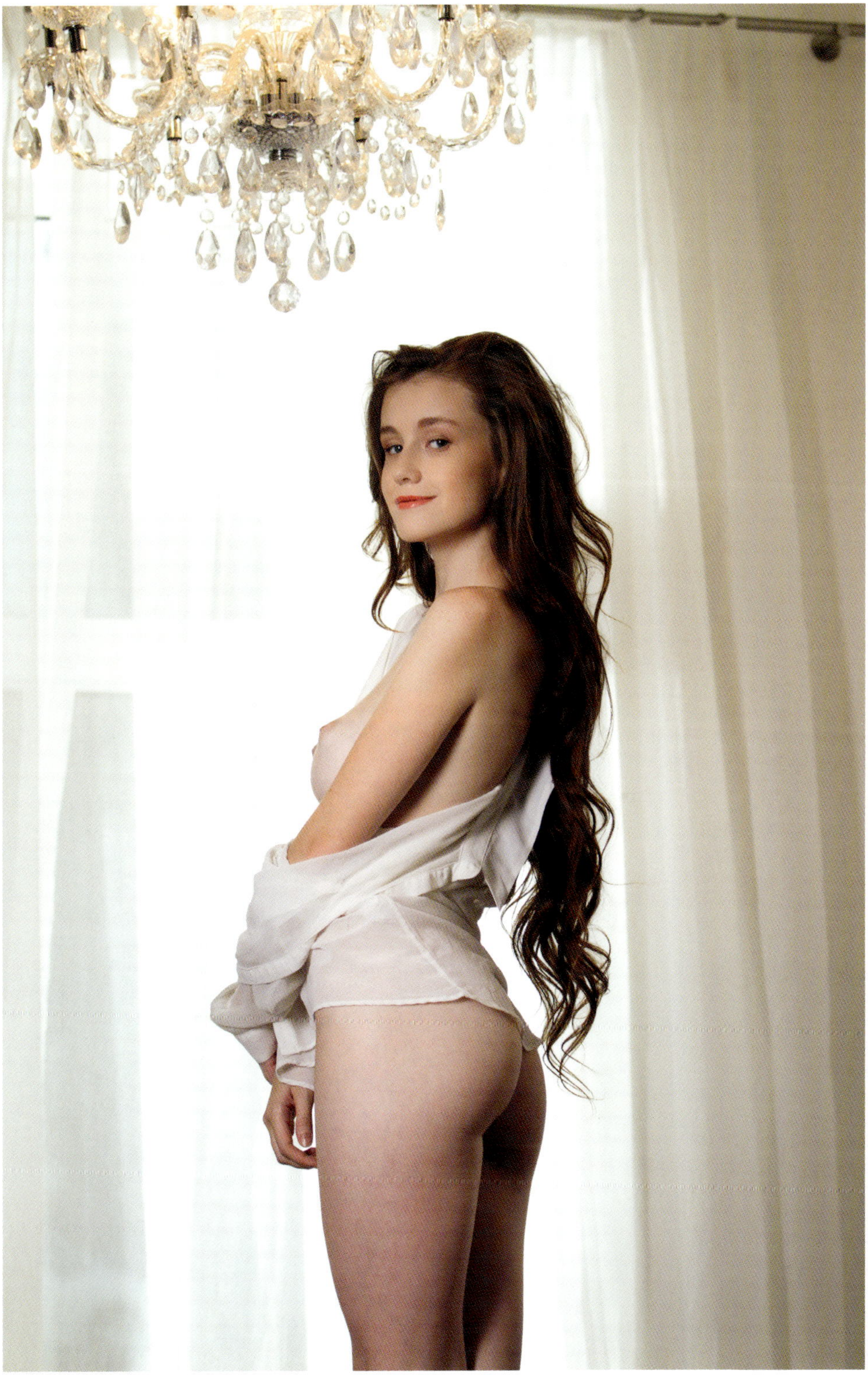

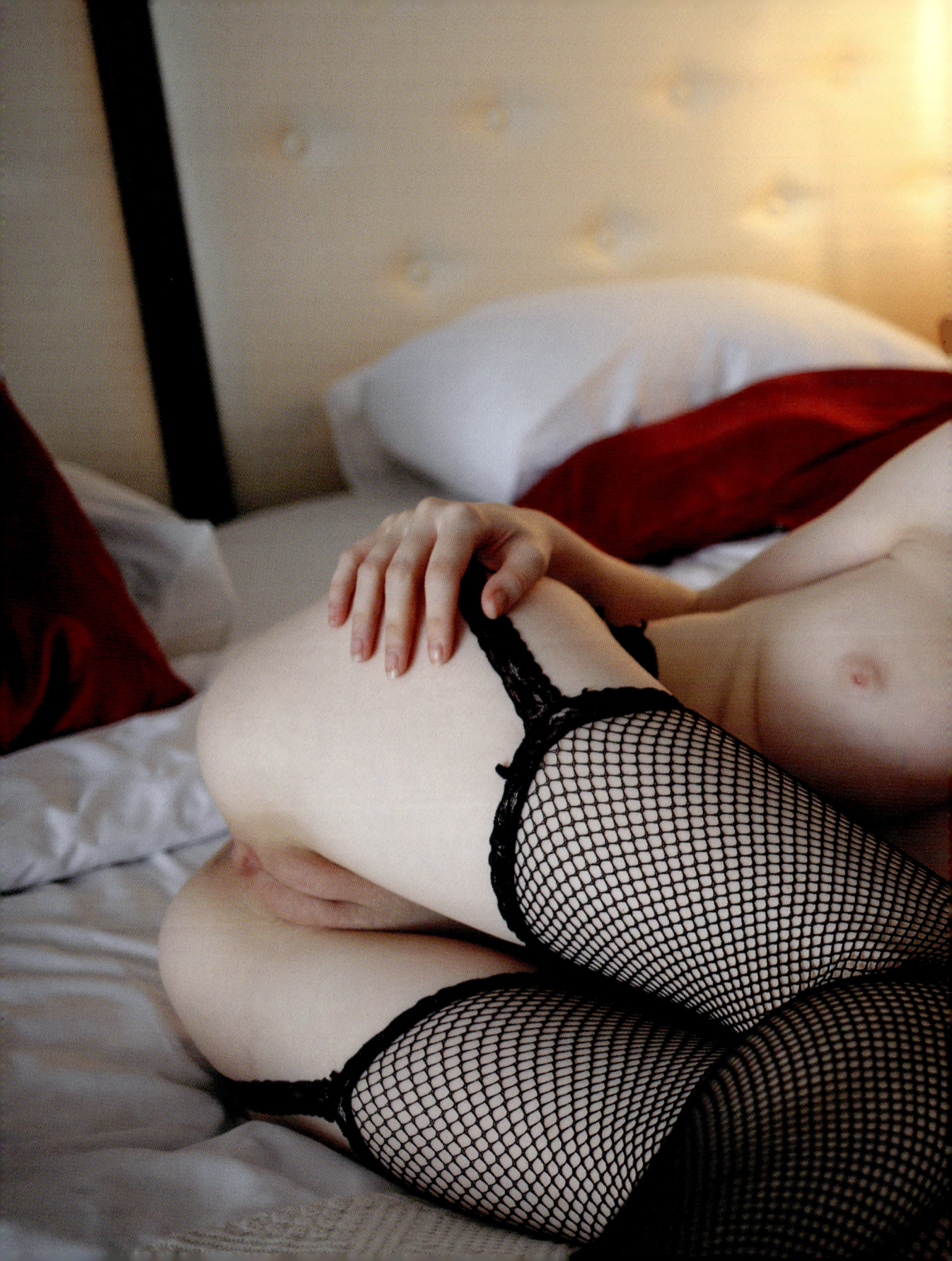

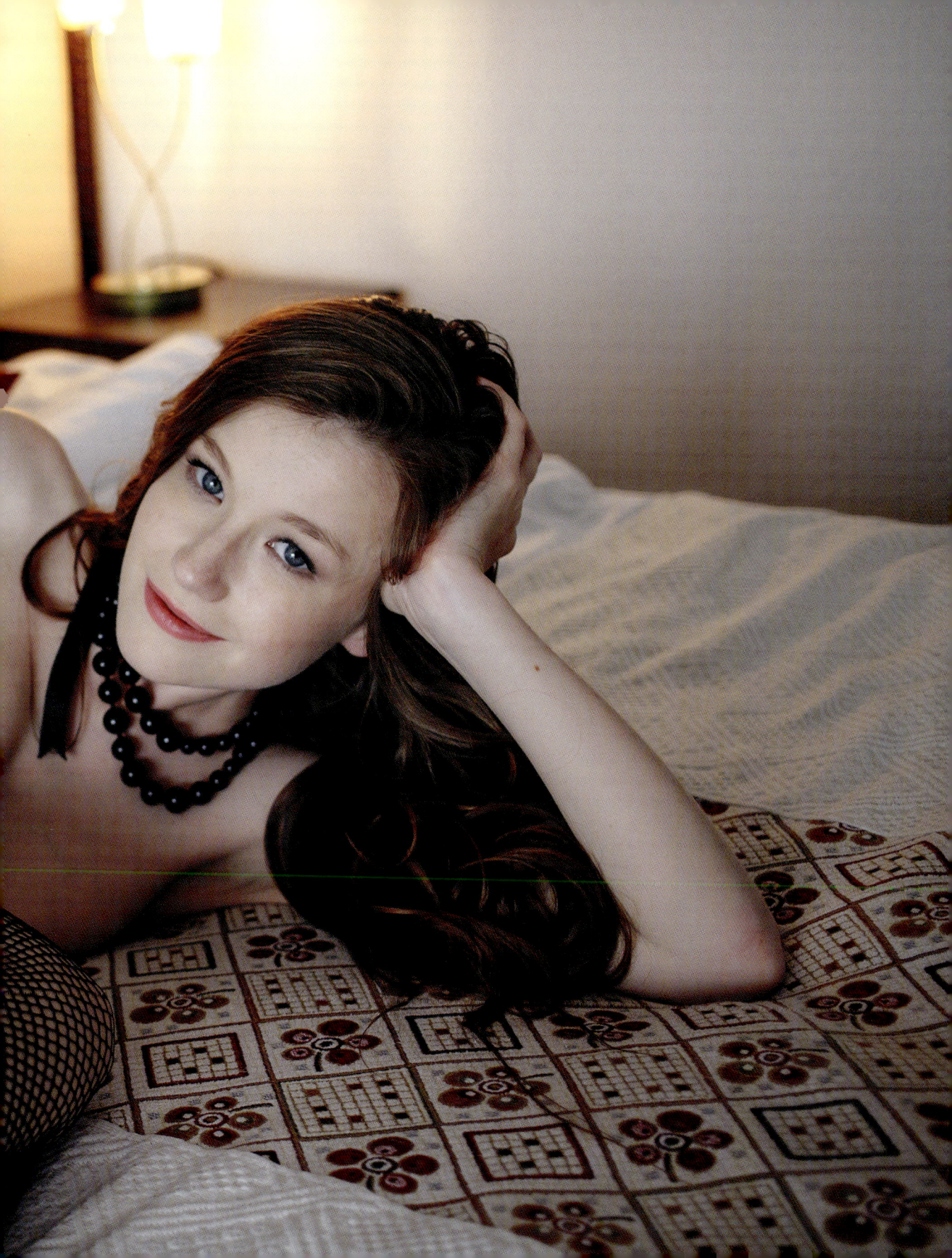

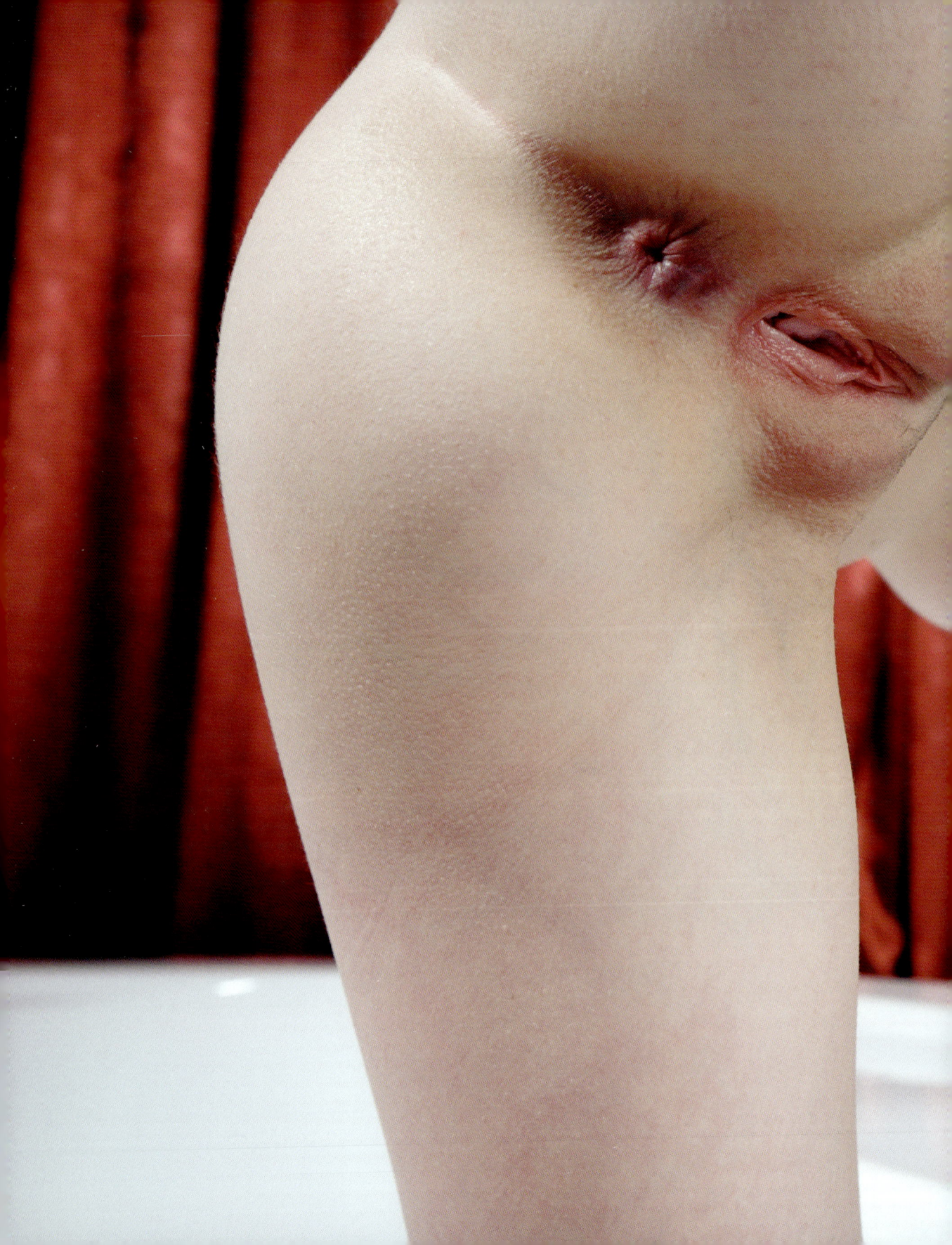

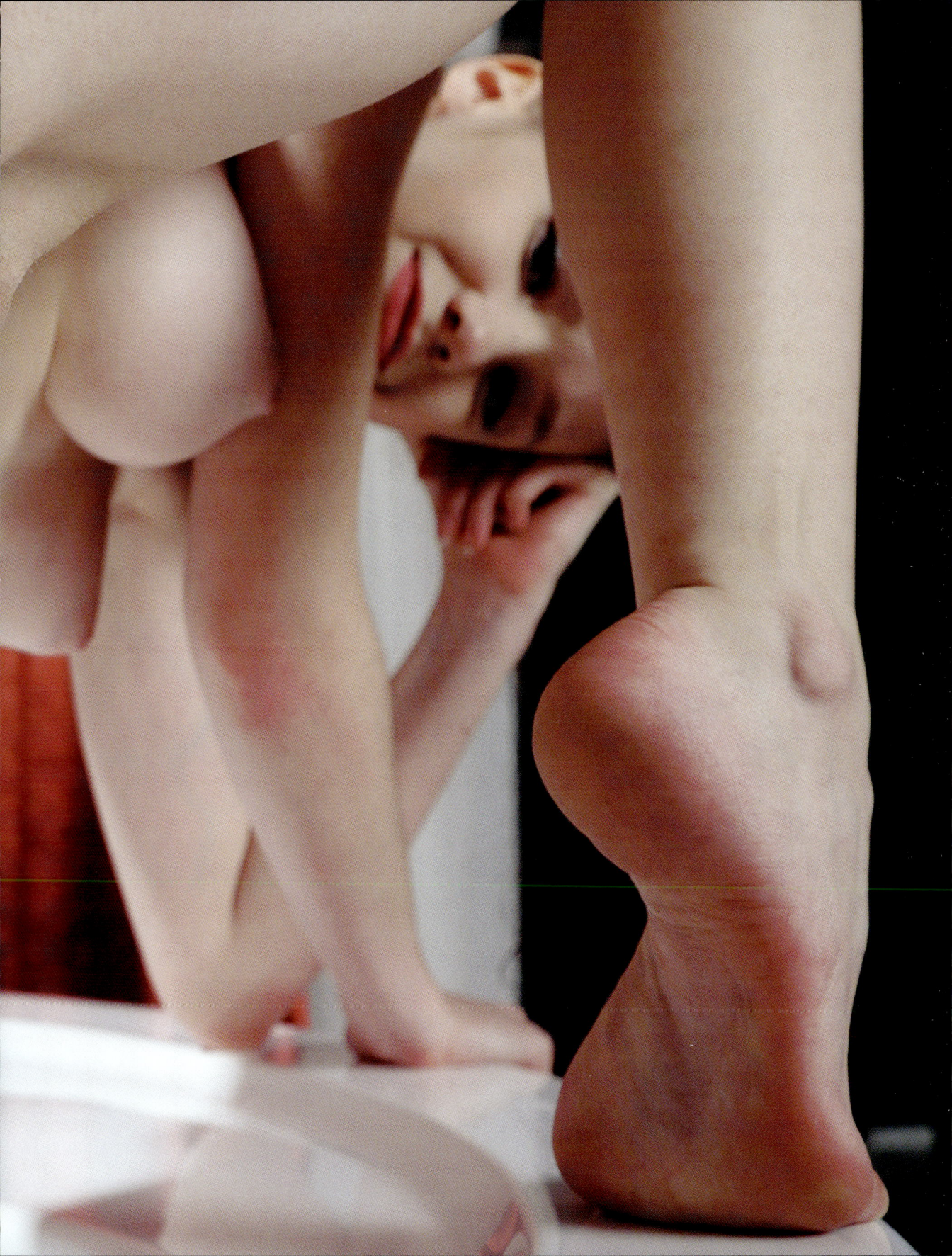

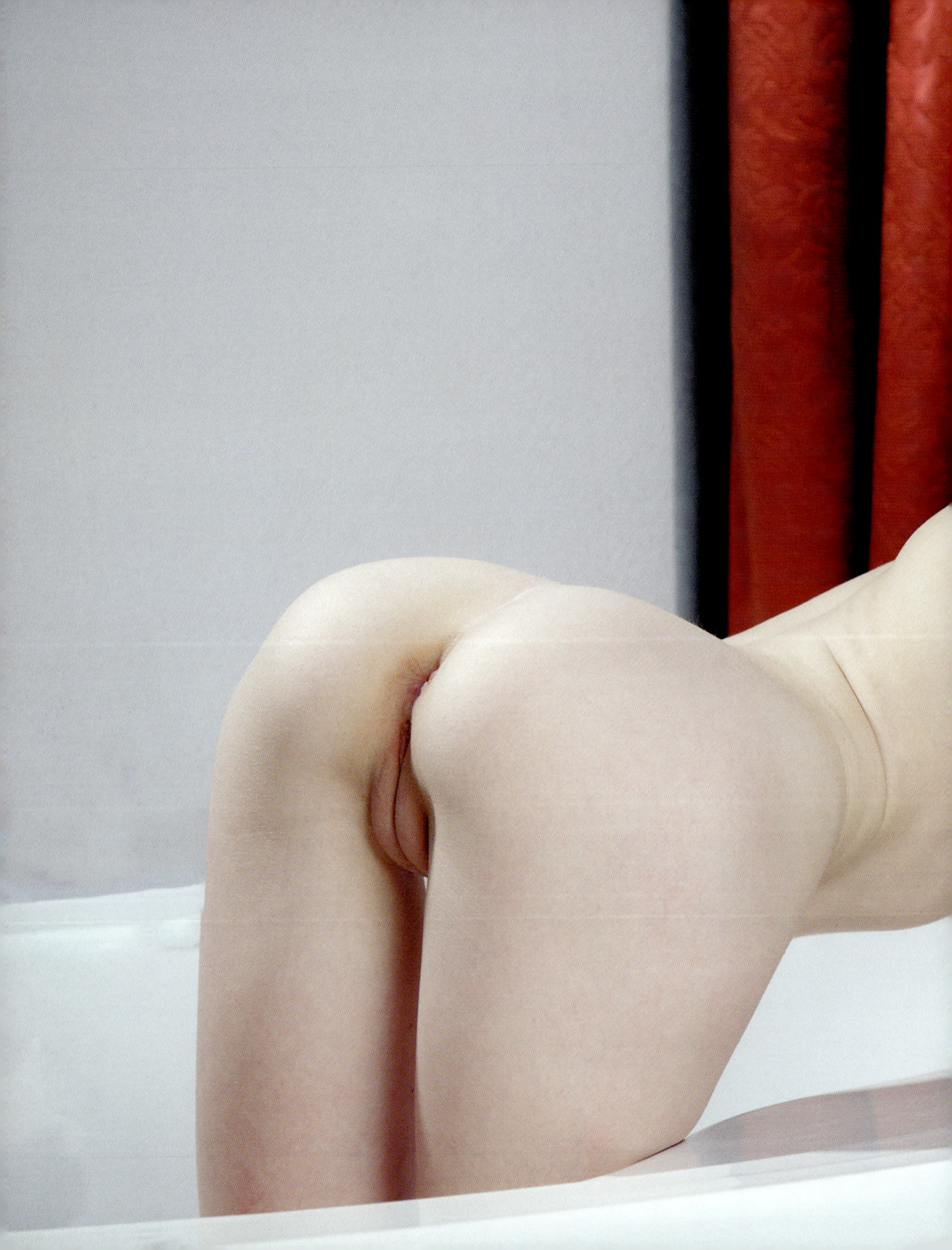

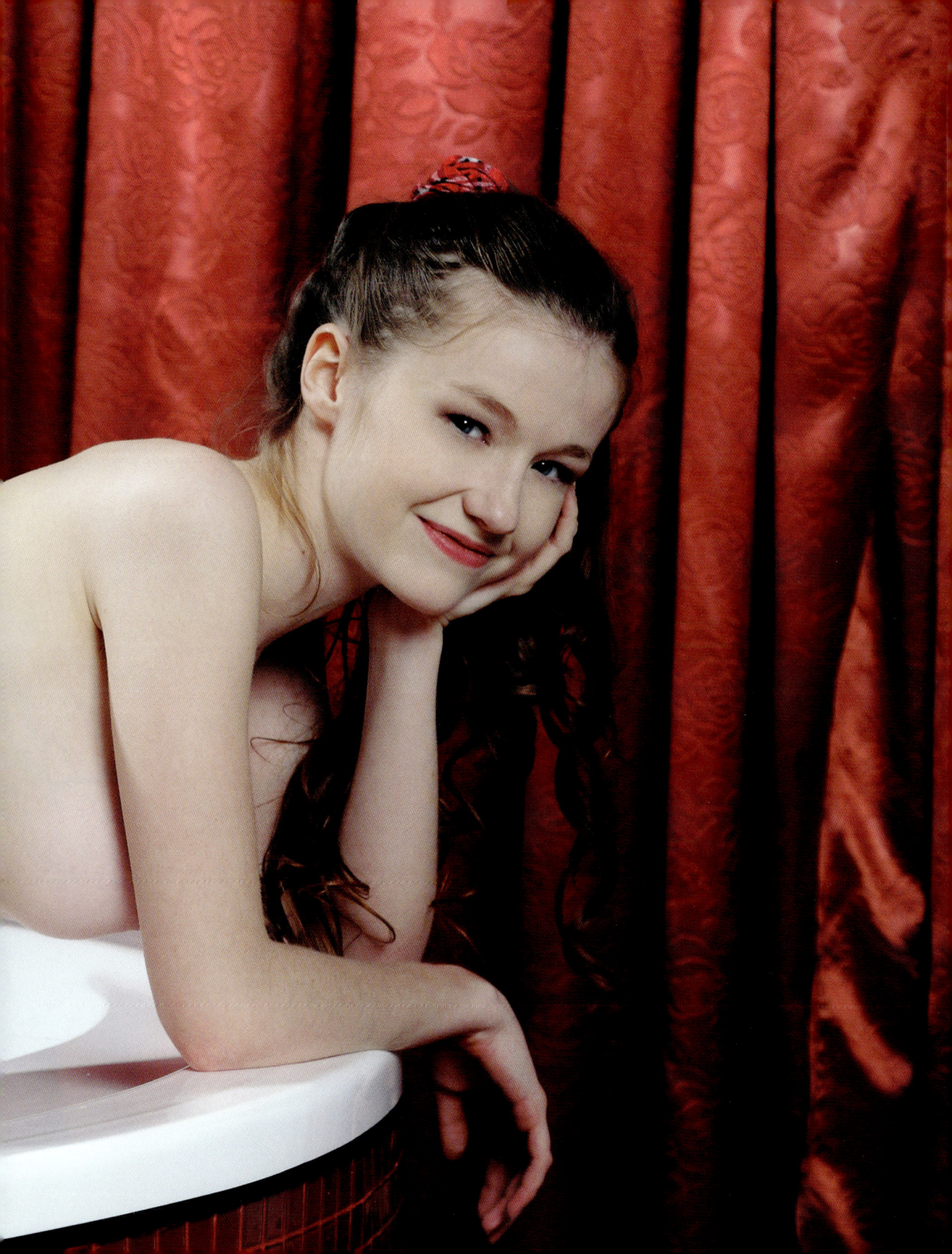

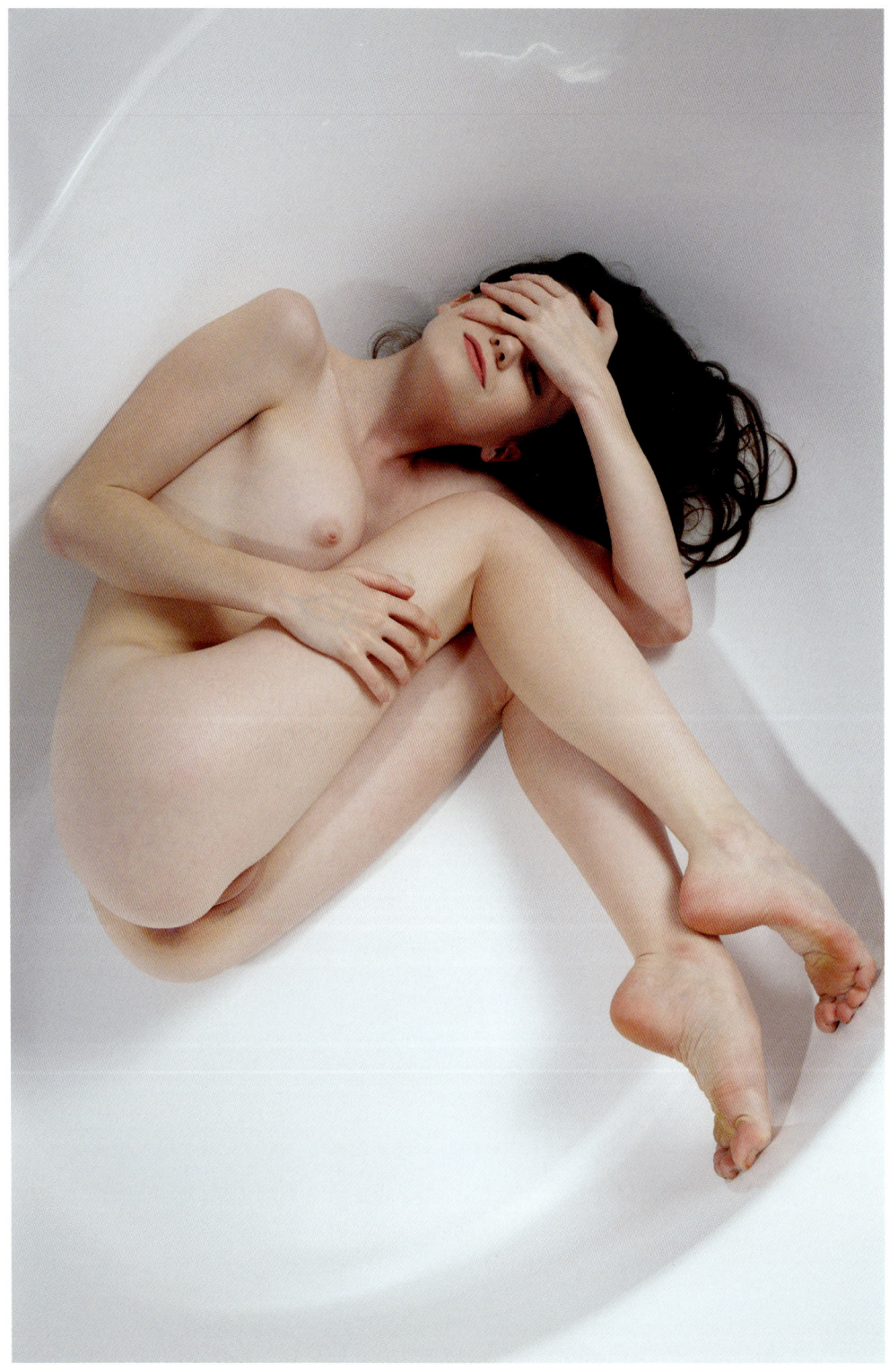

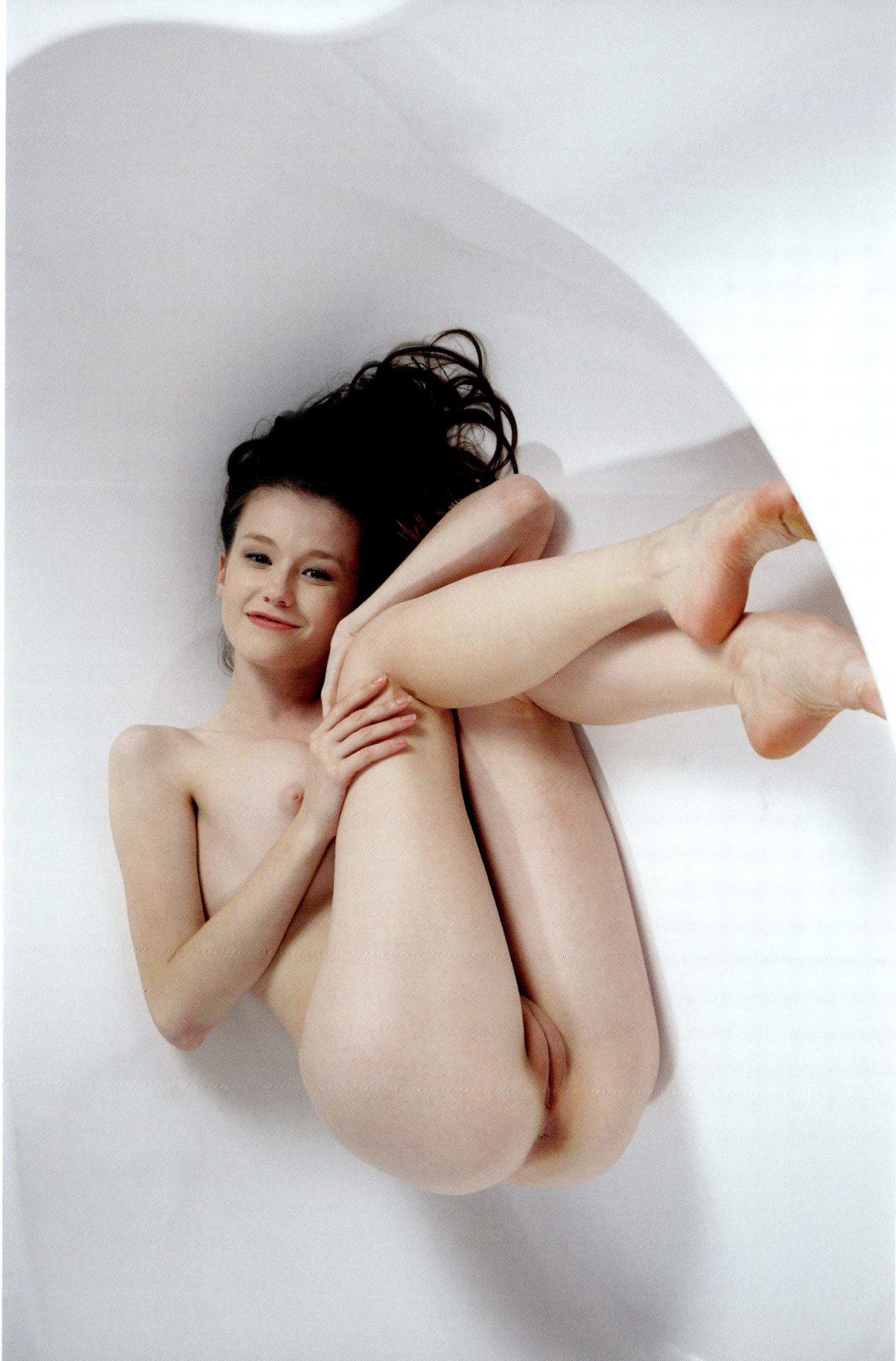

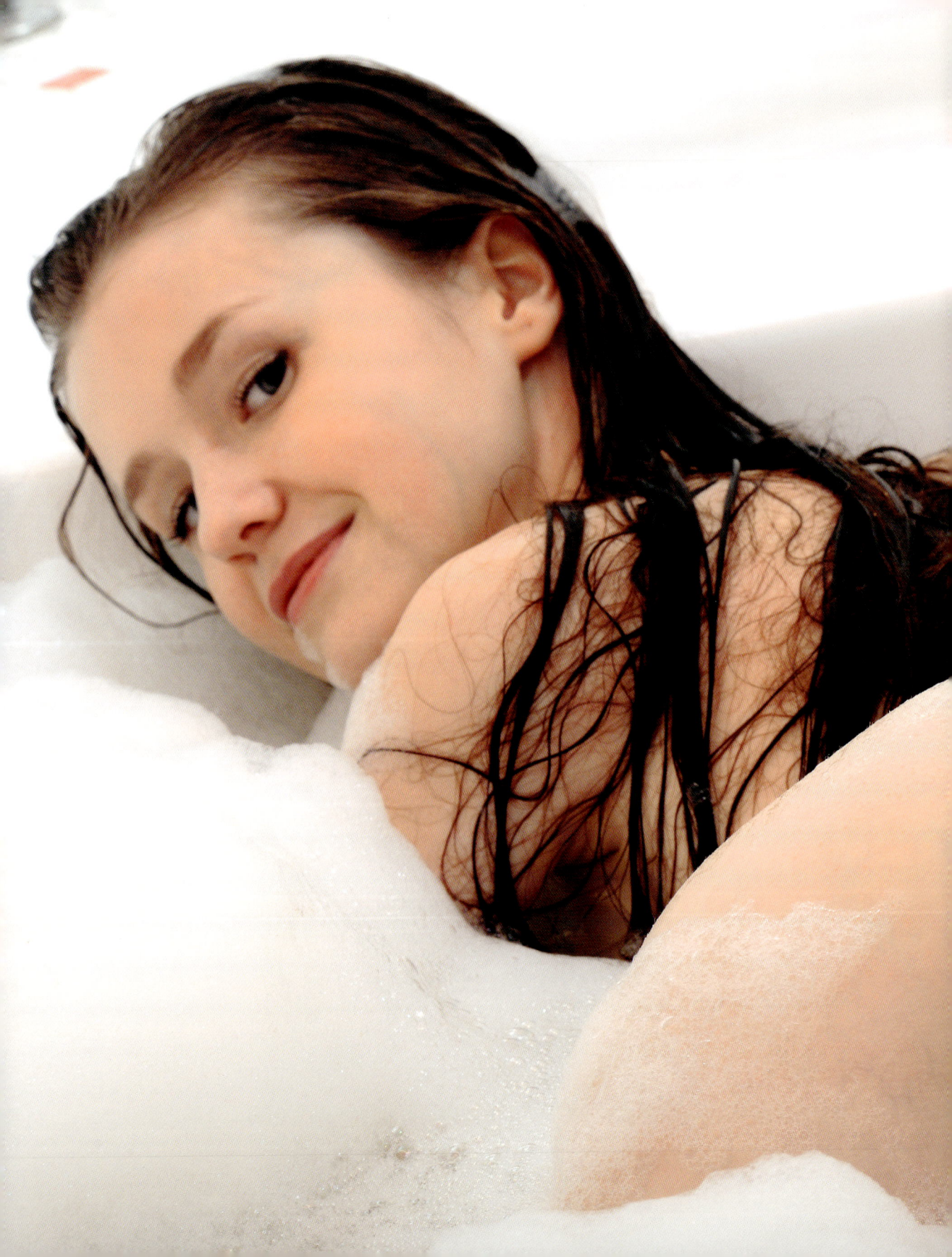

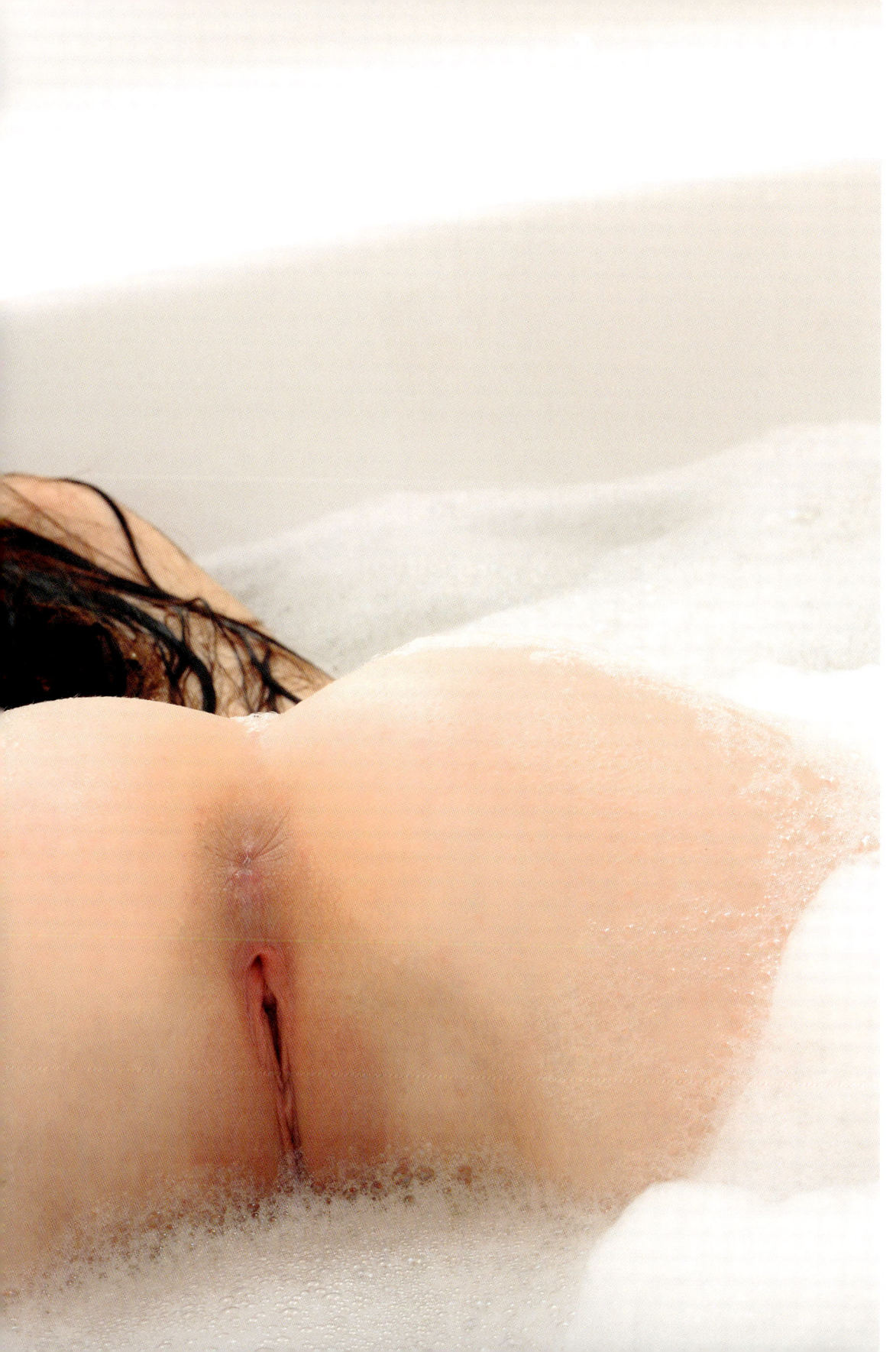

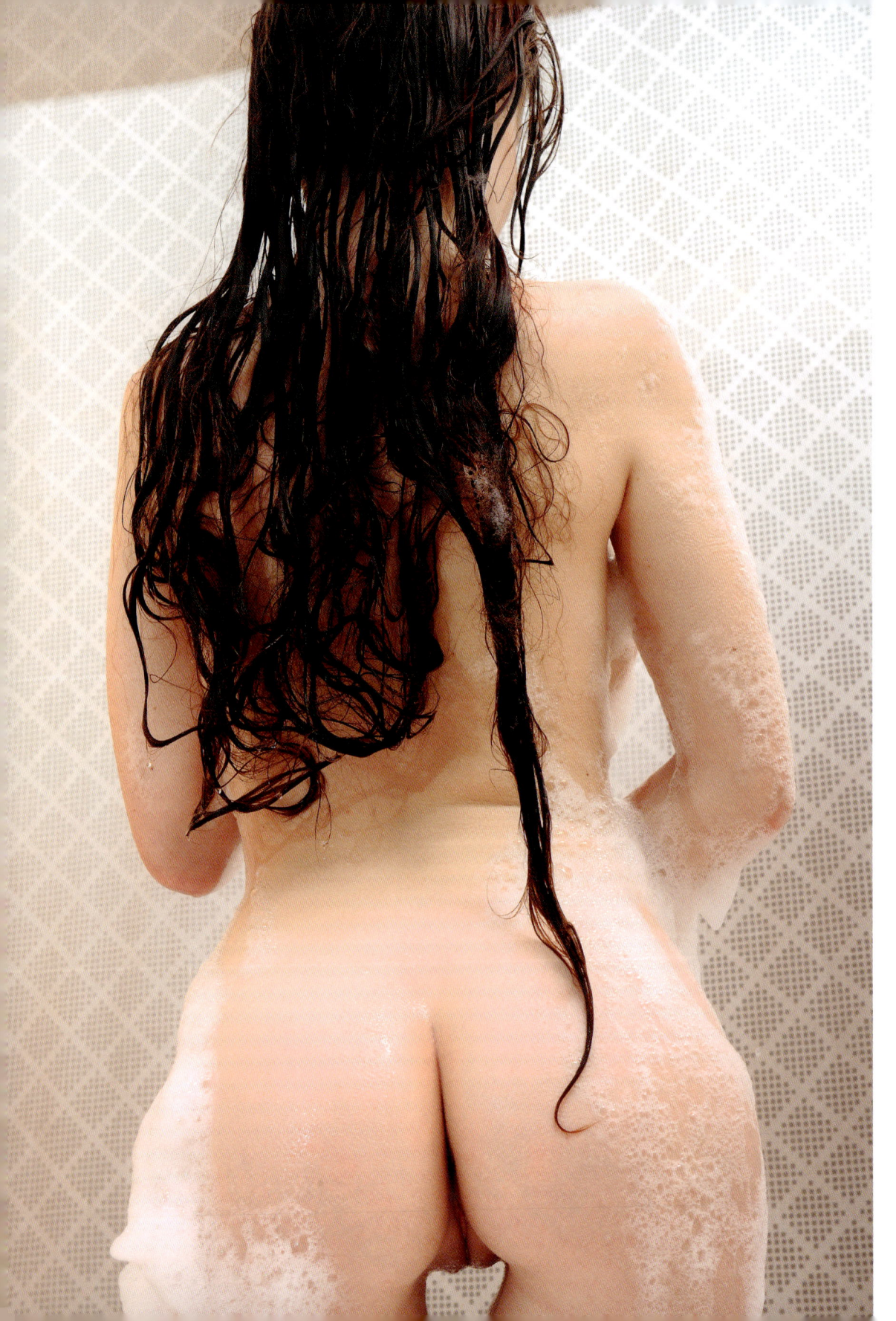

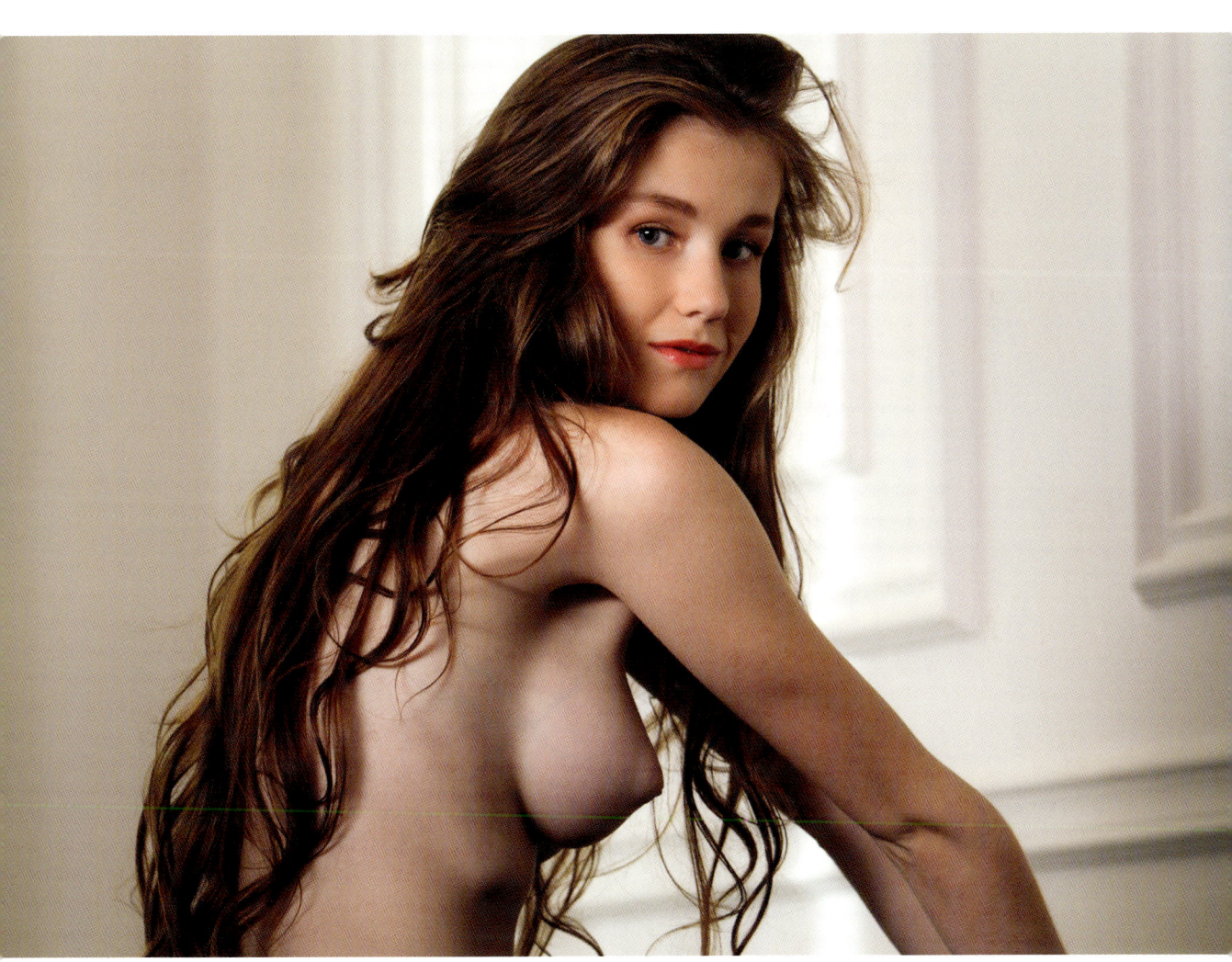

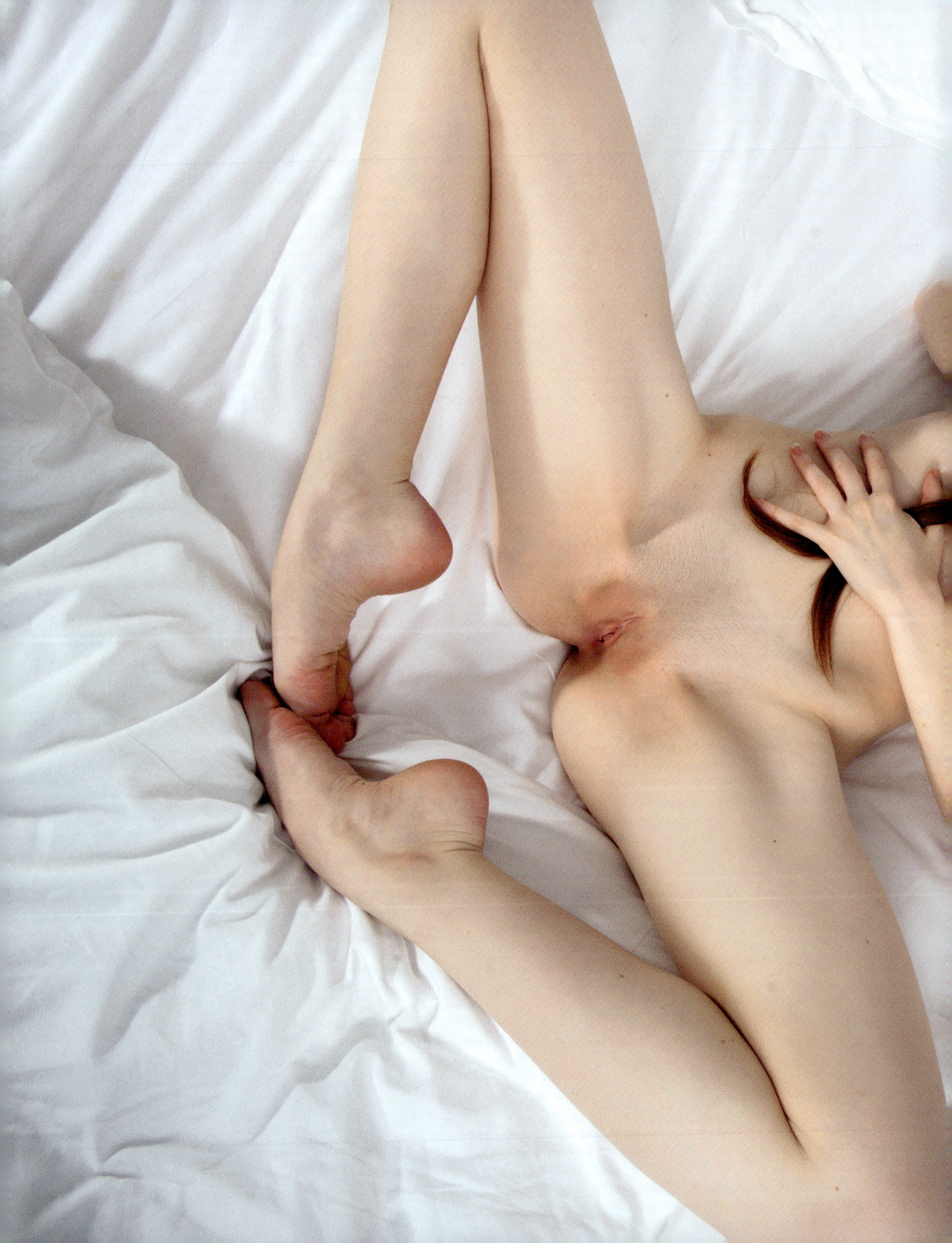

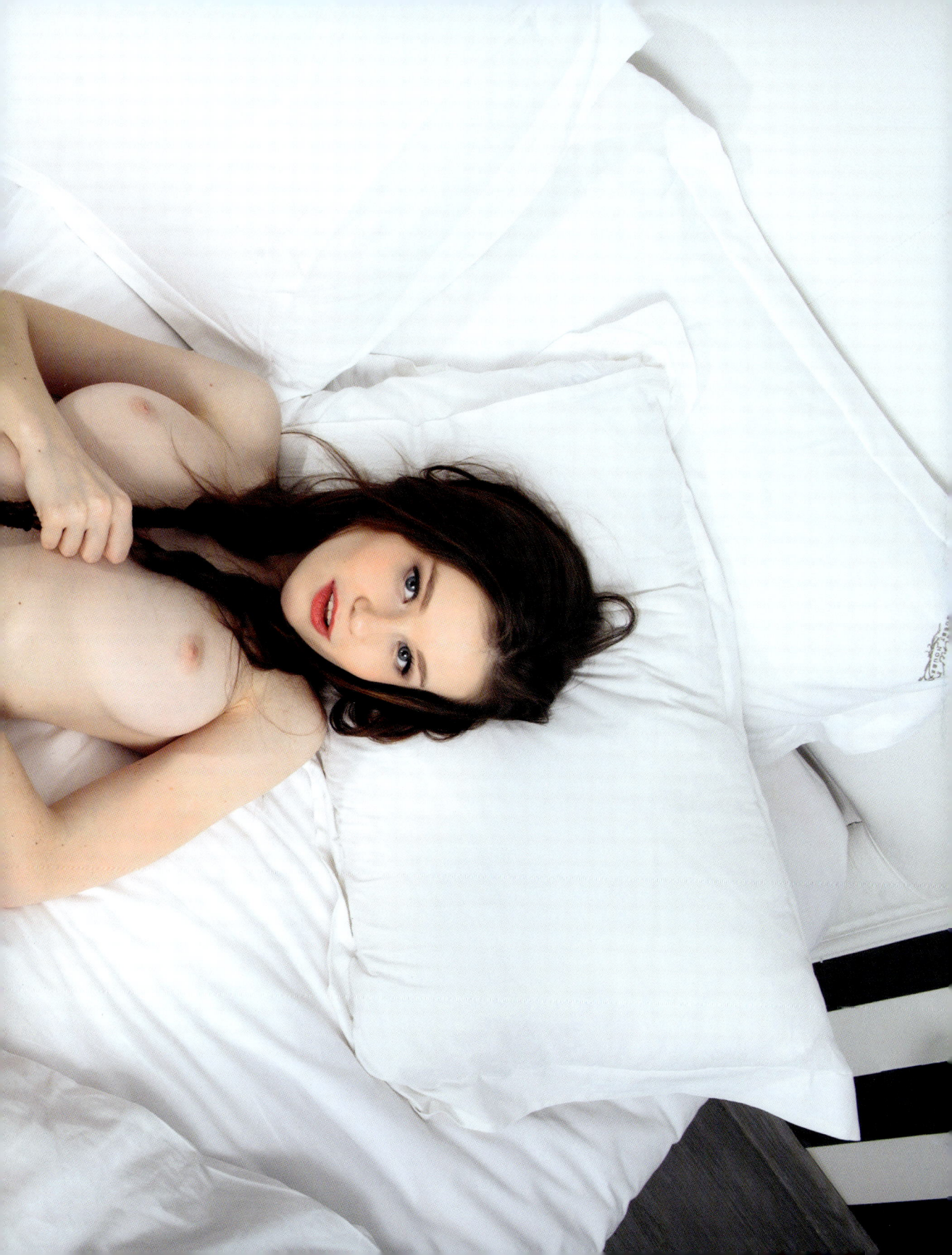

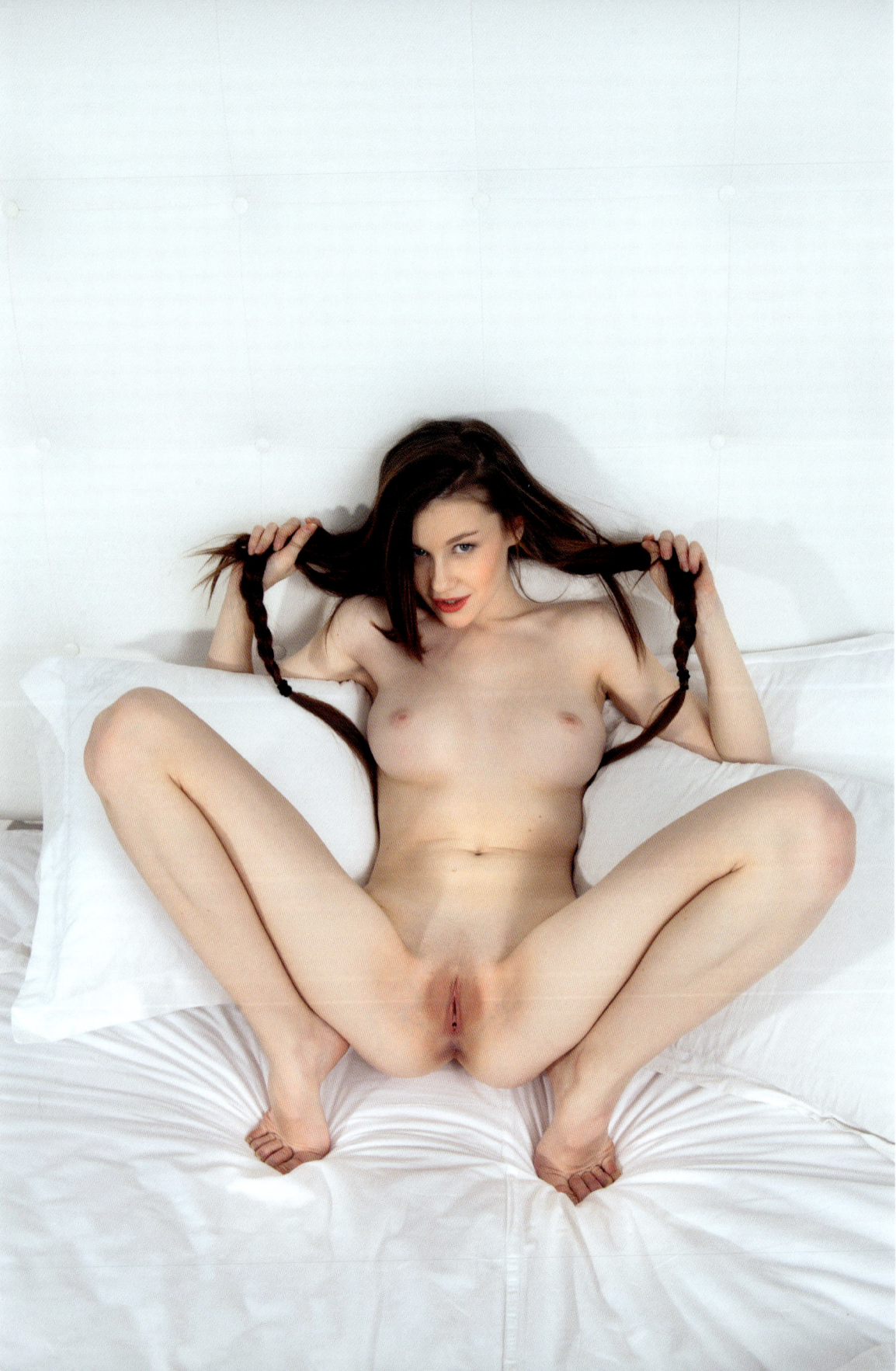

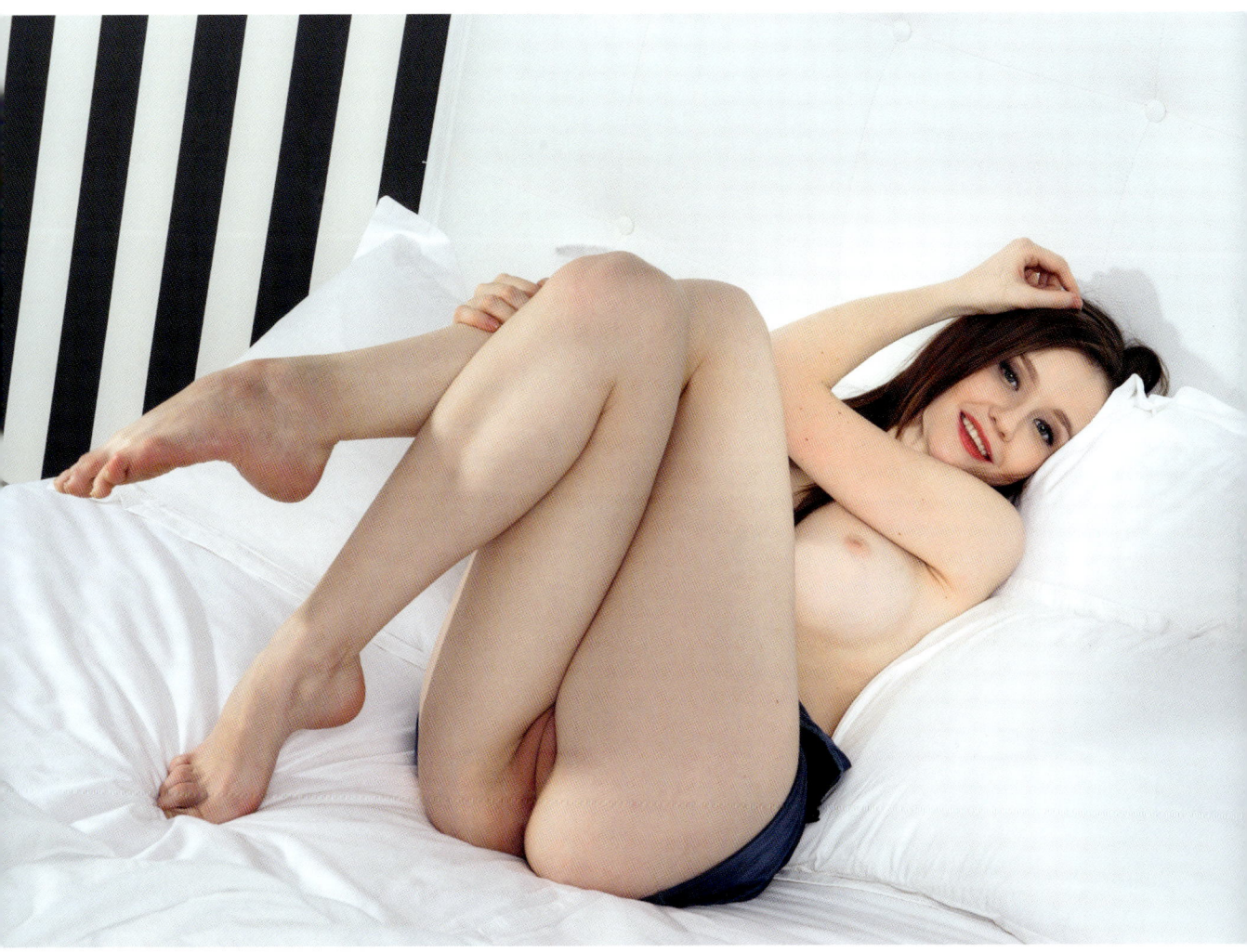

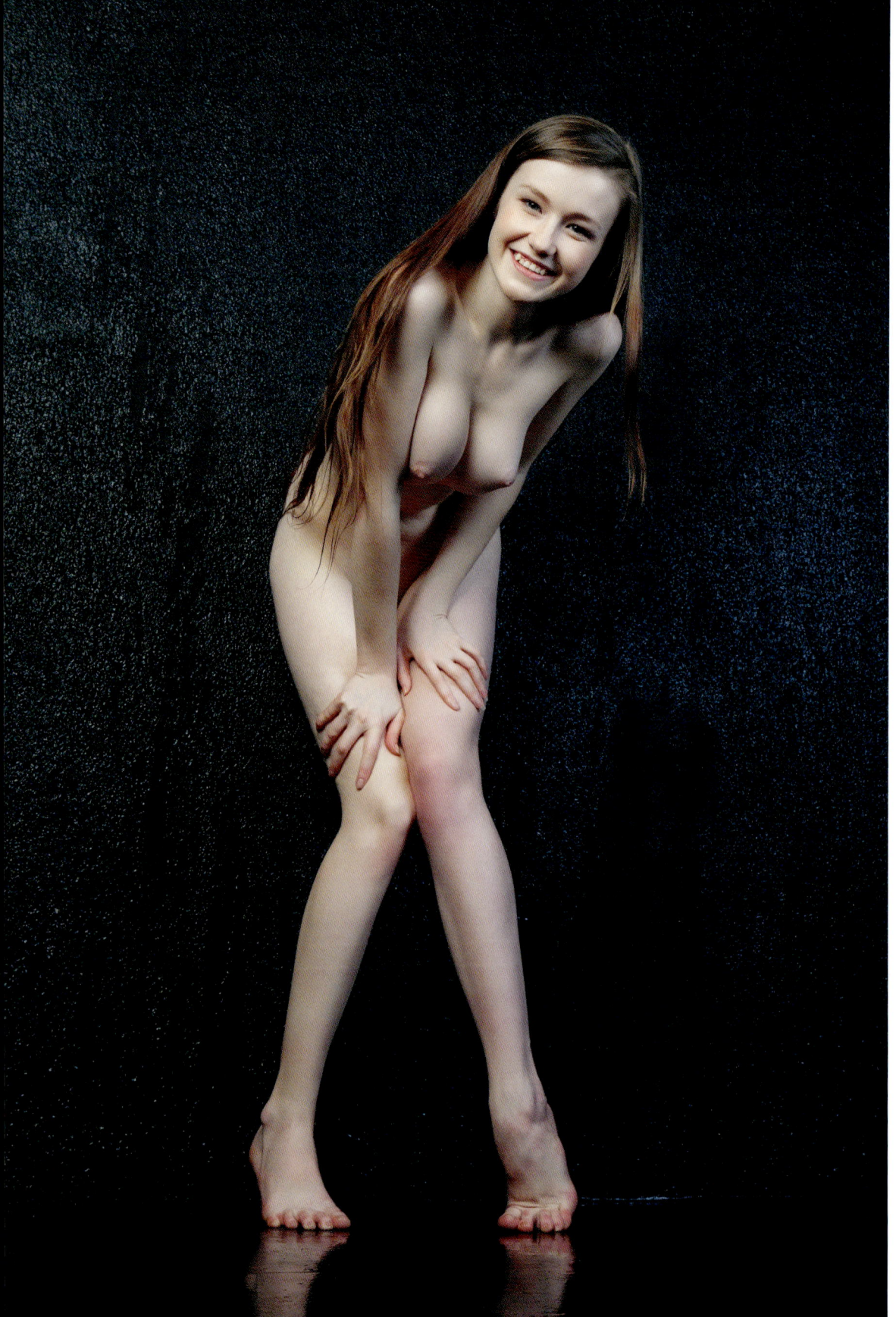

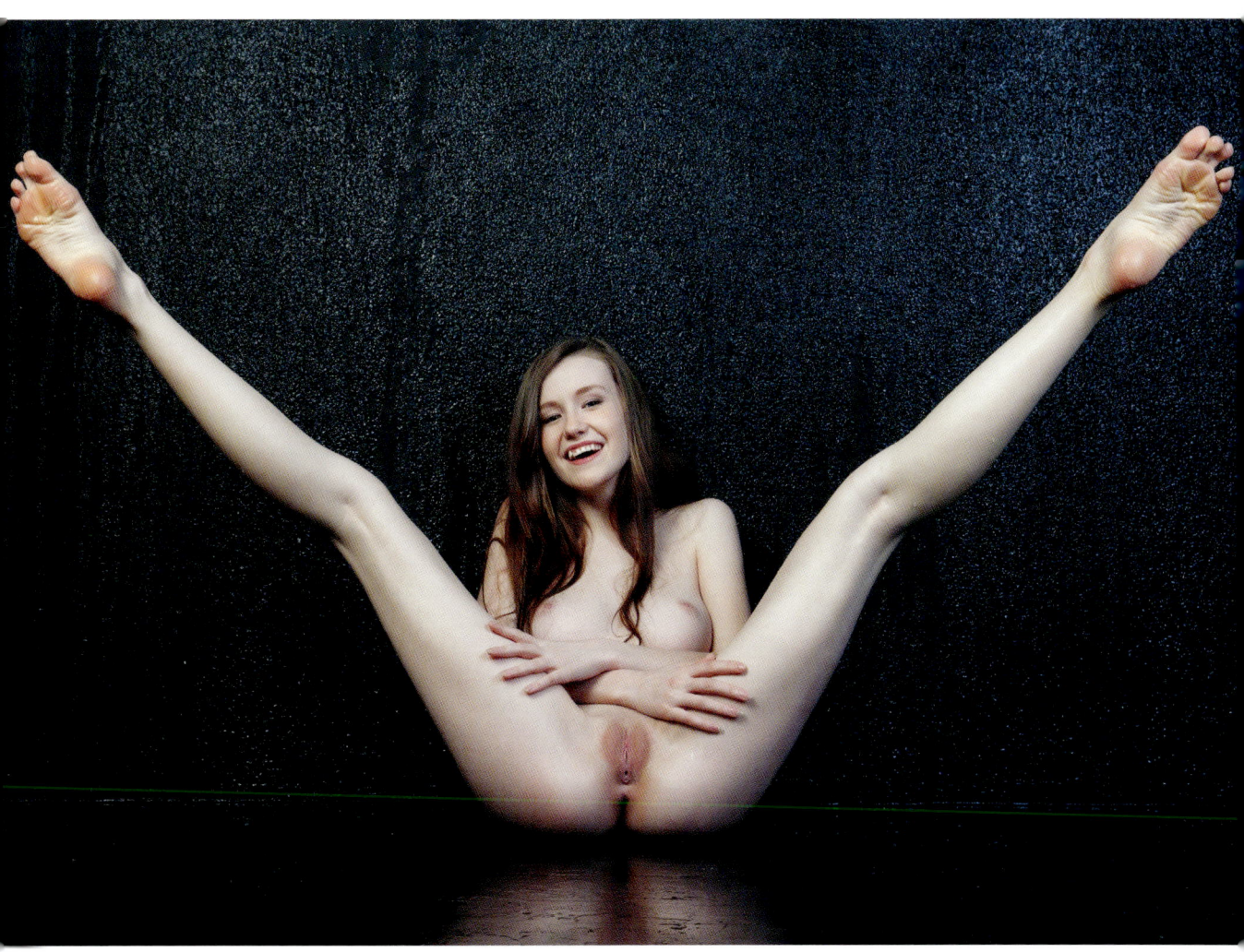

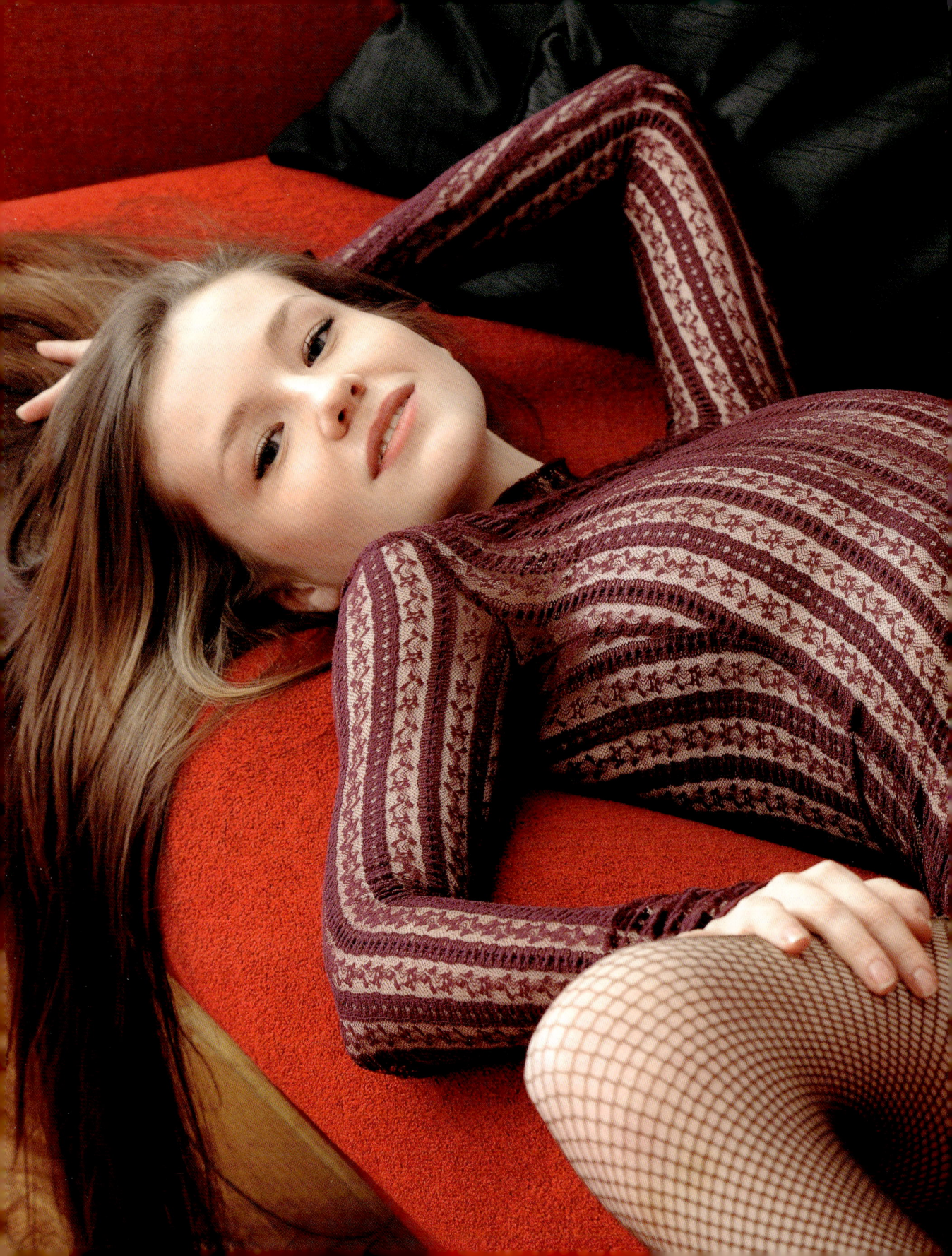

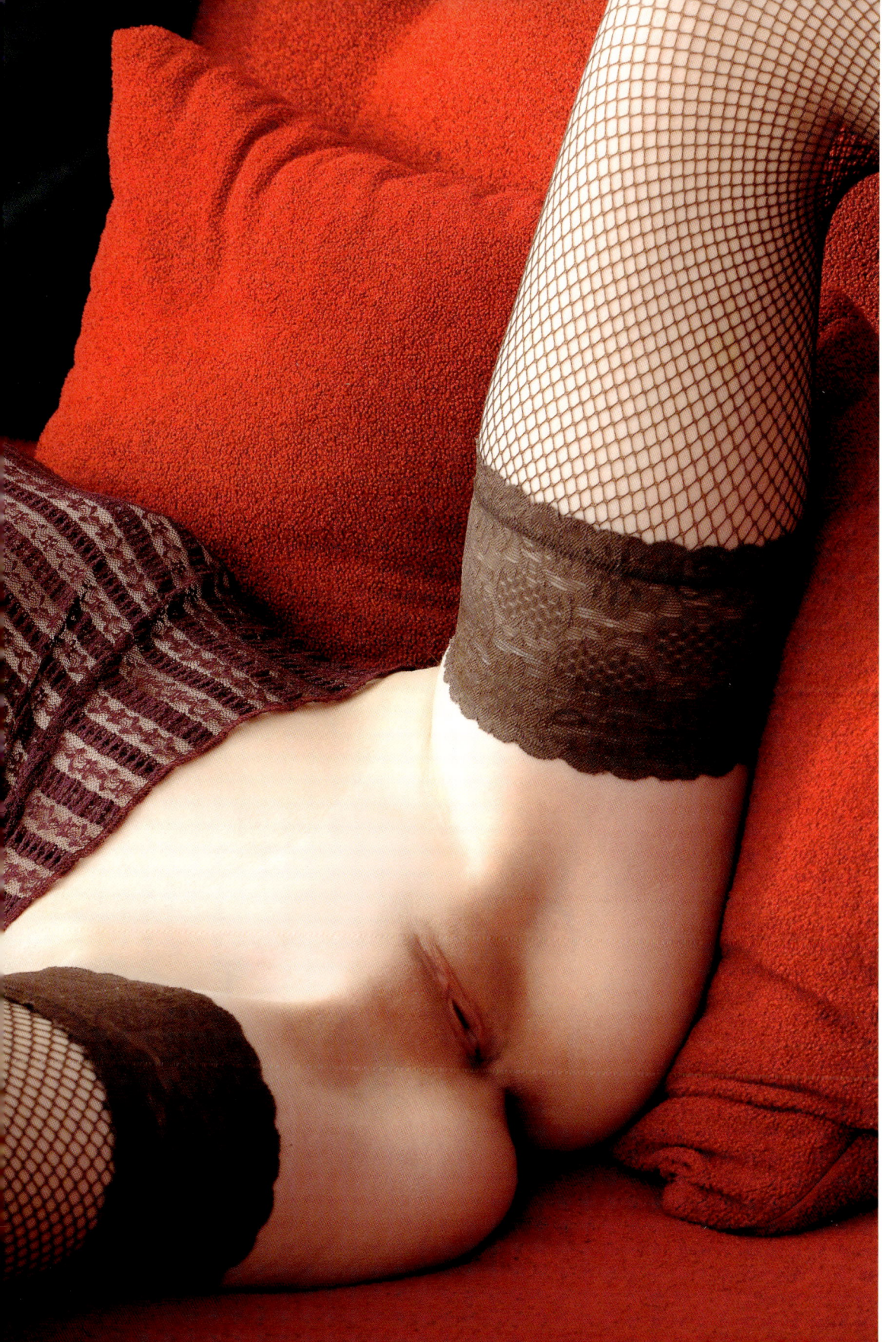

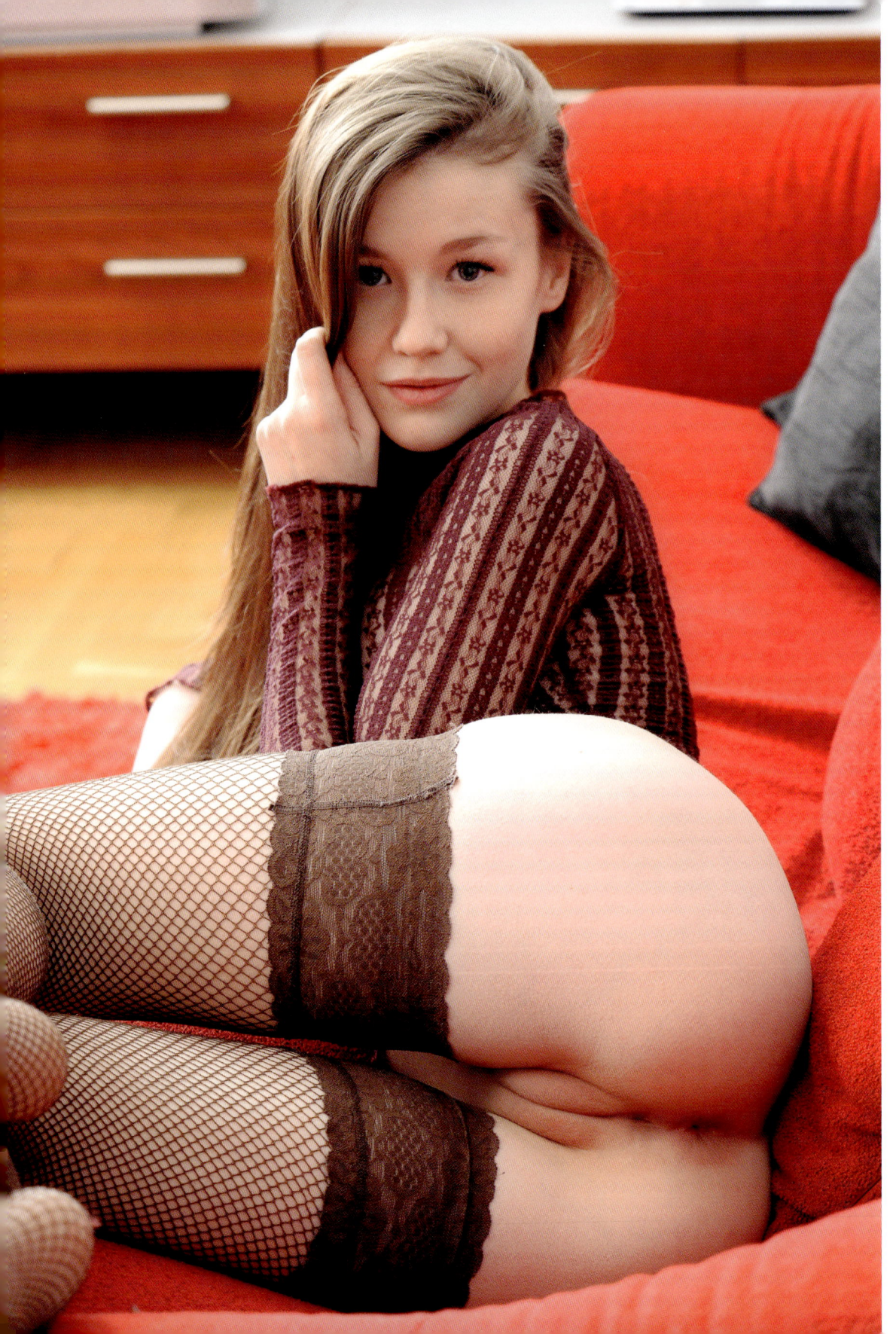

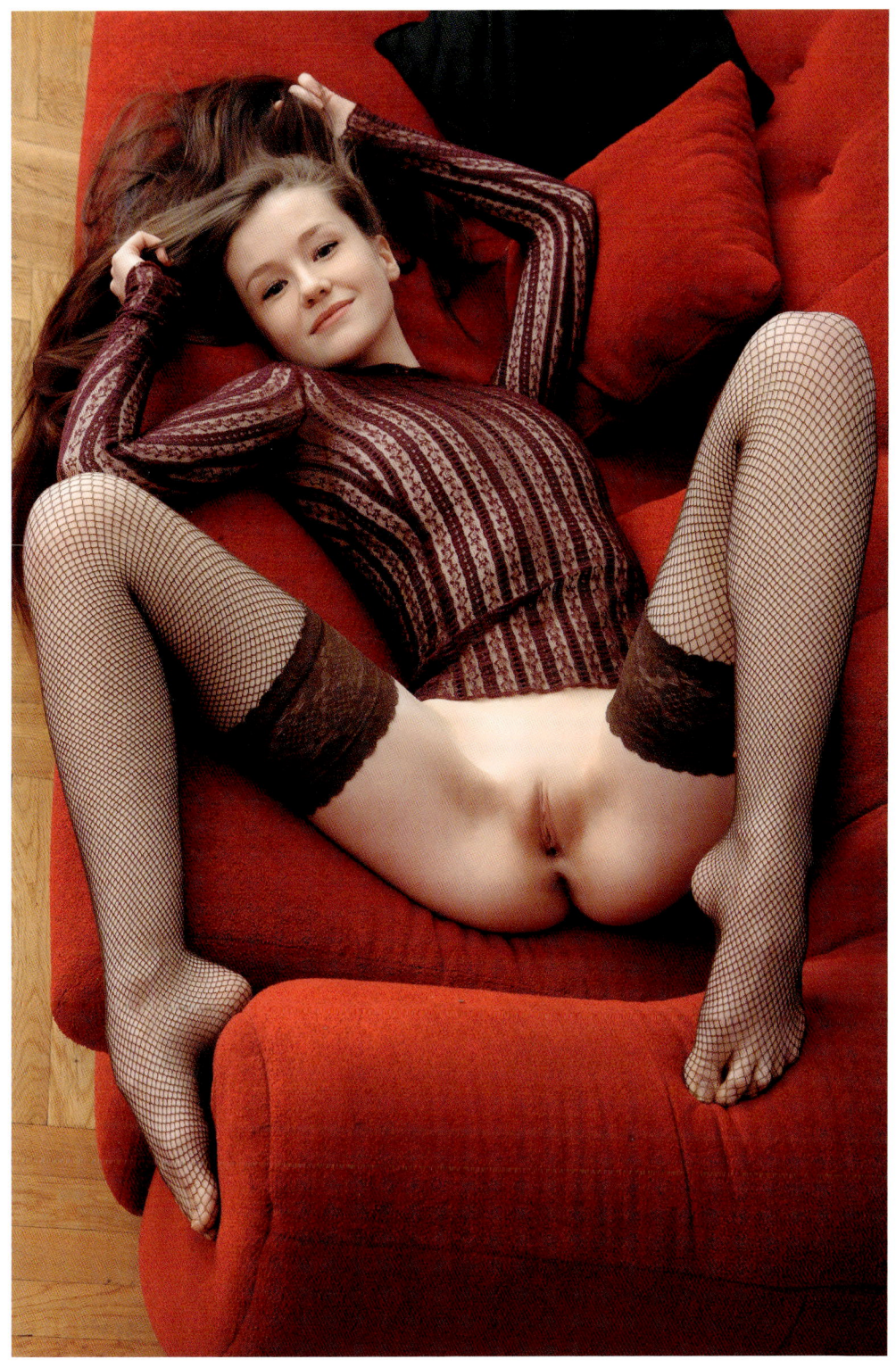

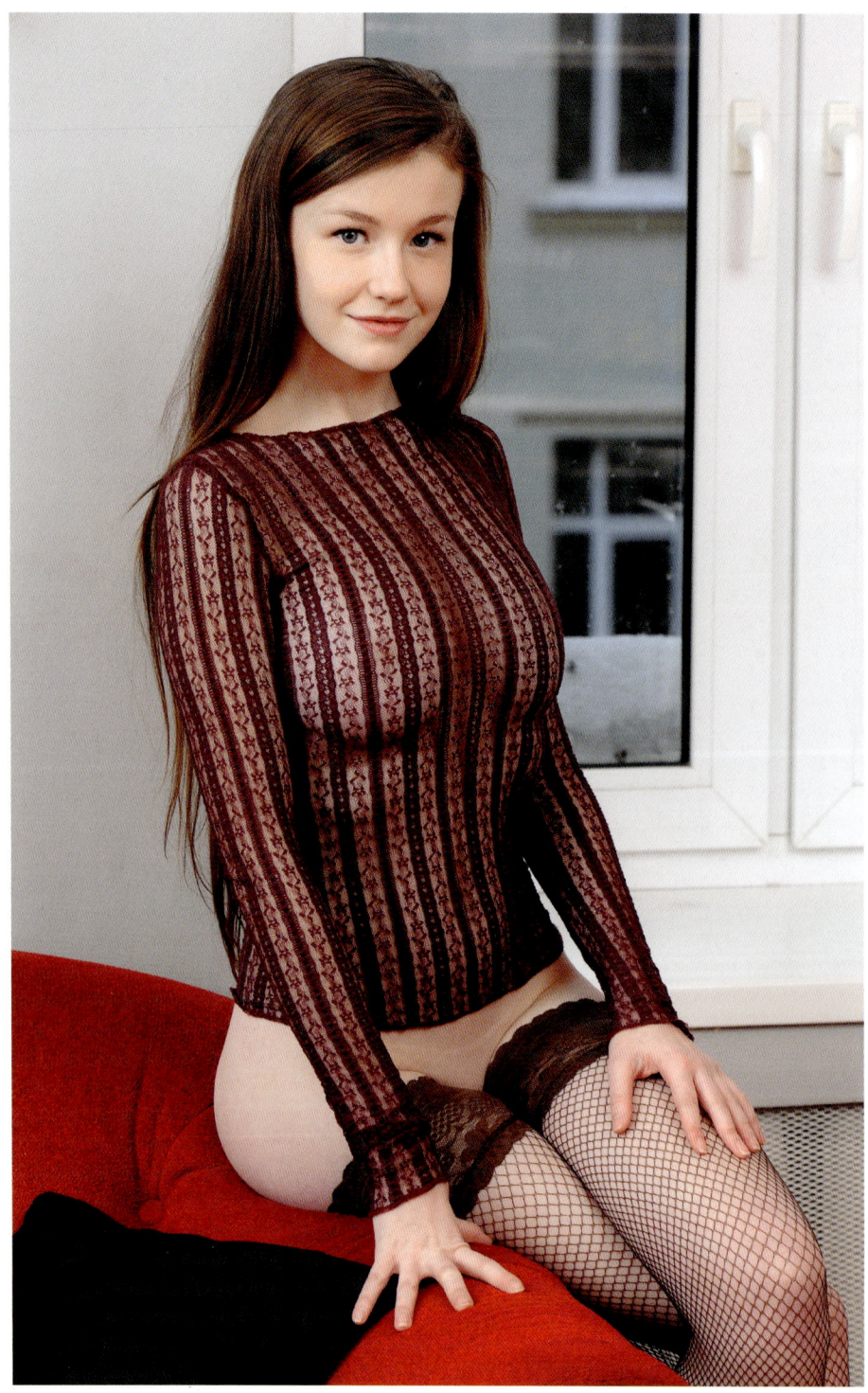

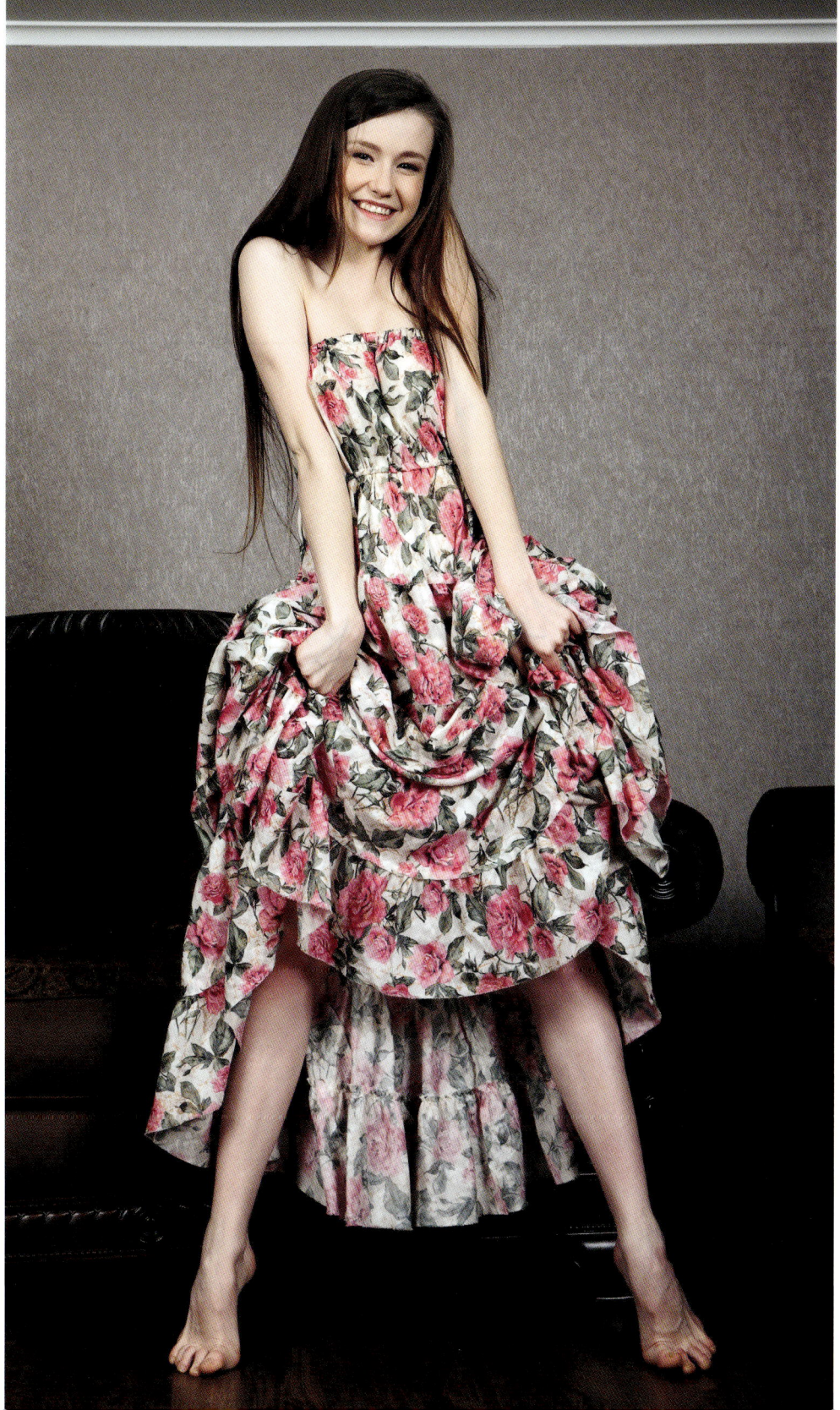

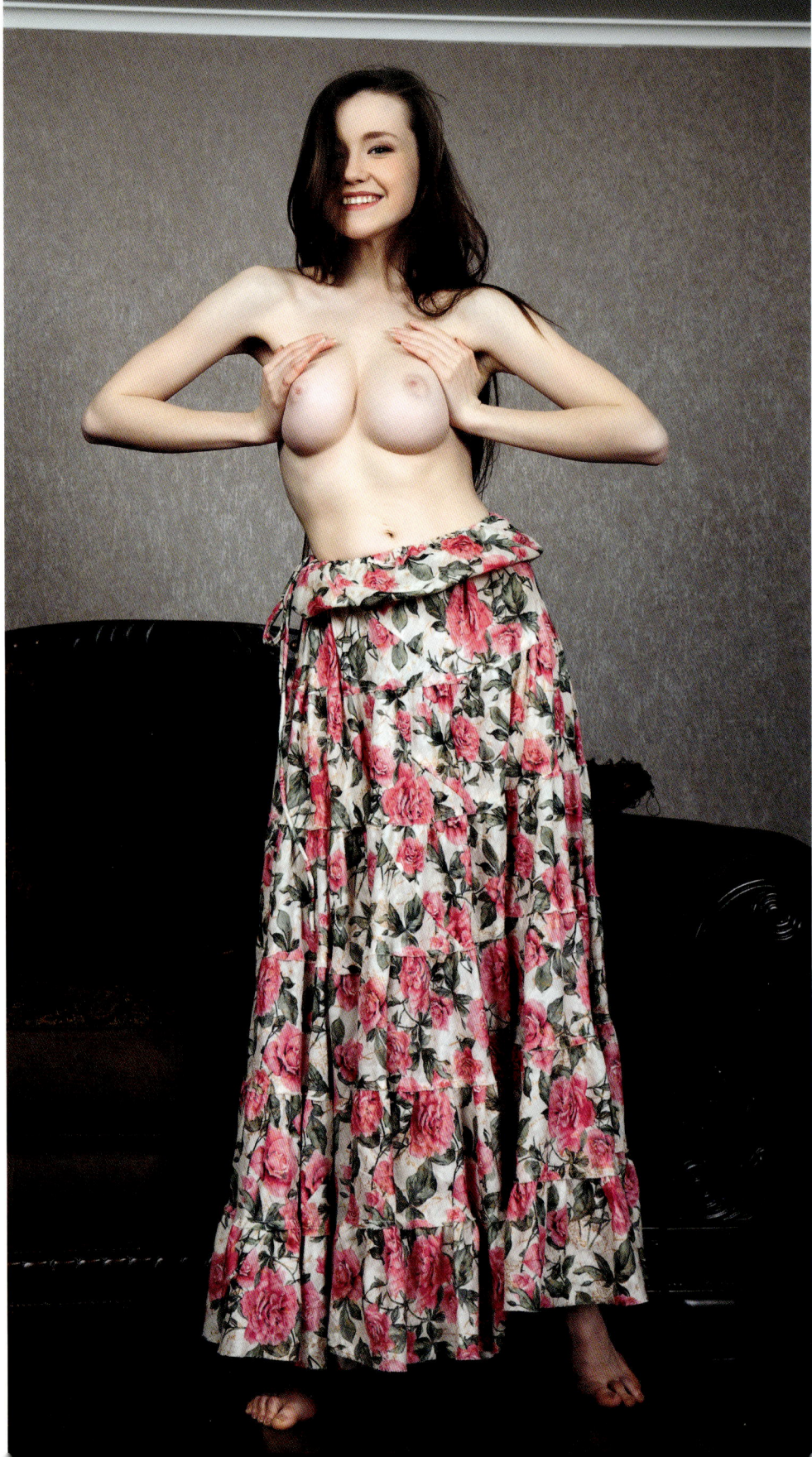

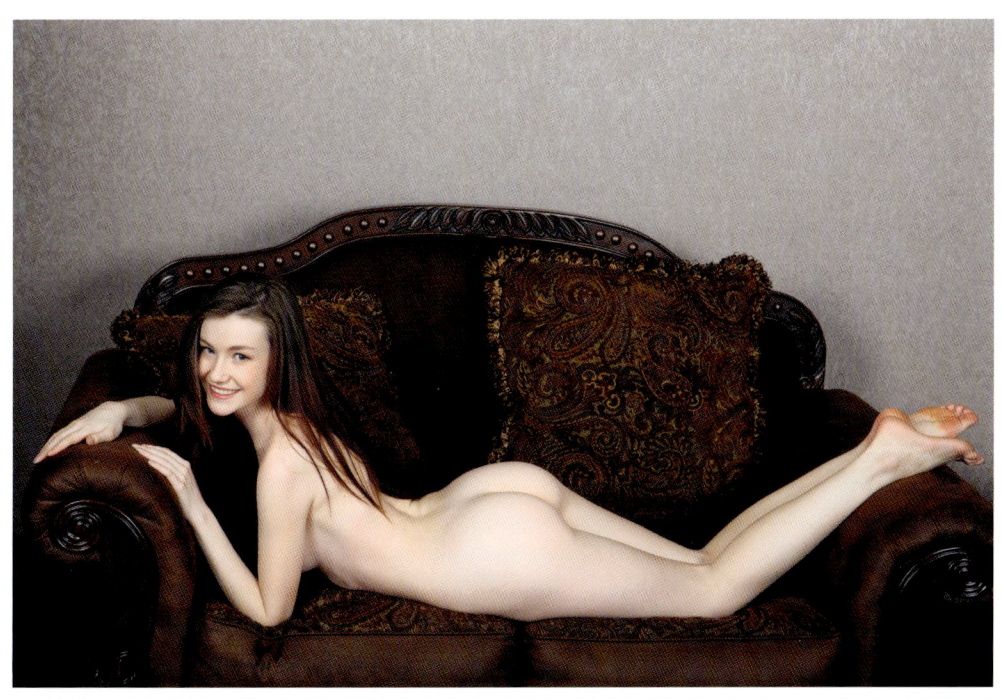

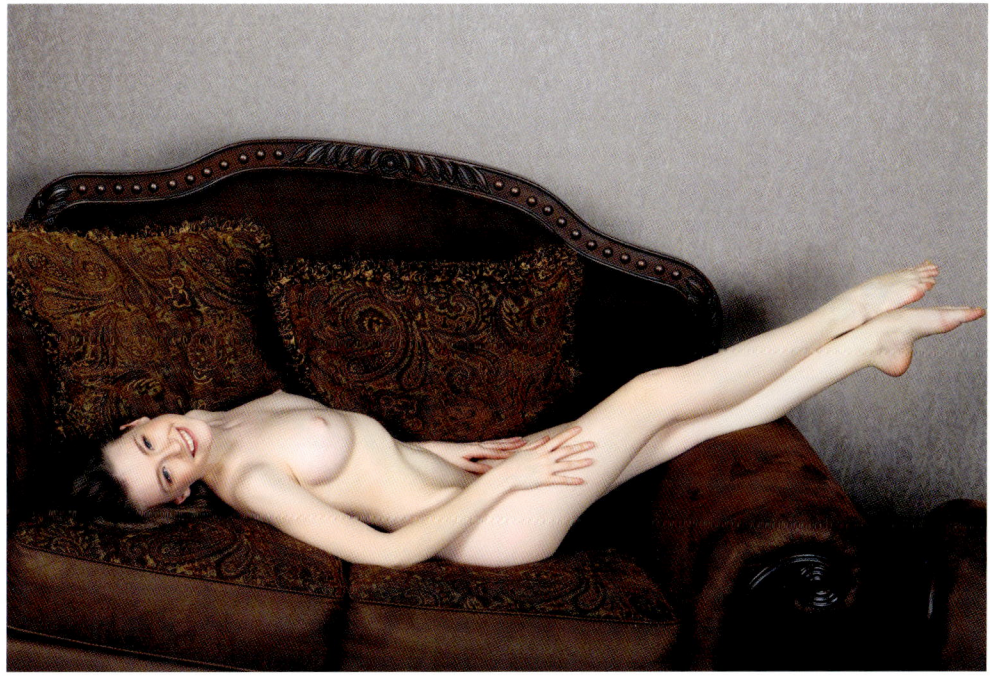

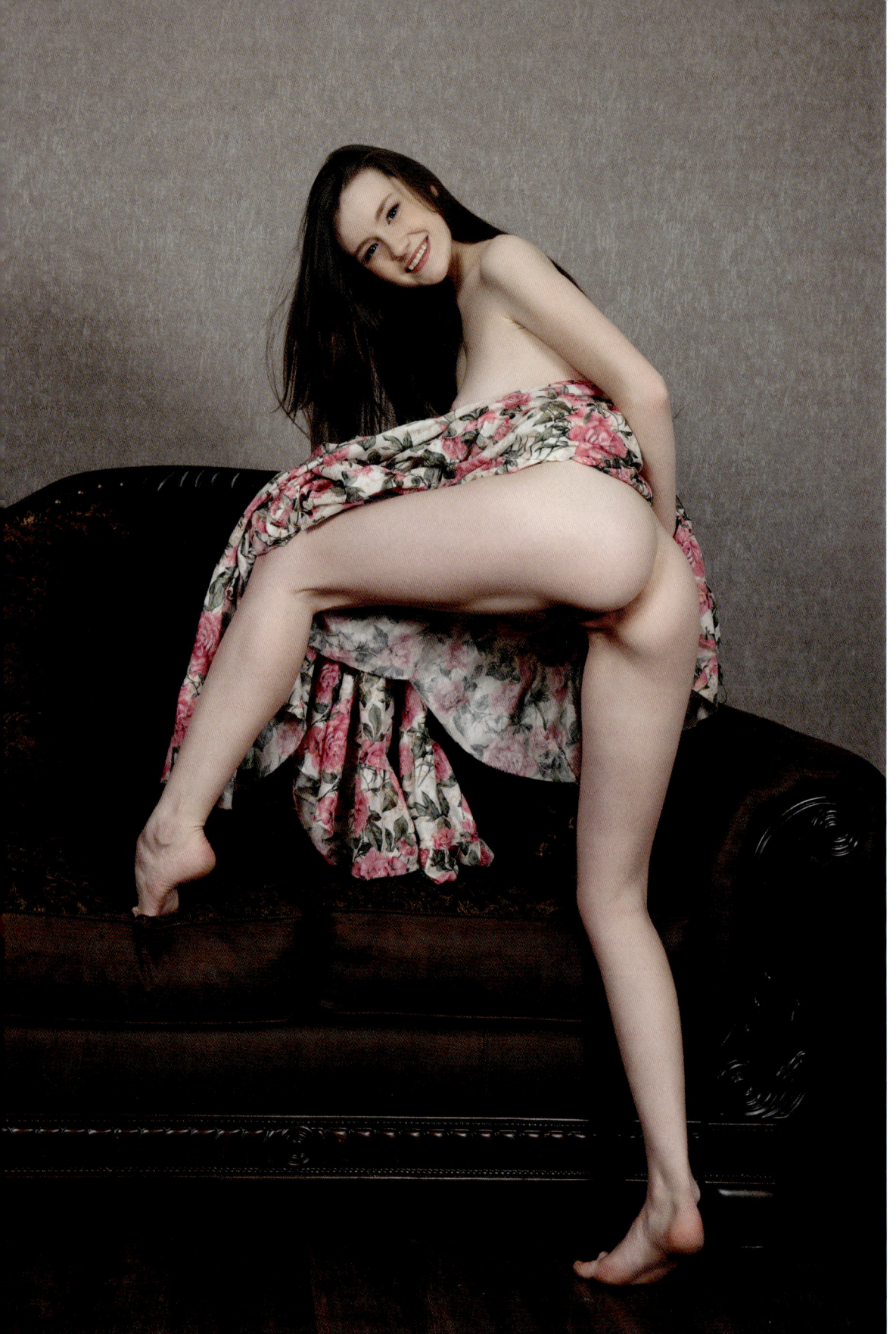

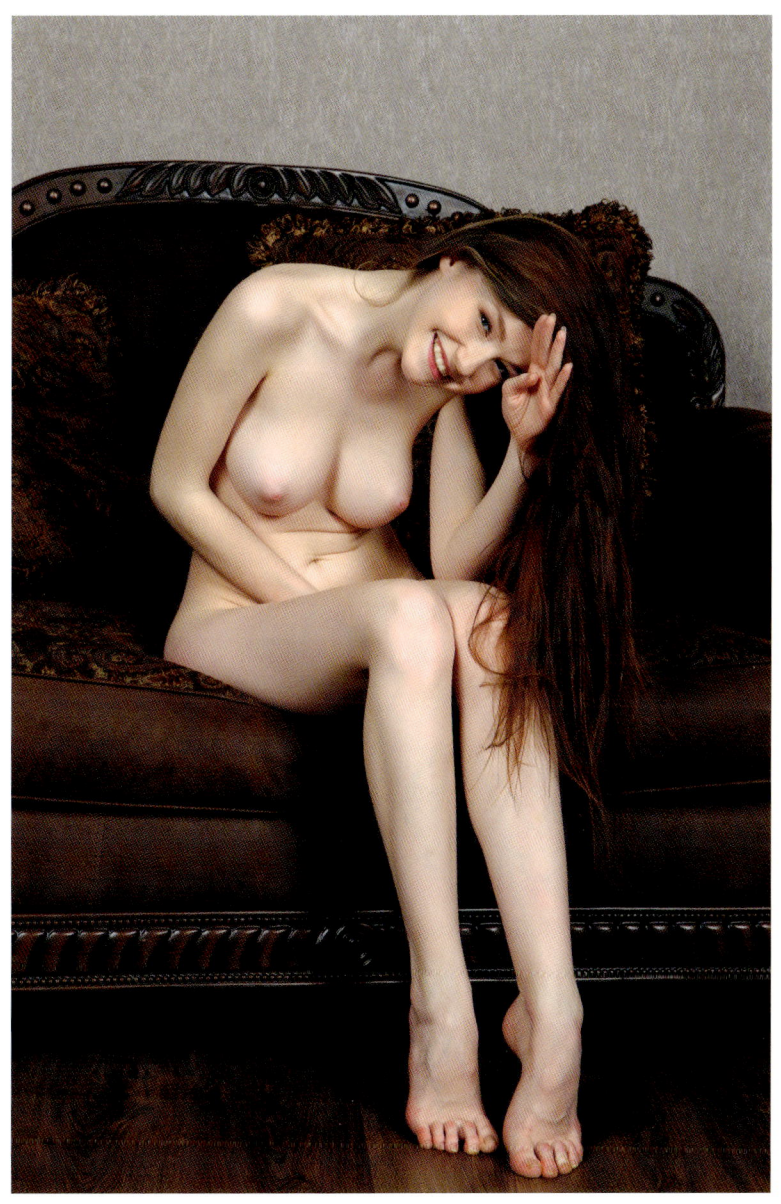

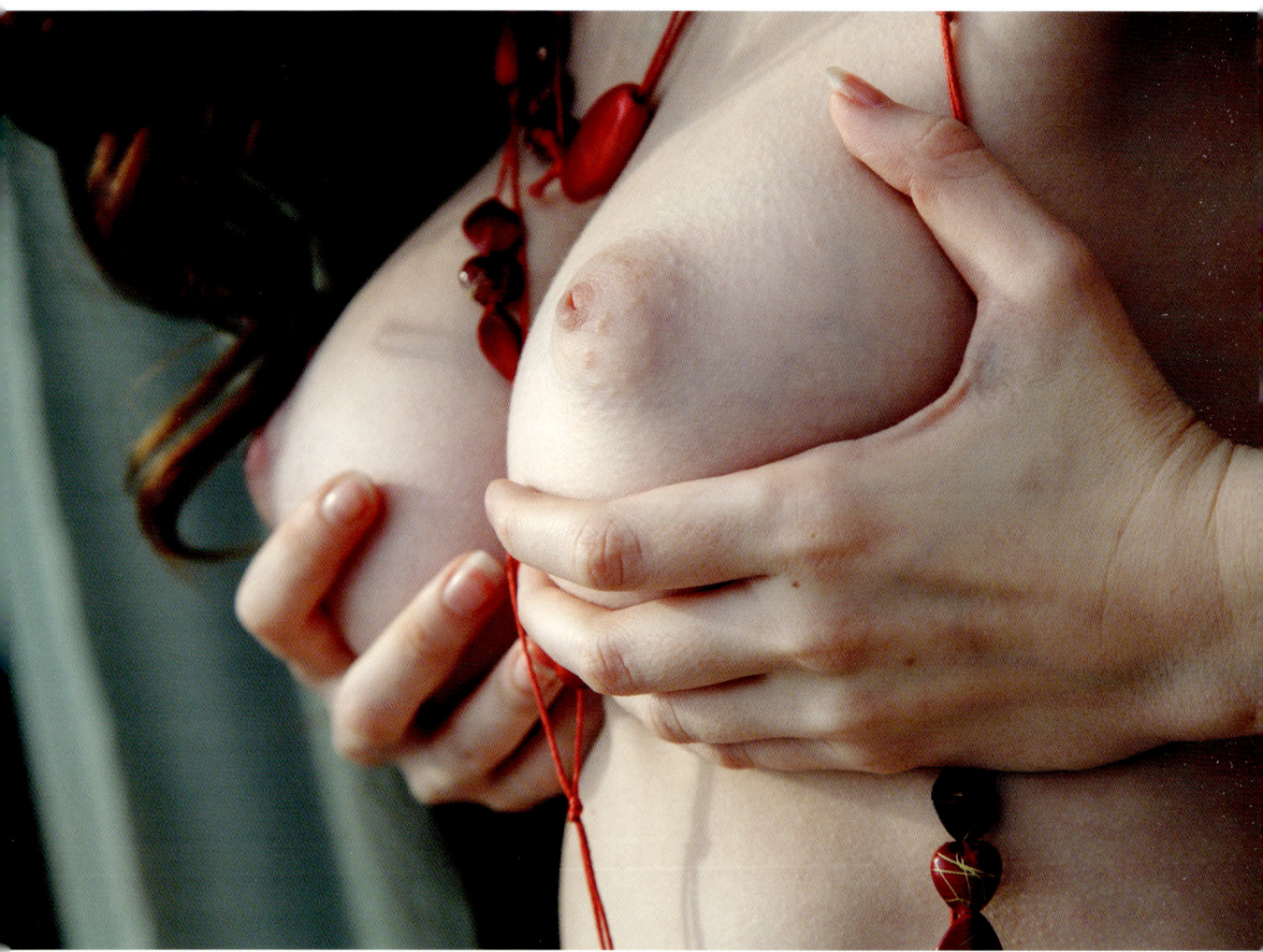

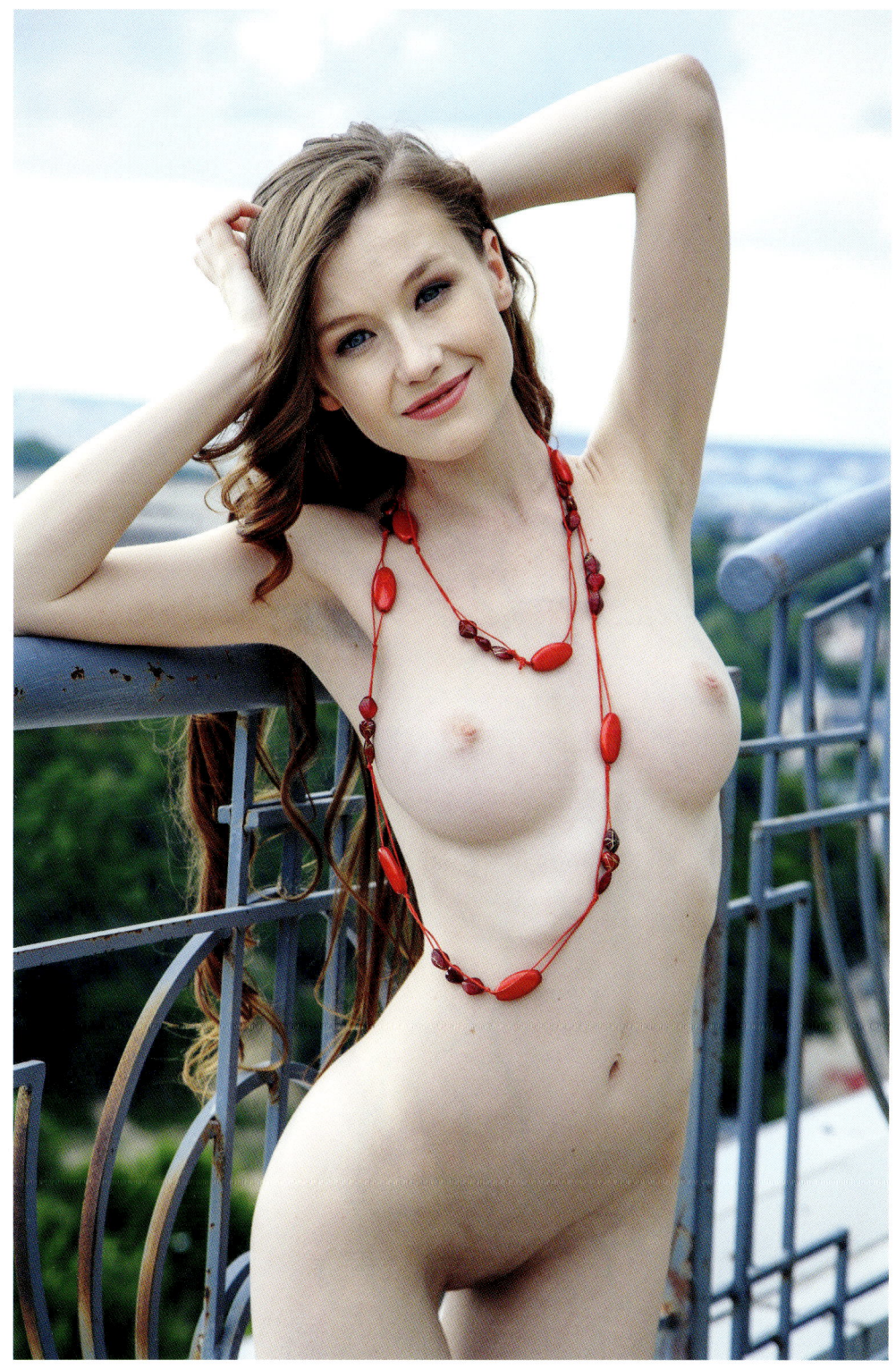

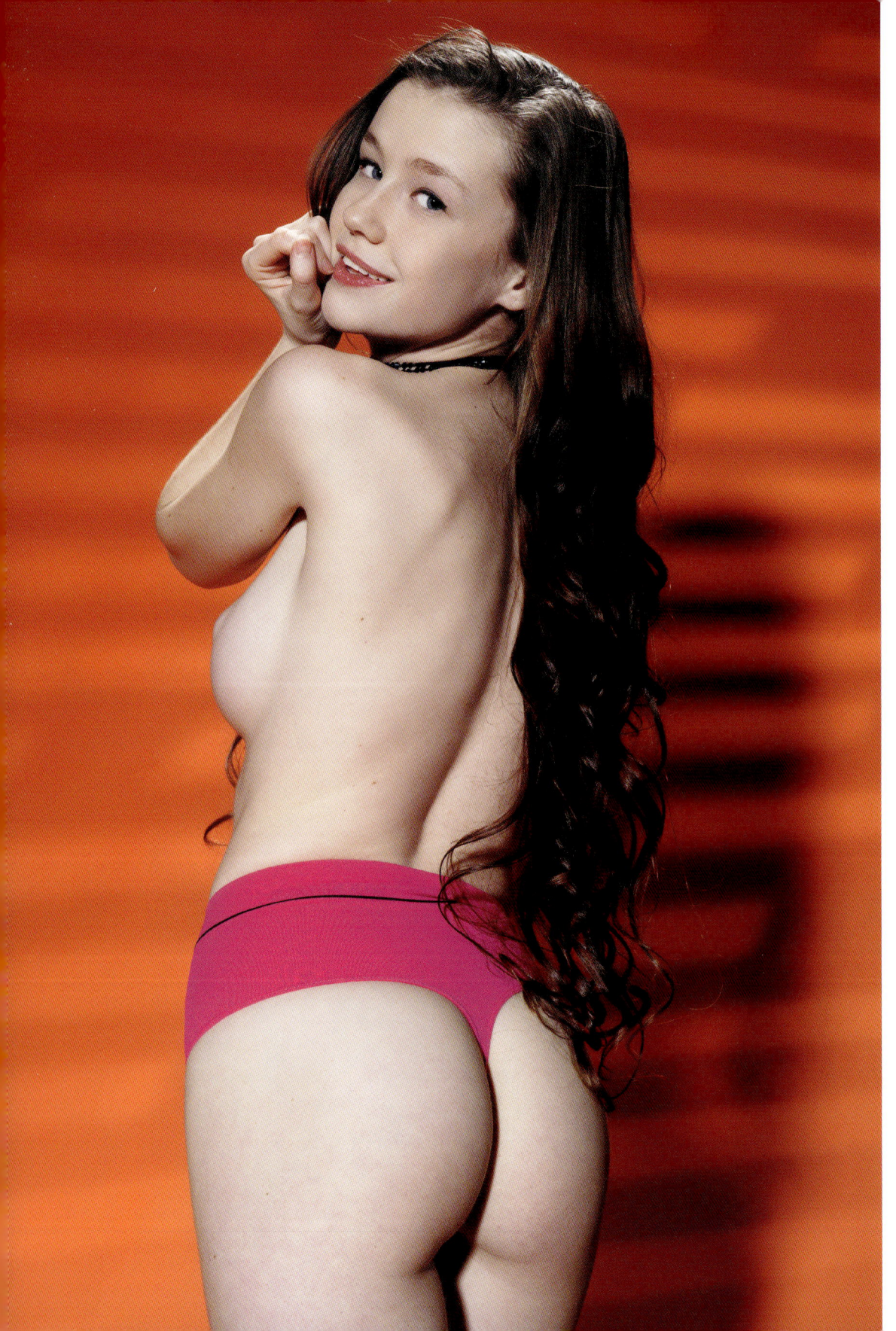

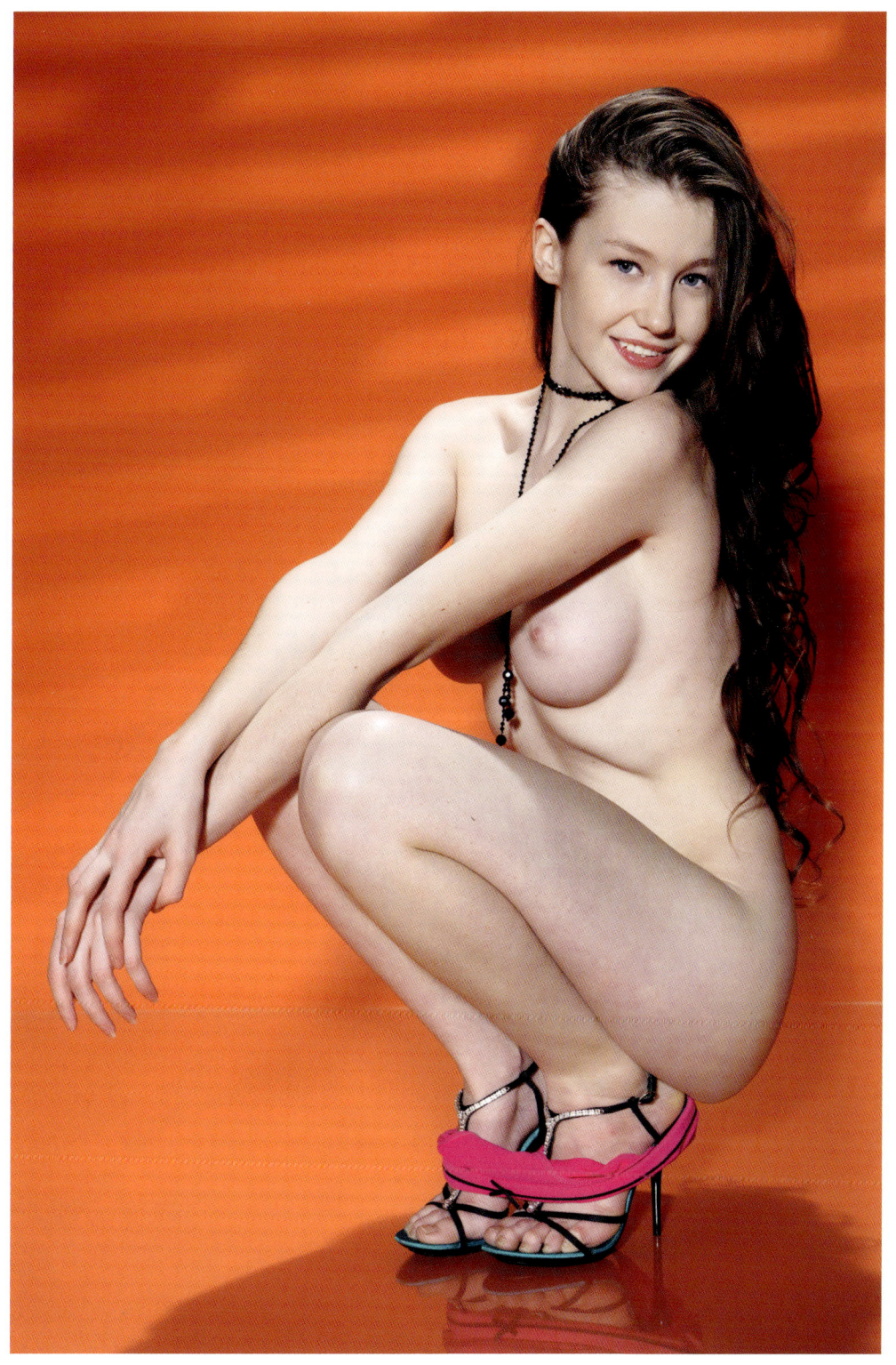

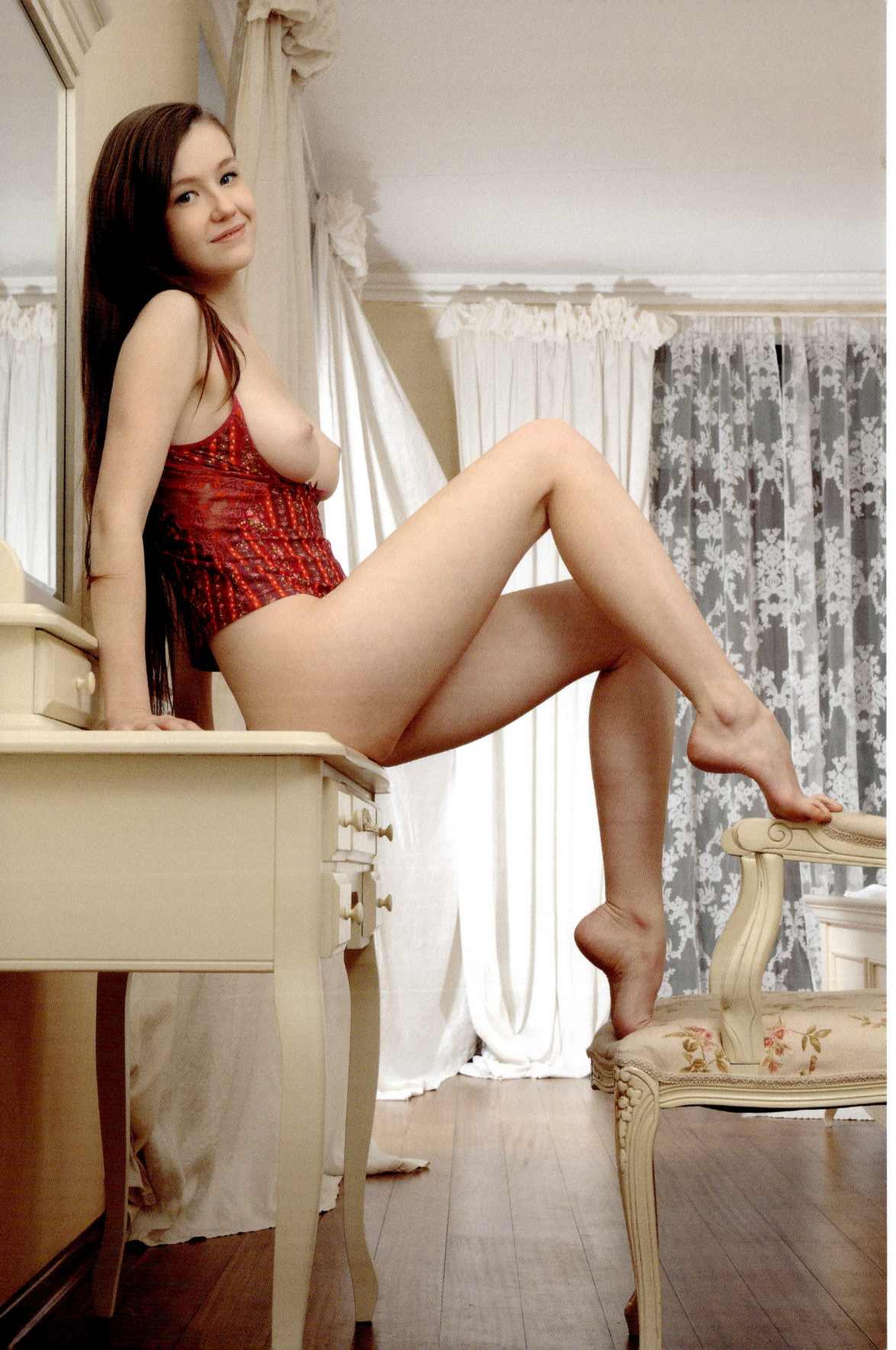

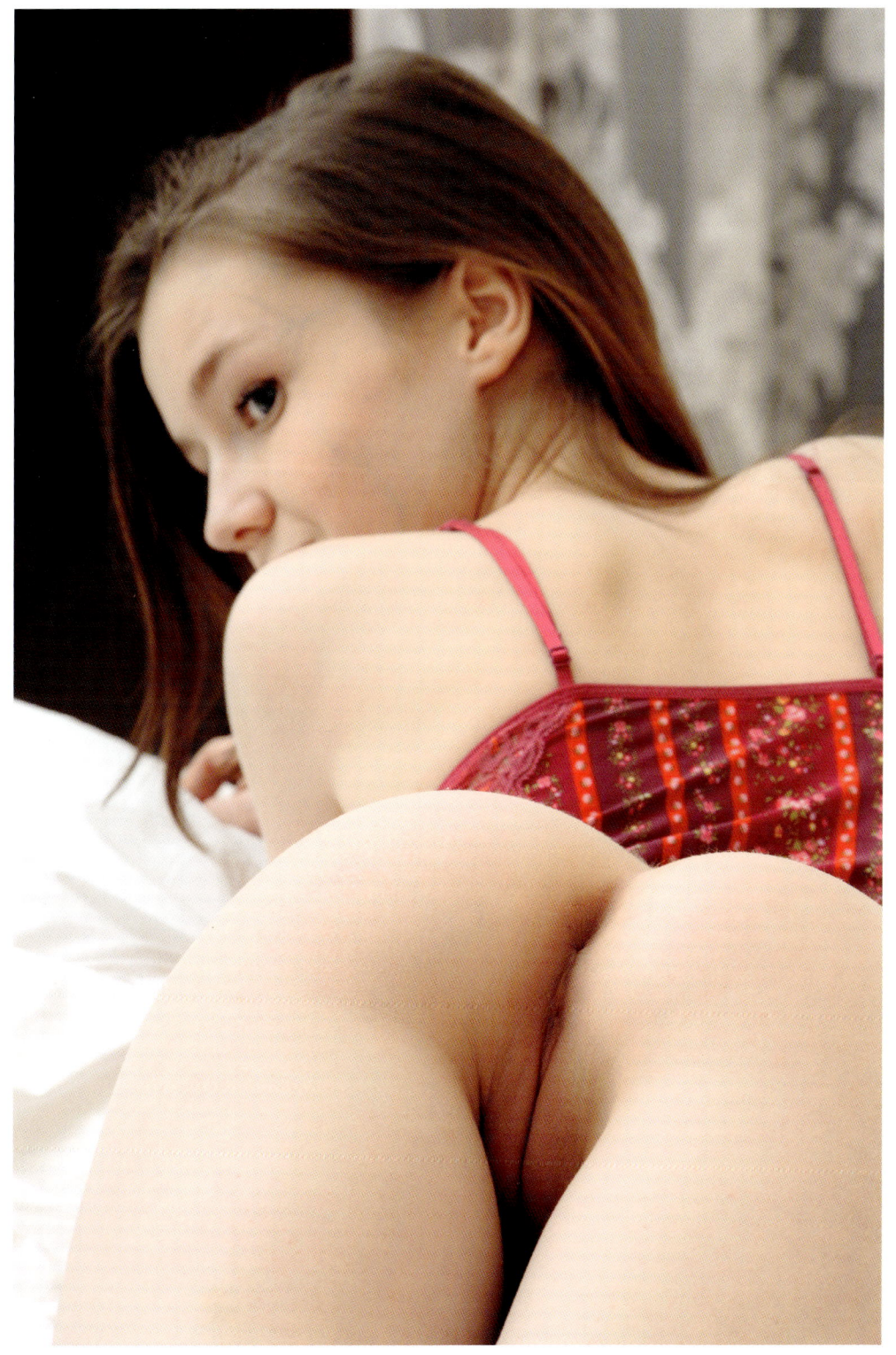

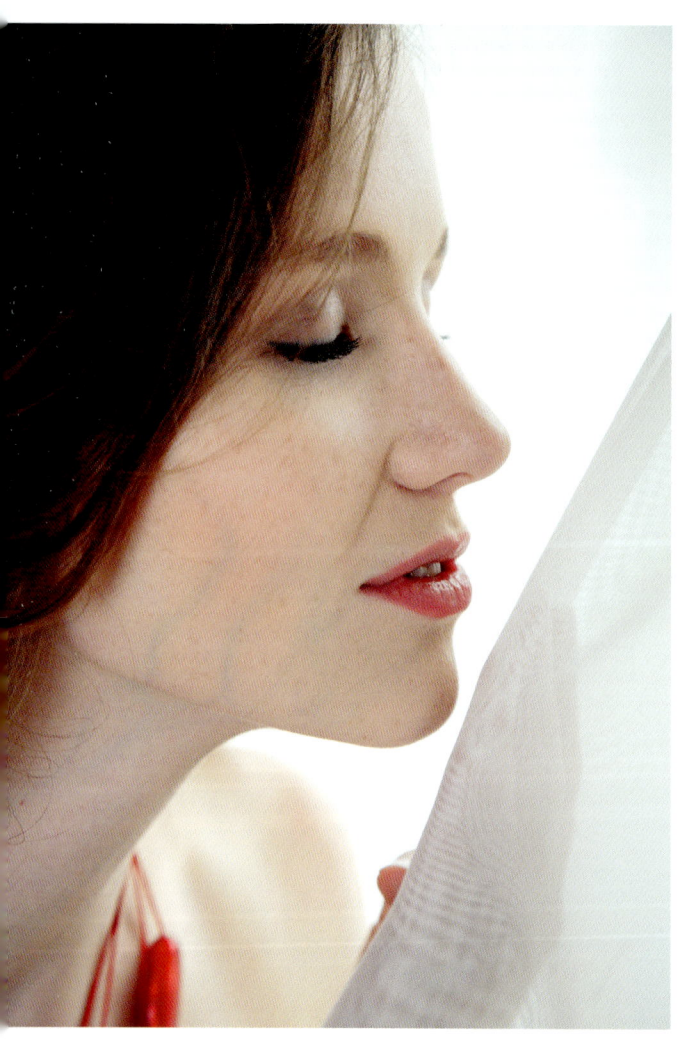
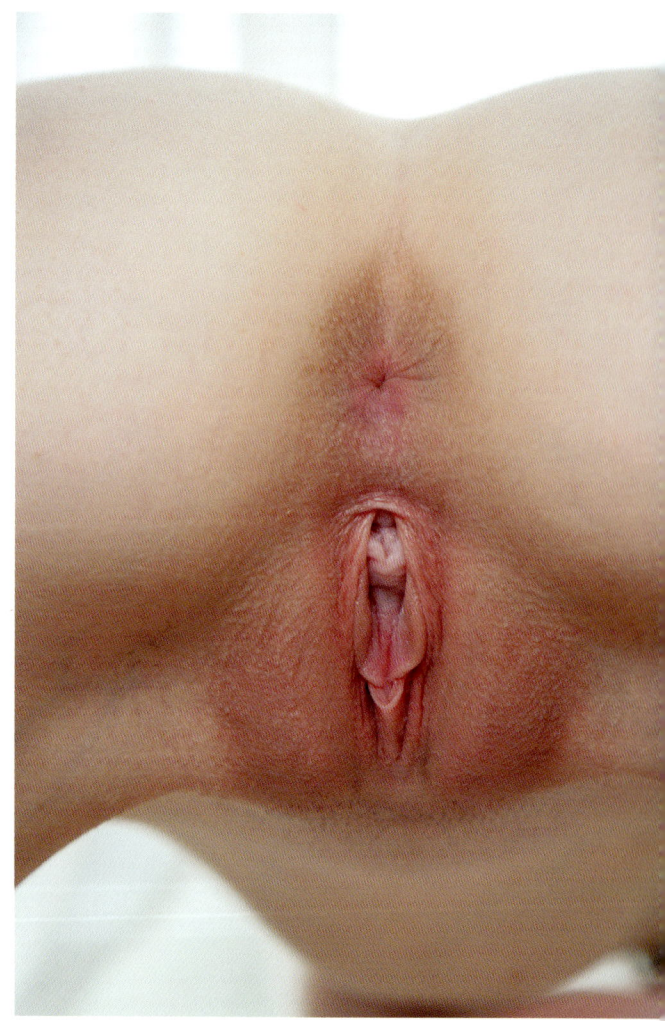

110

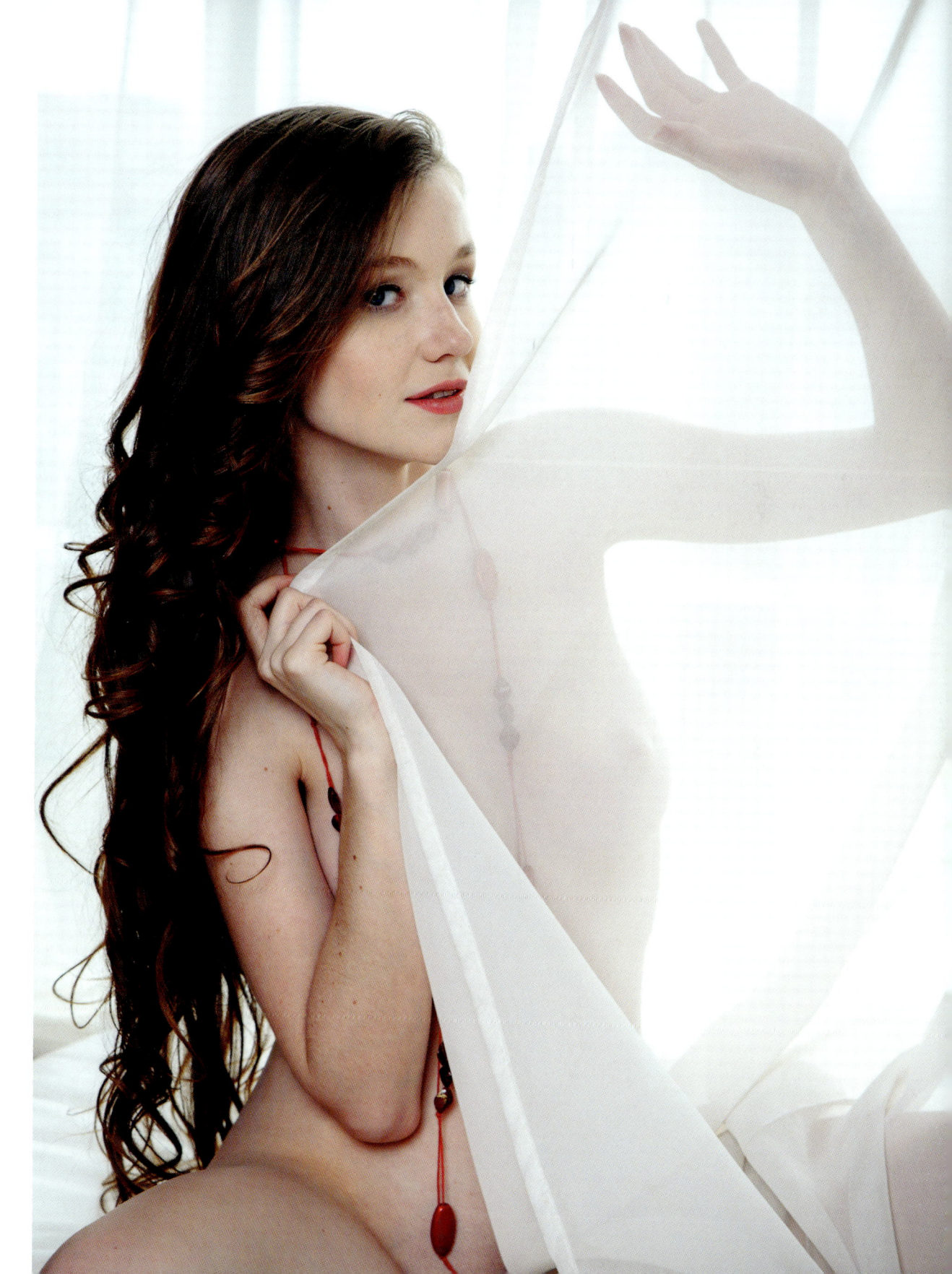

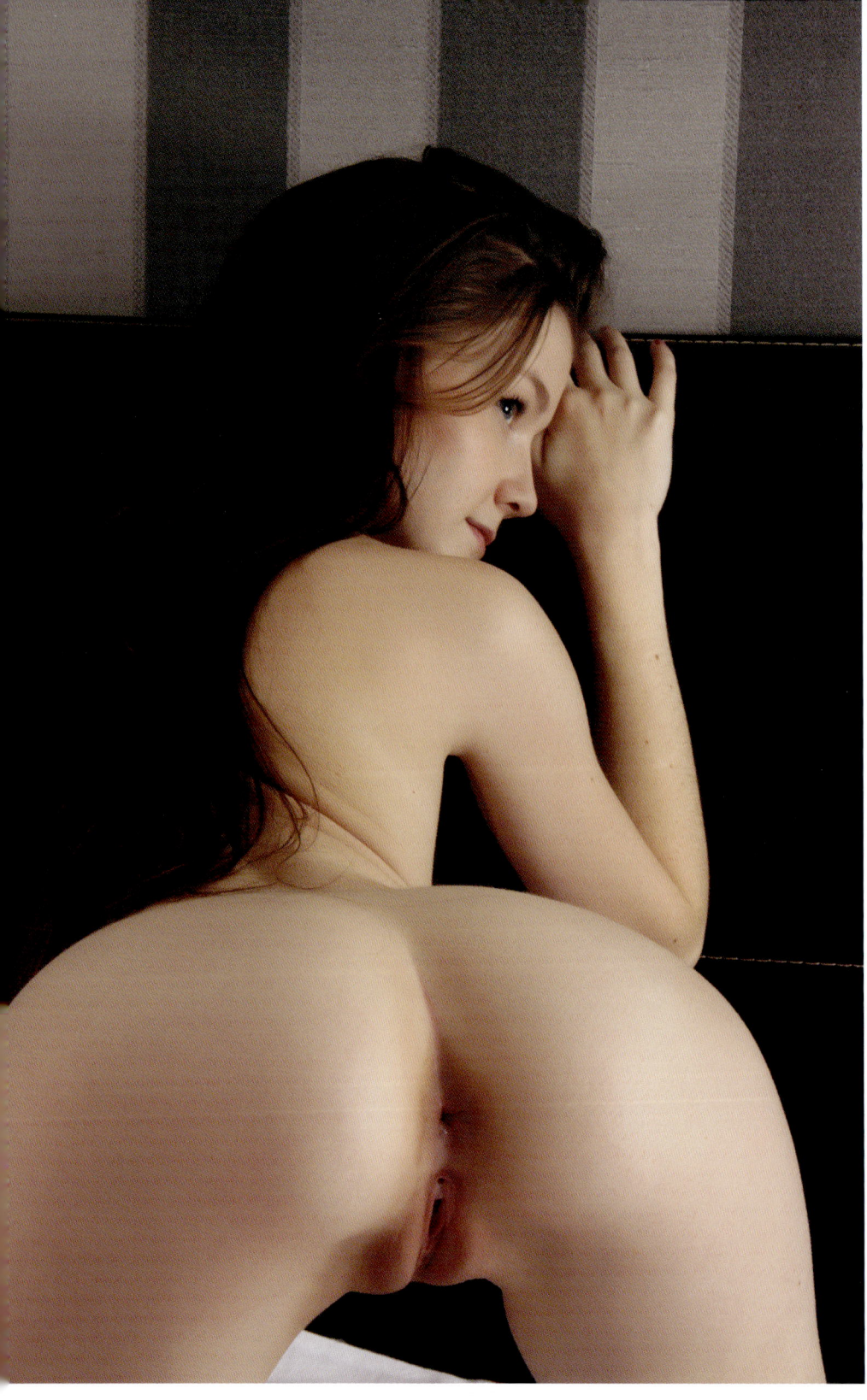

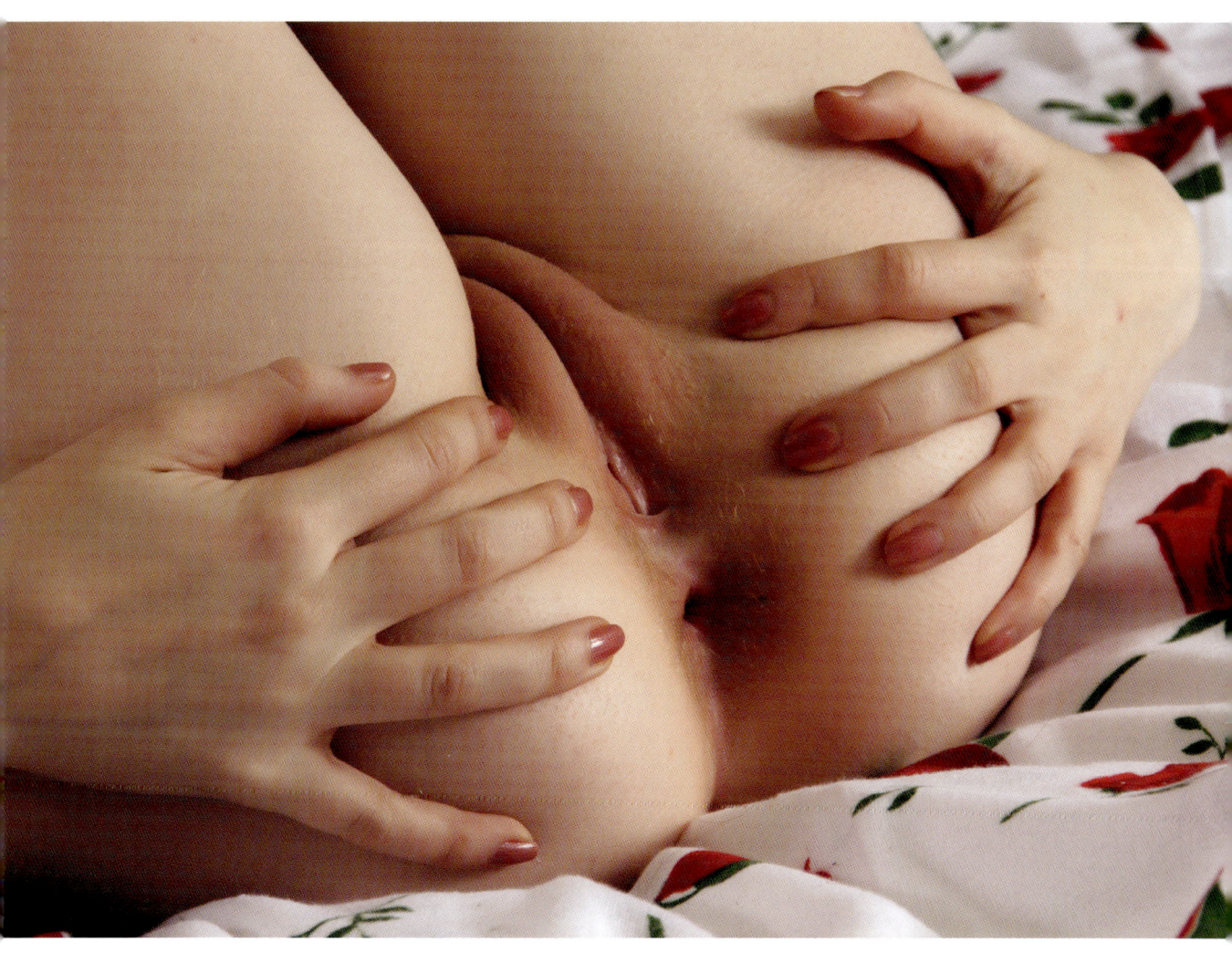

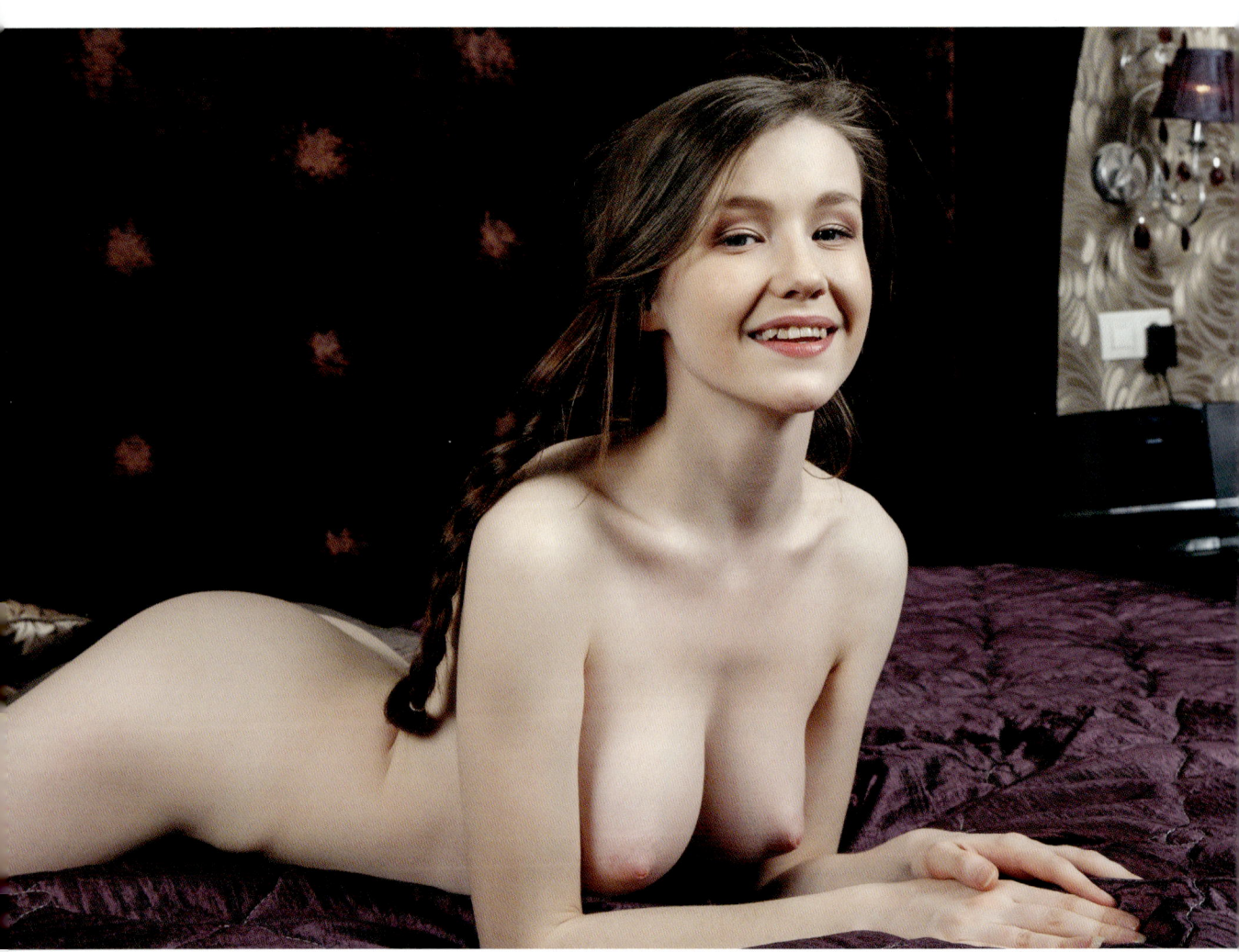

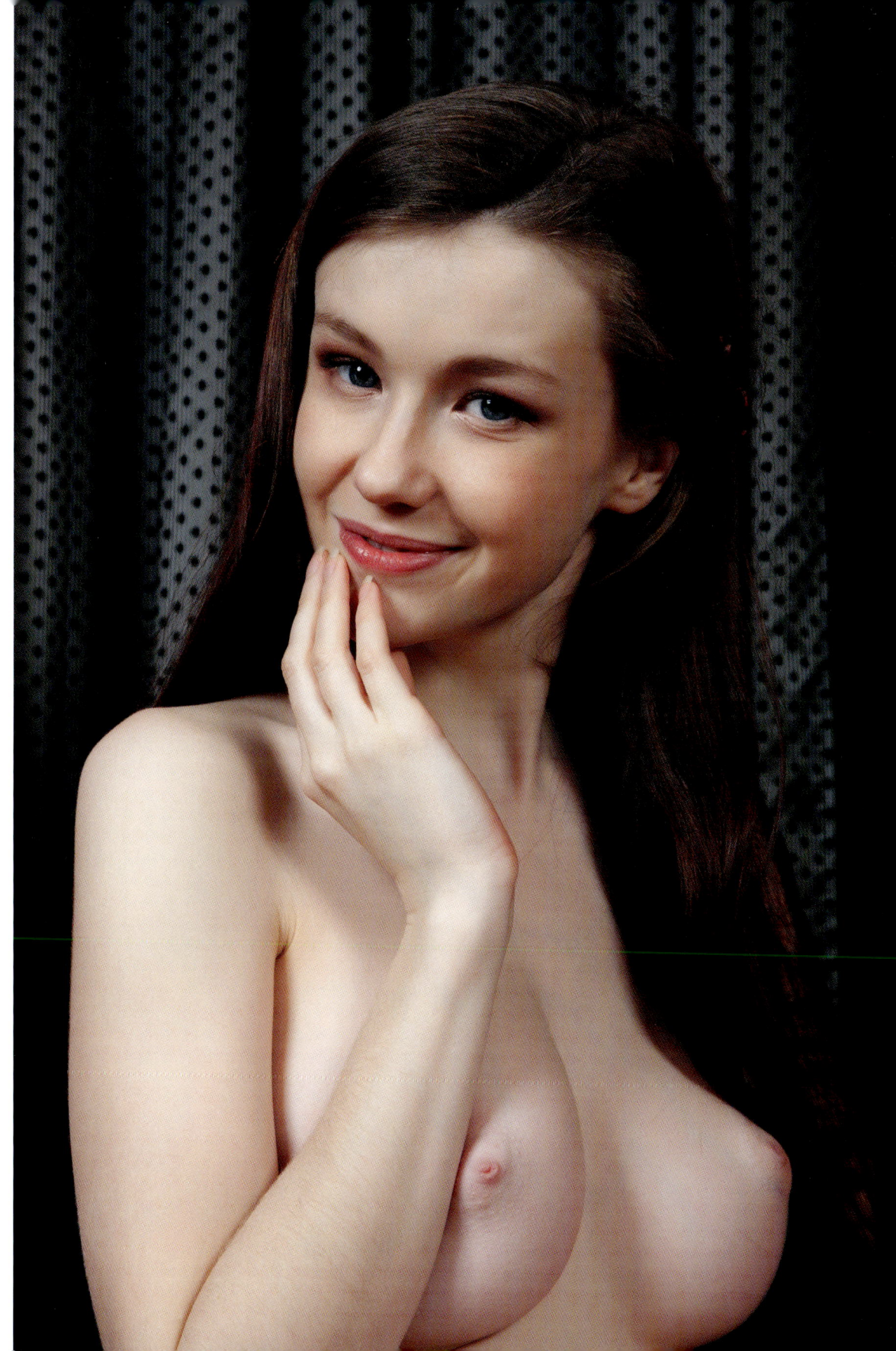

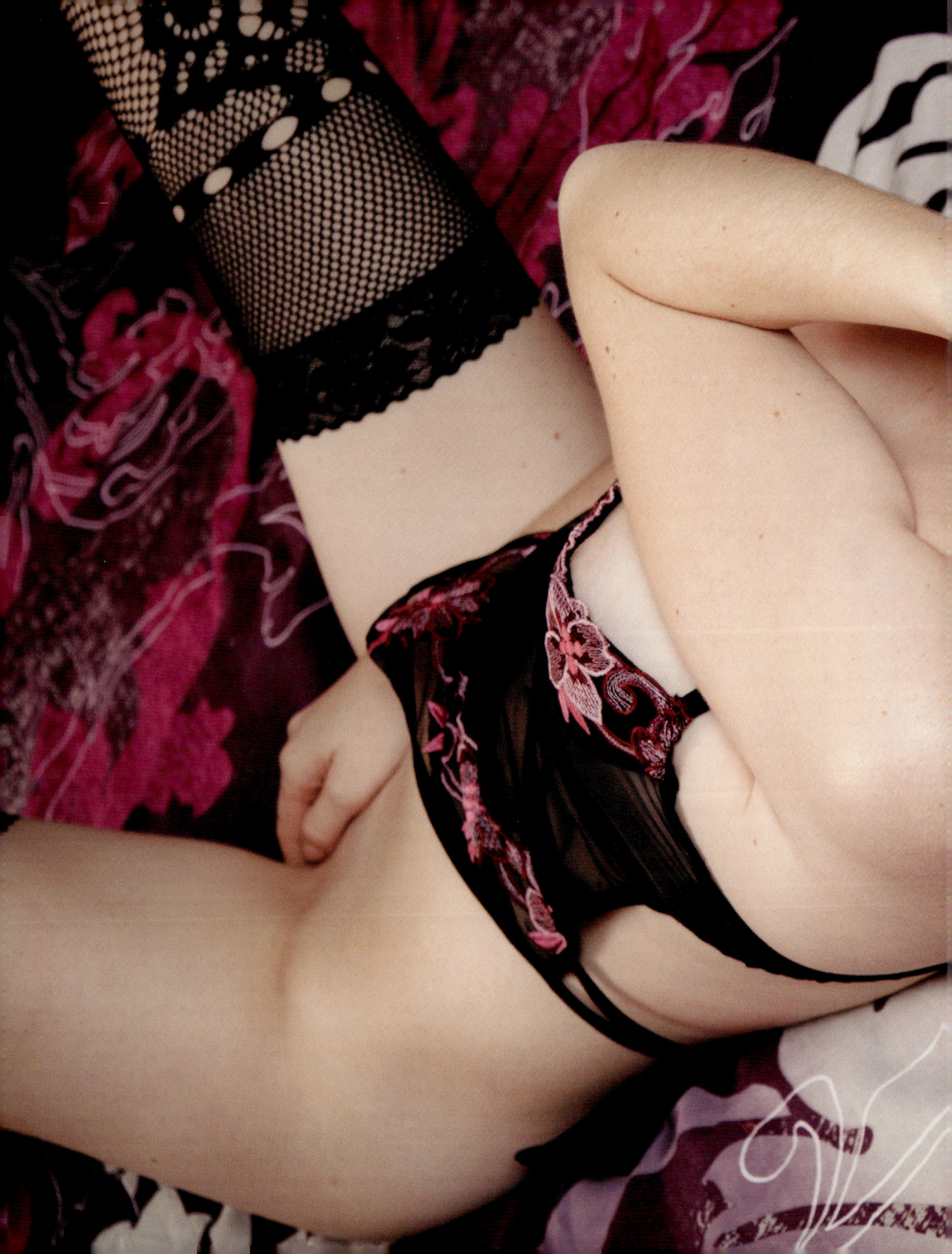

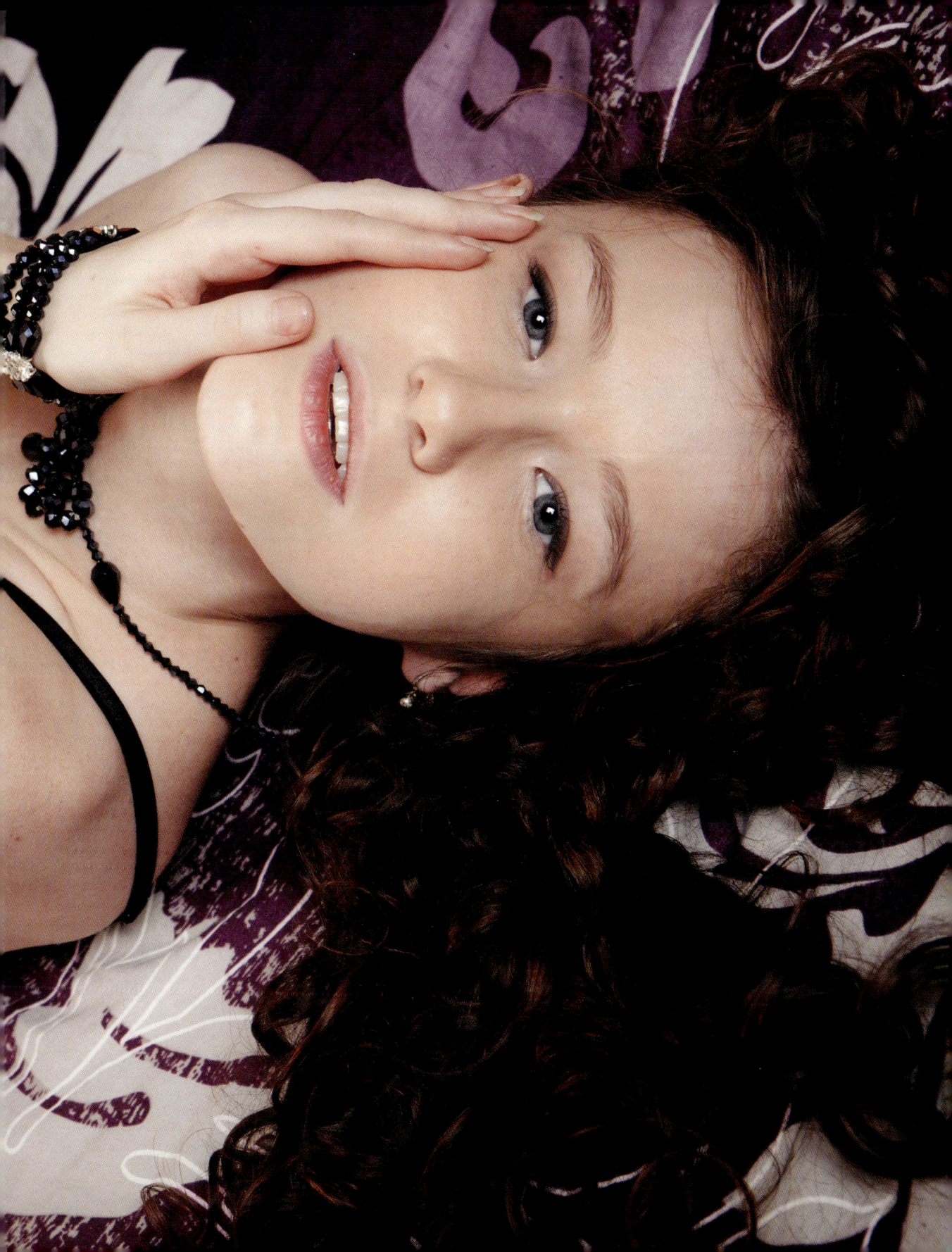

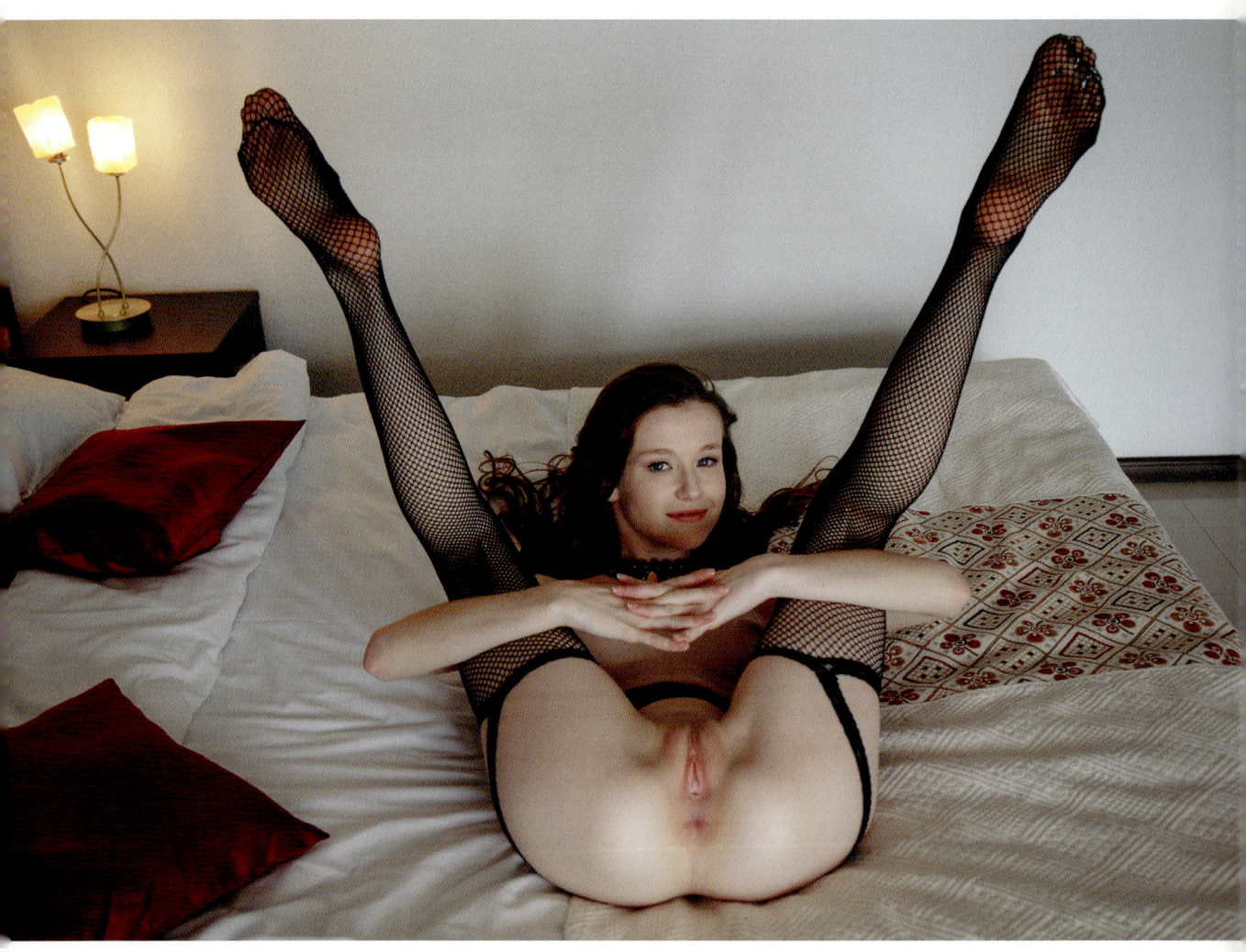

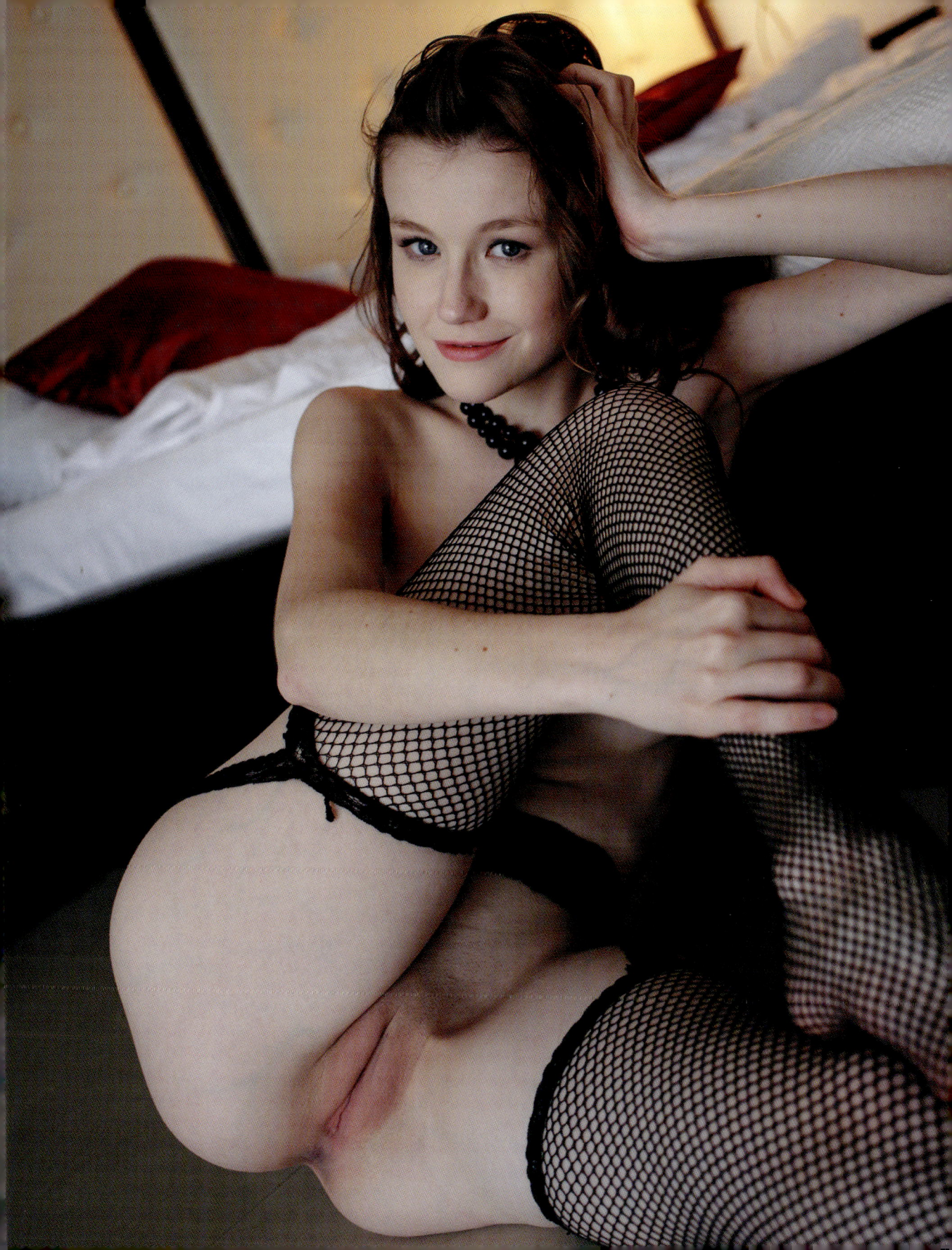

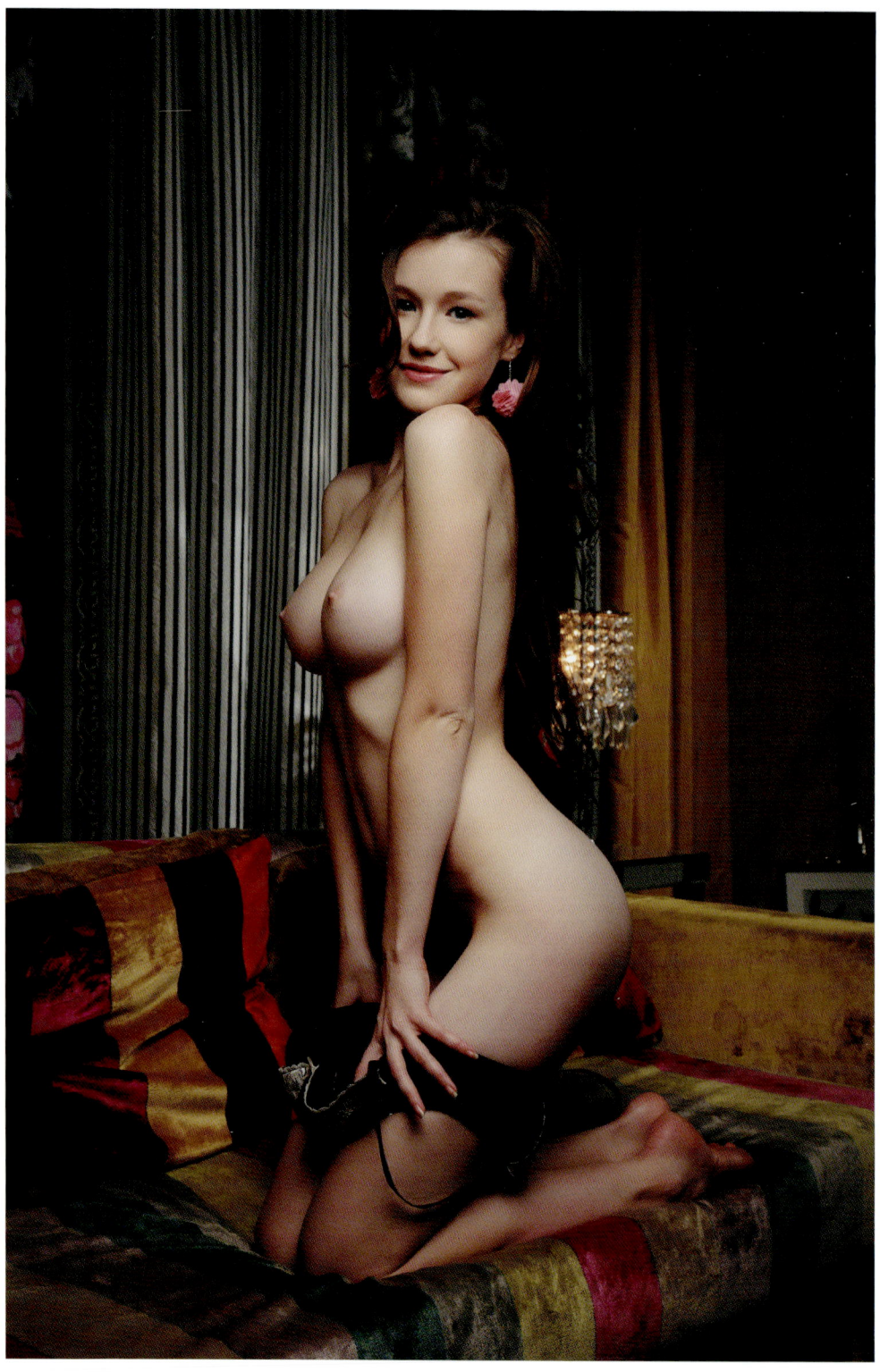

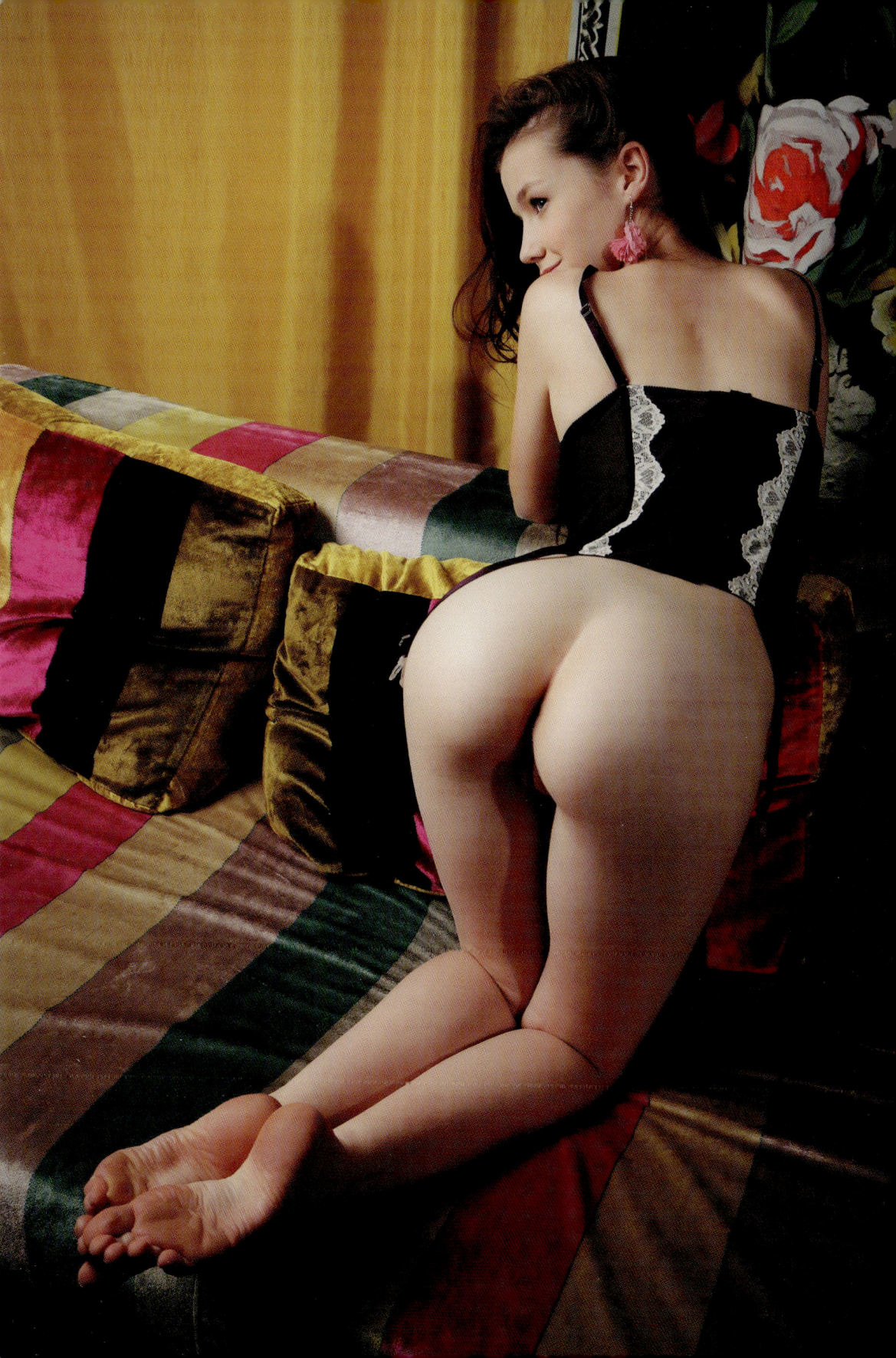

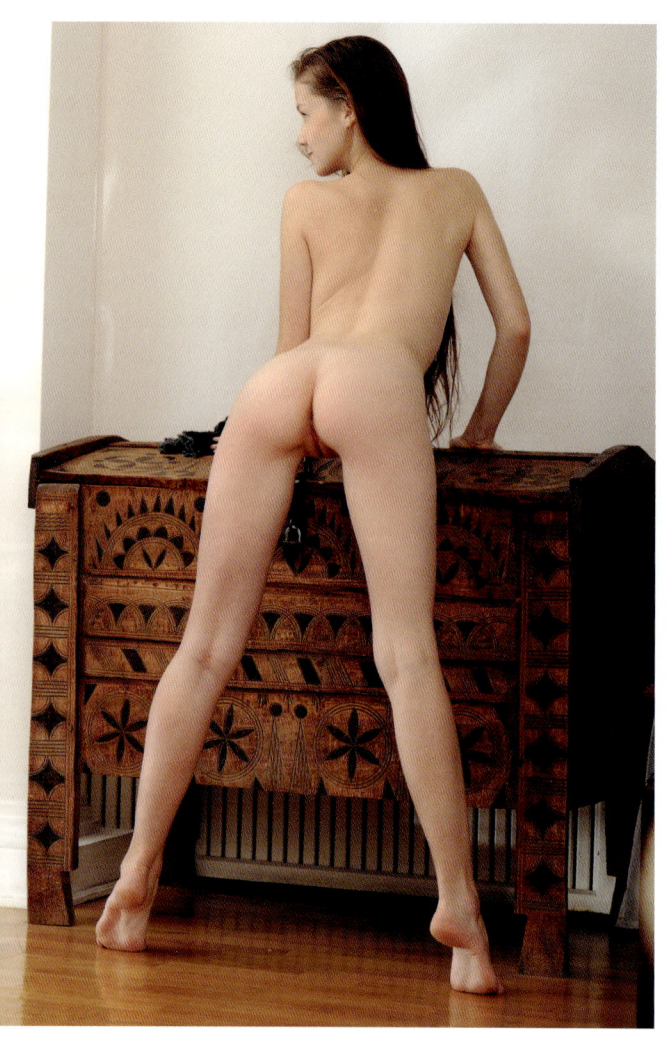
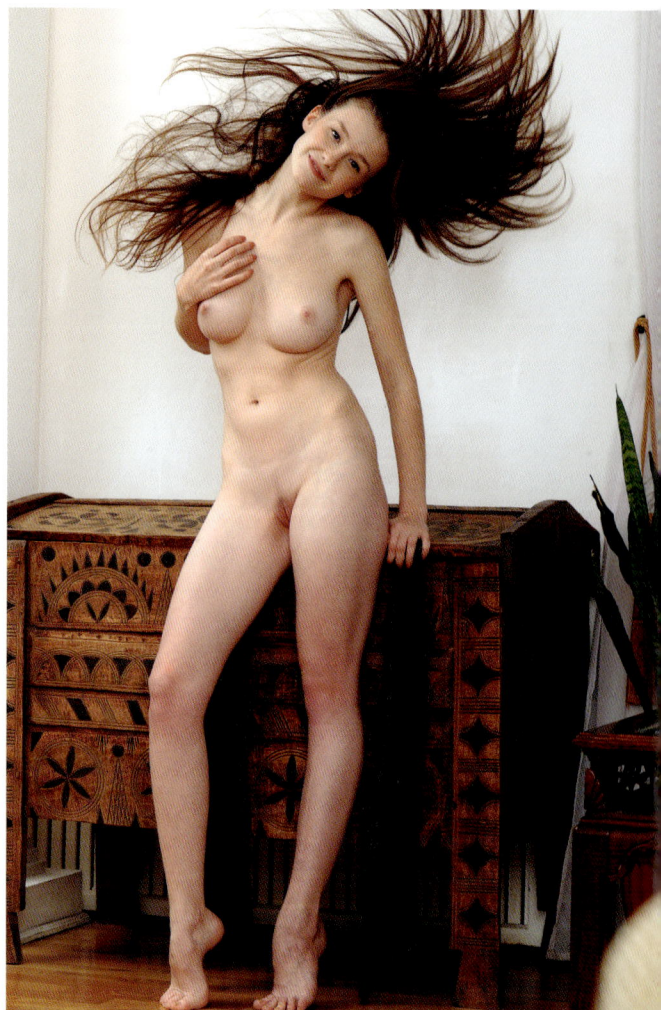

122

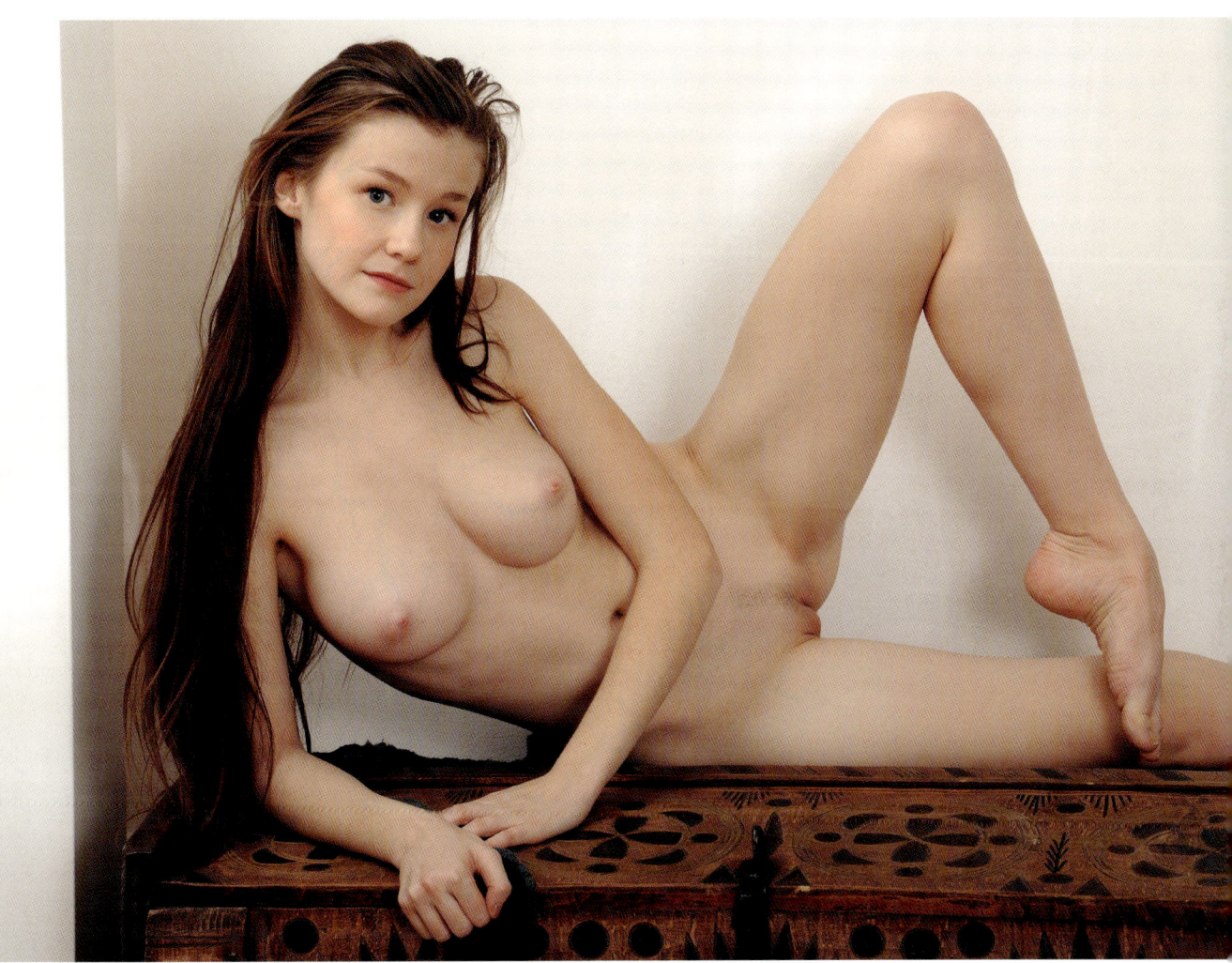

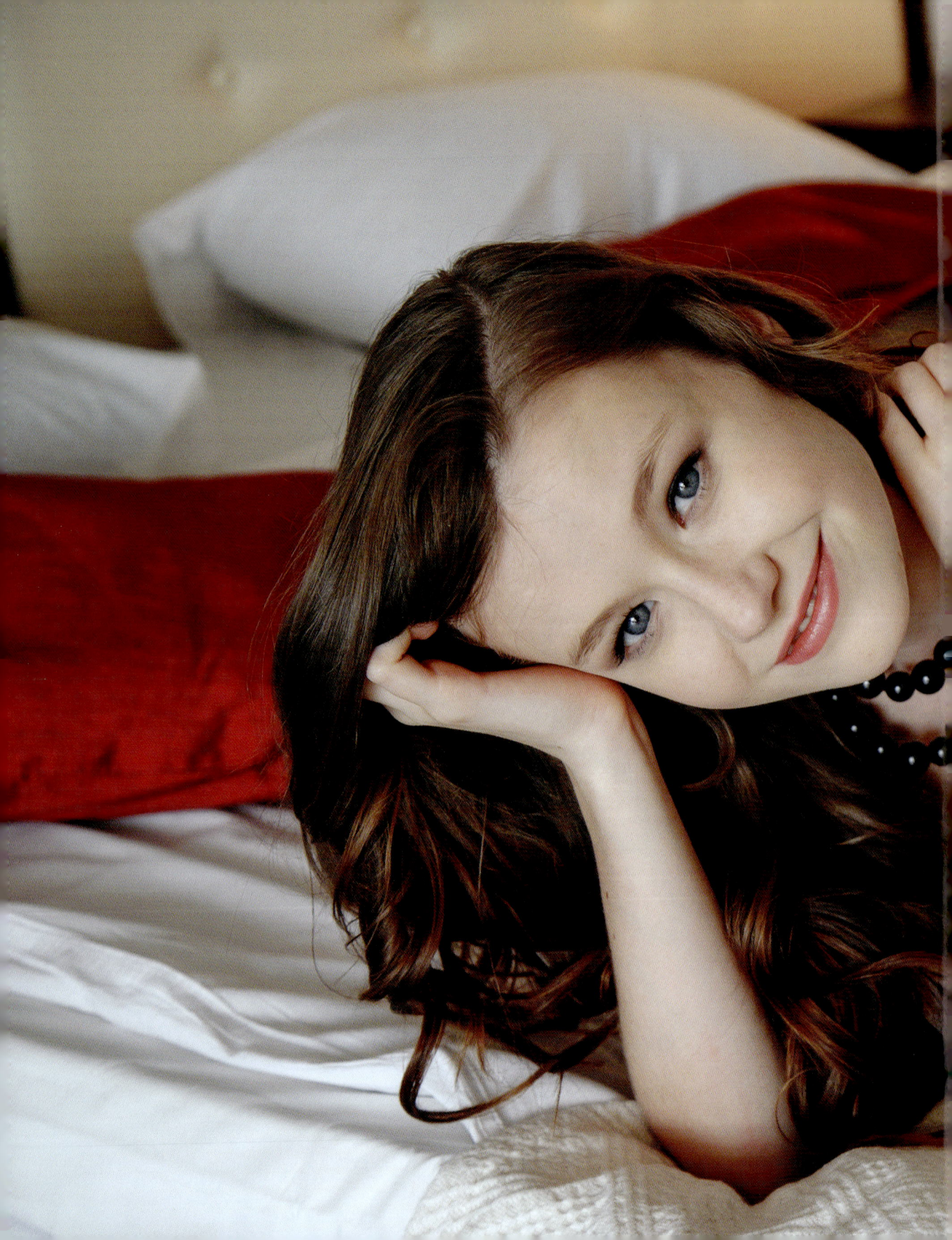

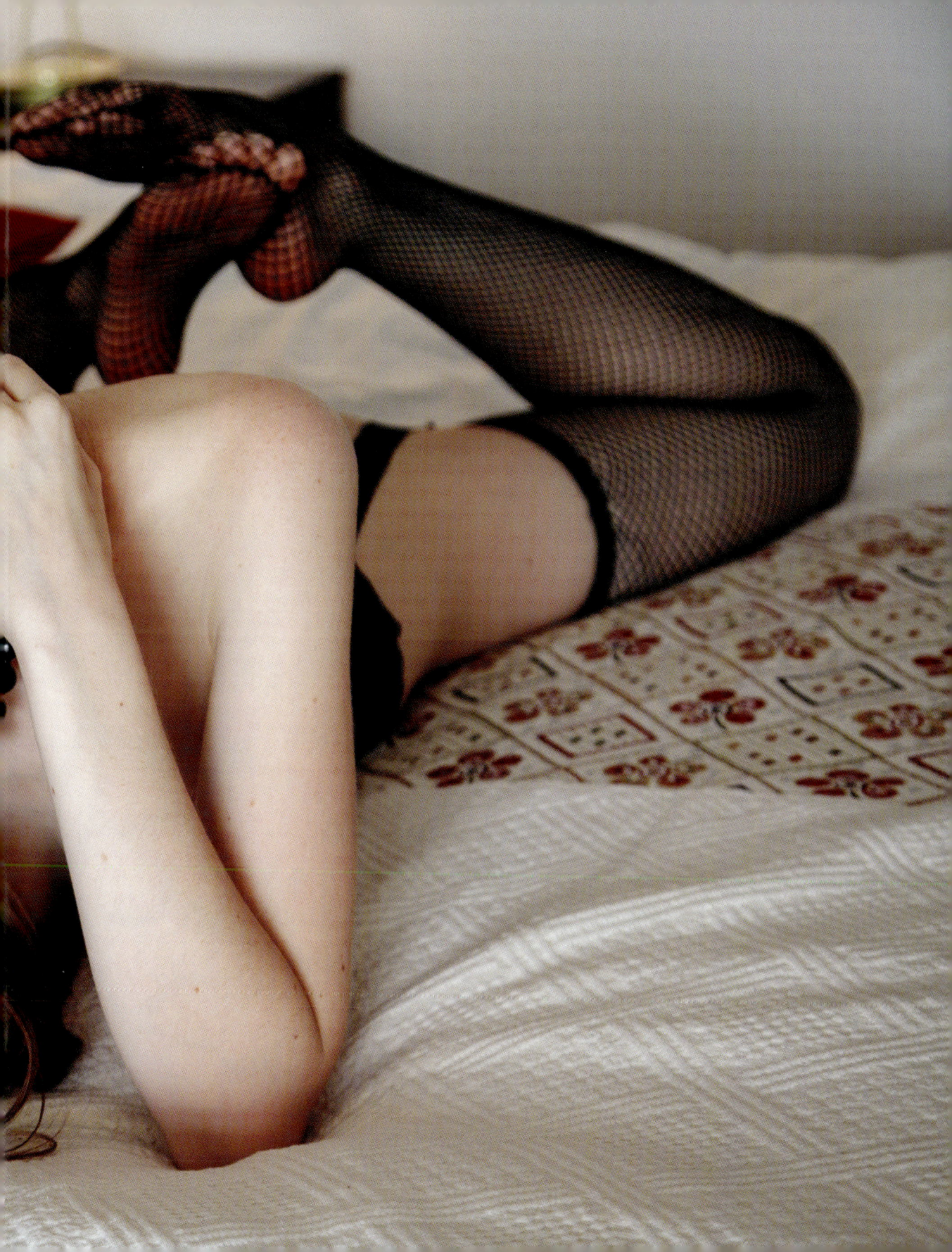

COLLECT THEM ALL: OUR MOST BEAUTIFUL

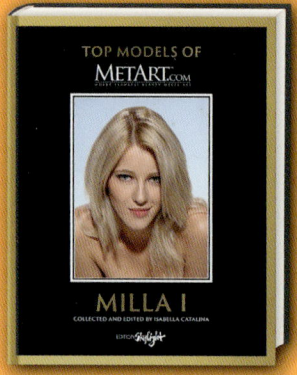
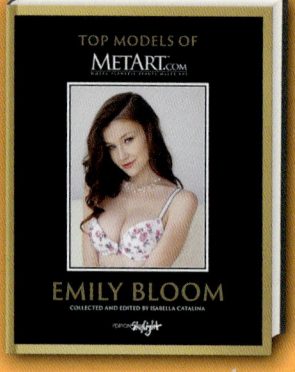
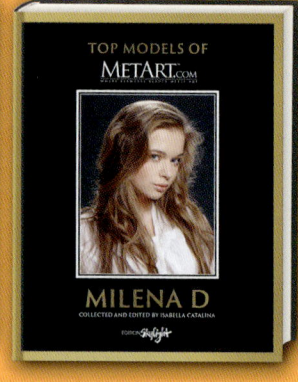
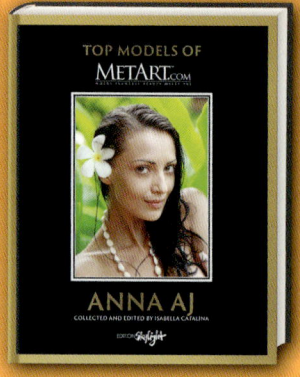
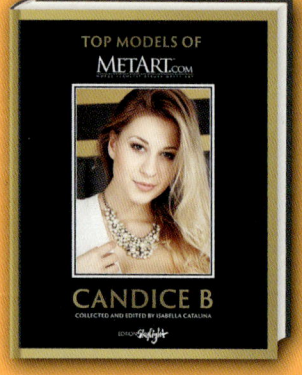
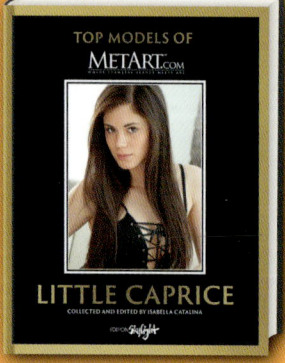
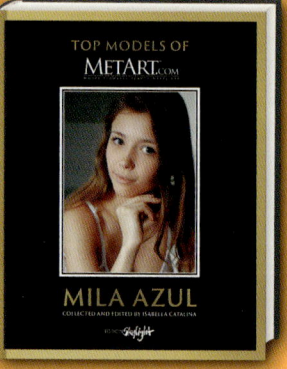
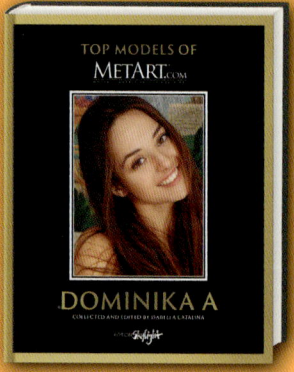
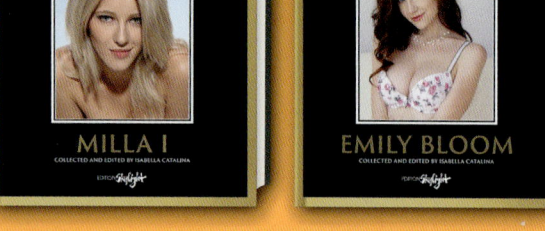
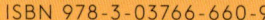